The Pottery of
San Ildefonso Pueblo

This publication was made possible by generous support from the Weatherhead Foundation whose program in the Southwest is concerned with the promotion of new knowledge, the creative arts, the perpetuation of traditional crafts, the ecology of the region, and the improvement of the human condition.

The Pottery of San Ildefonso Pueblo

BY

KENNETH M. CHAPMAN

SUPPLEMENTARY TEXT BY
FRANCIS H. HARLOW

Published for the SCHOOL OF AMERICAN RESEARCH

UNIVERSITY OF NEW MEXICO PRESS   *Albuquerque*

Number 28
School of American Research
Monograph Series
DOUGLAS W. SCHWARTZ, GENERAL EDITOR

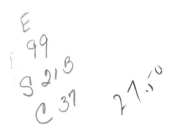

First Edition, 1970
Reprinted 1977

An Appreciation

IT IS APPROPRIATE that this second volume in the series on Pueblo Indian pottery should contain a few words about its author, Dr. Kenneth M. Chapman.

Born in Indiana in 1875, he spent five years as an apprentice commercial artist in St. Louis, Chicago, and Milwaukee engraving shops. In 1899, he came west for his health, as did so many young men in those days, and settled in Las Vegas, New Mexico, where he became art instructor at the Las Vegas Normal School (later, Highlands University). There, under Dr. Edgar L. Hewett, then the School's President, he became fascinated by the first Pueblo pottery specimens he had seen, and began to transcribe their painted decorations onto his sketch pad. These drawings were to be the forerunners of his book, *The Pottery of Santo Domingo Pueblo*, and the present volume, *The Pottery of San Ildefonso Pueblo*.

He had the distinction of being a founding member of the staff of the Museum of New Mexico and the School of American Research (then the School of American Archaeology) when they were jointly organized in 1909; as Executive Secretary, his activities included, among many others, that of archaeology and the continuing study of Indian design.

In 1915, after several years as a science illustrator and at work in various art associations in the East, he returned to Santa Fe to help paint the murals for the new Fine Arts Building, completed in 1917. He brought his lovely new wife (Katherine Müller) with him, and from that time on, they made New Mexico their permanent home.

In following years, he participated with the Museum of New Mexico researchers in restoration projects in the Frijoles and Chaco Canyons, where he could study firsthand the pottery designs of the ancients. He became increasingly aware of the importance of the post-Spanish period in the design of Pueblo pottery, and never lost an opportunity to stress this development. It was he who influenced Julian Martinez, then employed by the Museum, and his wife Maria (both of San Ildefonso) to use native designs and the traditional black polished ware technique in making their pottery, thereby sparking a revival of excellence in the making of Indian pottery.

In 1923 he joined the founders of the Pueblo Pottery Fund, which later became the Indian Arts Fund, in starting what has become one of the great collections of post-Spanish Pueblo Indian Art. Through it, he influenced his friends, Mr. and Mrs. John D. Rockefeller, Jr., to establish the Laboratory of Anthropology in Santa Fe, of which he later became Director and with which his life became identified.

He was a gifted and enthusiastic teacher. One of his first classes in Indian Art was held in the Palace of the Governors as far back as 1910. He lectured at the School's summer field camps in Frijoles and in the Jemez, and in 1926 at the University of New Mexico, where he became the first teacher of anthropology. Dr. Hewett started the University's Department of Anthropology later that fall. He also taught at the U.S. Indian School in Santa Fe, where he influenced Pueblo pottery by his insistence on quality of design. This in turn led to his long association with the U.S. Indian Arts and Crafts Board.

In addition to many articles and pamphlets, he wrote *Pueblo Indian Pottery*, in two volumes, published abroad in 1933-36; it is now a collector's item. In 1936, he wrote *The Pottery of Santo Domingo Pueblo*, to which the present *The Pottery of San Ildefonso Pueblo* is a sequel.

Before he died at the age of 92, Kenneth Chapman received many tributes for his study and preservation of Indian designs. The University of Arizona, the University of New Mexico, and the Chicago Art Institute awarded him honorary doctoral degrees. From the United States Government, he received a special citation for his achievements in helping to establish the high standards of Indian craftsmanship.

It is fitting to close these remarks by quoting from a Memorial Resolution adopted by the Board of the School of American Research, expressing ". . . its sense of personal loss at the passing of one who, through his life-long devotion to the conservation of Pueblo Indian Art, contributed so much and so richly to our knowledge and enjoyment of the culture of our fellow citizens, the Pueblo Indians."

JOHN G. MEEM, *Member of the Board*
School of American Research
Santa Fe, New Mexico

Contents

Illustrations

FIGURES

PLATES

Foreword

THE STUDIES FOR THIS BOOK on the pottery of San Ildefonso were begun as early as 1900, when several specimens from that Pueblo were used by the author in a course on Indian design at the New Mexico Normal University (now New Mexico Highlands University) in Las Vegas.

Ten years later, on joining the staff of the newly created School of American Archaeology (now School of American Research) and Museum of New Mexico in Santa Fe, on a part-time basis, there came further opportunities to examine a greater variety of Pueblo pottery types. Such examinations were carried on mostly in the shops of dealers in Indian goods, for at that time the activities of the School-Museum were directed entirely toward archaeology.

Thus, it was not until 1920 that means were found for beginning a systematic study of the arts of the modern pueblos and particularly those of the nearby Rio Grande groups, in several of which the ceramic craft still flourished. Research in the homes of the potters themselves would have been invaluable, but for various reasons it was limited almost entirely to contacts during the occasional brief visits of potters to Santa Fe.

Fortunately, beginning in 1920, a photographic record was made of all the Pueblo pottery available in the shops and in private collections of Santa Fe and neighboring towns. Within a few years, over 700 specimens were listed, nearly half of them from San Ildefonso. This list provided the only record of the current production of that period, and most of the specimens themselves have long since disappeared.

The actual collecting of a fully representative group of Pueblo ceramics, however, began in 1923, with the organization of the Indian Arts Fund by a voluntary association impressed with the need of immediate action to preserve the indigenous arts of the Indians of the Southwest for the benefit of future generations of Indian craftsmen and for the enjoyment of all Americans.

The efforts of the Fund won ever-increasing support from sources far beyond the Southwest. As a result, the Indian Art Fund's superb collection of pottery from sixteen pueblos now includes well over 2500 specimens, of which 300 are from San Ildefonso. Owned by the School of American Research, it is presently housed and used by the Museum of New Mexico in Santa Fe. Between this pottery collection and the Fund's collection of photographs from many sources, a total of almost 1000 specimens of San Ildefonso wares is available for study.

With collecting as the prime activity in the early years, very little time could be devoted to publication, but since then considerable progress has been made, largely with the generous help of several volunteer assistants. Finally, through the cooperation of the University of New Mexico, I was relieved of all other duties and have been free to continue with the preparation of this publication and other long-deferred works.

The delay, however, has not been without its compensations. The steady accumulation of material and data at the Laboratory of Anthropology has provided a far better representation of Pueblo ceramics than had been conceived in the early 1920s. And, furthermore, the delay has made possible a considerable section on the more recent developments of pottery styles at San Ildefonso in which, for better or for worse, I have had a hand.

KENNETH M. CHAPMAN

Preface

WHEN KENNETH MILTON CHAPMAN DIED in February 1968, his book, *The Pottery of San Ildefonso Pueblo,* was not quite completed. The drawings were finished, and much of the text had been drafted. All that remained was to add a chapter on recent historical discoveries, to organize the manuscript into a cohesive whole, and then to carry through all the innumerable editorial tasks that lead to final publication.

To me has come the honor of being assigned the first two of these processes. Since 1960, I had been working on studies similar to those of Dr. Chapman, and had enjoyed a number of stimulating conversations with him about these investigations. His emphasis in Pueblo pottery studies was always on design, artistry, and the personalities of the craftsmen, while mine has been on pottery history, technology, and design evolution. Thus, our work was complementary, so that the addition of my efforts to this monograph is hopefully useful and appropriate.

In assembling the various portions of Dr. Chapman's manuscript and organizing the final text, I have been guided by two principal aims:

1. To retain as much as possible of Dr. Chapman's own wording and, where discernible, his desired order of presentation.
2. To make additions only as required for continuity, or where recent data have shed additional light on matters of pertinence.

I believe that the result comes very close to the final book that Dr. Chapman himself would have completed. As such, it stands as a great monument to the infinite patience and skill of a dedicated man, a true pioneer in the studies of the Pueblo Indians and their magnificent crafts. To the extent, however, that this book may fail to fulfill the vision that "Chap" had carried for so many years, the fault is mine alone.

FRANCIS H. HARLOW
Los Alamos, New Mexico

Acknowledgments

TO RECORD FULLY my indebtedness and appreciation of the many instances of encouragement and assistance afforded me in conducting this study through the many years since its inception, would be a most agreeable and heartwarming task, but the limitations of space make necessary the mere mention of institutions and individuals whose cooperation has been extended so freely. These are as follows:

The museums of the universities of Arizona, California, Colorado, Michigan, Nebraska, New Mexico, New Mexico Highlands, Oklahoma, Pennsylvania; and the Museum of Girard College, Philadelphia.

Museums — Public, and Privately Conducted: The American Museum of Natural History, New York; Arizona State Museum, Tucson; Brooklyn Museum; Chicago Natural History Museum; Colorado State Museum, Denver; Davenport Public Museum; Denver Art Museum; Gila Pueblo, Globe, Arizona; Grand Rapids Public Museum; Illinois State Museum of Natural History and Art, Springfield; Laboratory of Anthropology, Santa Fe; Los Angeles County Museum of History, Science and Art; Milwaukee Public Museum; Minnesota Historical Society Museum, St. Paul; Museum of the American Indian, Heye Foundation, New York; Museum of Fine Arts of Houston; Museum of New Mexico, Santa Fe; Peabody Museum of Archaeology and Ethnology, Harvard University; Peabody Museum of Natural History, Yale University; Philbrook Art Museum, Tulsa; Robert S. Peabody Foundation for Archaeology, Andover, Massachusetts; Rochester Museum of Arts and Sciences; Royal Ontario Museum of Archaeology, Toronto; Santa Barbara Museum of Natural History; San Diego Museum of Man; School of American Research, Santa Fe; Society of Liberal Arts, Joslyn Memorial, Omaha; Southwest Museum, Los Angeles; United States National Museum, Washington; and Vancouver City Museum and Art Gallery, British Columbia.

The Officers and Staffs of the School of American Research, Laboratory of Anthropology, Inc., and the Indian Arts Fund, Inc., Santa Fe.

Volunteer Assistants: Margaret Blecha, Anne Harding, Miriam Marmon, Nellie O. Matthews, Eleanor C. Rawlings, Anna O. Shepard, Beula M. Wadsworth, Jane Walstrum, and Yvonne Zacharias.

New Mexico Dealers: the late J. S. Candelario, Santa Fe; Fred Harvey, Inc., Albuquerque; Old Santa Fe Trading Post, Santa Fe; the late Juan Olivas, Santa Fe; Southwest Arts and Crafts, Santa Fe; Spanish and Indian Trading Co., Santa Fe; the late A. F. Spielgelberg, Santa Fe; and C. G. Wallace, Zuñi.

xv

Special Mention: Rose Dougan, Bruce T. Ellis, Jane Evans, Clark Field, Laura Gilpin, Joe H. Herrera, Hester Jones, Dr. A. V. Kidder, Eleanor C. Rawlings, Dr. David H. Stevens, and Verra von Blumenthal.

And finally, the list would not be complete without a special mention of the cordial cooperation afforded by the officials and the potters of San Ildefonso Pueblo during the many years in which the work has been in progress.

The study has been furthered by grants from the Rockefeller Foundation.

Publication was made possible through a contribution from the late Mr. John D. Rockefeller, Jr.

K. M. C.

THE PUEBLO OF SAN ILDEFONSO

The pueblo of San Ildefonso is an Indian village of Tewa linguistic stock, situated on the east bank of the Rio Grande about 20 miles northeast of Santa Fe.

The Indian name for San Ildefonso is Powhoge, meaning "where the water cuts through" in reference to the Rio Grande. The Pajarito Plateau is the legendary home of the San Ildefonso people.

The site of this Pueblo is especially beautiful, with the Jemez Mountains on the west, the Truchas on the east, and the Black Mesa directly north. The daily life of the inhabitants continues much as it has for many decades.

Other Tewa pueblos include San Juan, Santa Clara, Tesuque, Nambe, and Pojoaque in the Rio Grande valley. Hano, also of Tewa linguistic stock, is located on First Mesa of the Hopi country. It was settled by Tewa refugees from the Rio Grande valley after the Pueblo Rebellion.

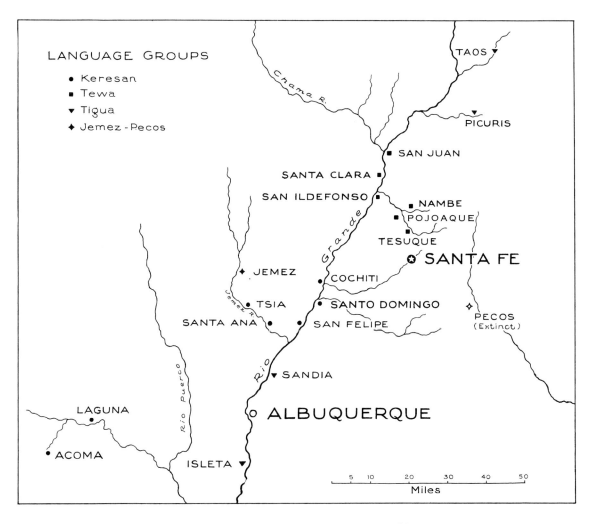

Figure 1. Map of the Rio Grande pueblos.

CHAPTER I
The Historical Setting

FOR NEARLY TWO THOUSAND YEARS the ancestors of the Pueblo Indians (the Anasazi, meaning "the ancients," a term used by their successors, the Navajo) had developed through gradual changes a culture well adapted to temperate, semiarid areas centering in northern Arizona. Depending at first mainly upon food gathering and hunting, they had turned by degrees to a more settled life. The adoption of agriculture was partly responsible for more permanent dwellings as beans, squash, and maize were introduced, evidently from the south.

Throughout many centuries, depletion of the soil by erosion and overuse, lack of water in intermittent periods of drouth, scarcity of game, and the inroads of nomadic tribes led several groups to spread farther and farther in search of better living conditions.

Thus, by A.D. 1200 certain branches of two important language groups had made their way eastward to the Rio Grande region in northern New Mexico. Of these the Tewa branch of the Tanoan group settled in an area extending from the Sangre de Cristo Mountains on the east, to the Jemez range on the west, and from El Rito and Ojo Caliente on the north, some fifty miles south to the neighborhood of the present city of Santa Fe. The Tewa now name a score or more of villages occupied by their people in prehistoric times, of which but five remain, with a total population of less than two thousand. These, reading from north to south, are San Juan, Santa Clara, San Ildefonso, Nambe, and Tesuque.

The startling impact of the first visit by a European, Coronado in 1540, made a lasting impression upon the Pueblo Indians. However, during the Spaniards' stay of two years, they made only brief forays into the Tewa area; and after the return of the expedition to Mexico, forty years were to pass before the appearance of other parties, intent on further explorations.

Finally, in 1598, the first attempt was made to colonize the vast area, by then known as Nuevo Mexico. A party of settlers, under Oñate, chose a site at the confluence of the Rio Chama and the Rio Grande, giving it the name of San Gabriel. There the group, with later reinforcements, remained until 1609 when they abandoned their settlement, retired thirty miles southward, and founded their capital city at the more strategic site of Santa Fe.

During those ten years at San Gabriel the neighboring Tewa pueblos began to feel

[3]

the hand of oppression as they were subjected to enforced labor and were taxed for food, clothing, and other necessities required by the officials, the soldiery, the Franciscan fathers, and also for use by the servant class of Tlascalan Indians and mixed breeds from Mexico, some of whom had brought their families. From then on, life under the conquistadors became increasingly unbearable until 1680, when by concerted action the pueblos throughout all northern New Mexico rebelled, drove the intruders across the border, and kept them out for twelve years, until a strong armed force returned under de Vargas and regained Santa Fe without opposition. After many battles with the Indians, and by making certain concessions, the Spaniards again assumed control. By degrees they gave greater freedom to the pueblos in continuance of their own way of life on their own lands, which had been assured them in 1687 by grants from the King of Spain.

In this book, particular emphasis is given to one of these Tewa villages, San Ildefonso. The Pueblo, with a present population of less than 150, is situated on the east bank of the Rio Grande, some twenty miles northwest of Santa Fe. Known in the Tewa dialect as Powhoge, or Poqwoge (place where the water cuts through), the Pueblo was not mentioned by name in the account of Coronado's expedition of 1540-42, but presumably it was visited by members of his group in the course of explorations extending as far north as Taos.

The name of San Ildefonso was given the Pueblo as early as 1617, when it became the seat of a Spanish mission. The inhabitants took part in the Pueblo Revolt of 1680 and aided in driving the Spanish settlers from the Southwest. Following the reconquest of the province by de Vargas in 1692, the people of San Ildefonso were among the last to capitulate. In their defiance they at one time took refuge on Tunyo, the black basaltic mesa a short distance north of the Pueblo, and it was not until 1696 that they were finally resettled in their old home. Here, in comparative seclusion, they rebuilt their Pueblo and its mission, tended their flocks, and tilled their fields while watching, doubtless with considerable anxiety, the steady influx of Spanish-speaking rancheros on the eastern border of their grant. Year by year the rancheros reduced the available water from the Pojoaque creek, upon which the people of San Ildefonso depended largely for irrigation.

A more serious menace to the pueblos came with constantly increasing raids by the Navajo, Comanche, and other nomadic tribes. In self-defense, the San Ildefonsos invited certain families of Spanish descent to settle near them and provided them with lands to the south and west of the Pueblo. There the descendants of a few of the settlers still remain, with good titles to their holdings. With the American occupation in 1846, and the gradual subjection of roving Indian tribes, there came a more peaceful era among the northern pueblos. Even the building of a narrow-gauge railroad through the San Ildefonso grant brought little travel to the Pueblo, and it was not until 1924 that a highway bridge across the Rio Grande, two miles to the south, made San Ildefonso more accessible to tourists en route to the prehistoric cliff dwellings west of the Rio Grande.

Later, during World War II, the establishment of the "Atomic City" of Los Alamos in the heart of the cliff dwelling country has led to far greater changes in the life of all the Tewa pueblos. Since then the pace has quickened, but in spite of the introduction of electricity, radio, and television the people of San Ildefonso have maintained much of the charm of their old Pueblo.

The impact of all these trends upon the ceramic art of San Ildefonso is reflected in the development of pottery styles, from early to late, as set forth in the following chapters.

CHAPTER II

General Features of San Ildefonso Pottery

EARLY DESCRIPTIONS

POTTERY MAKING AT SAN ILDEFONSO, as among most of the Tewa pueblos, was practiced from early times by a considerable number of women mainly for their domestic use and for occasional bartering among the housewives of their own and neighboring villages.

The craft of San Ildefonso has rarely been mentioned, even in the accounts of government officials. The earliest available reference, dated June 1852, is by the regional Superintendent of Indian Affairs and reads as follows:

". . . visited San Ildefonso Pueblo all getting along well, crops look fine, Indians working their fields, women making tinajas. . . ."[1]

During two decades following, the casual accounts of Pueblo arts and crafts by travelers make no references to San Ildefonso. Finally, in 1879, matters took a turn for the better when the newly organized Bureau of Ethnology of the Smithsonian Institution turned its attention to the Southwest, thus making possible a study of the Pueblo Indians, including in its second year considerable field work among the Rio Grande pueblos.

The resulting descriptions of San Ildefonso pottery appear in a detailed report of the Smithsonian expedition by its leader, James Stevenson, covering collections acquired particularly during 1880.[2]

Apparently two visits were made to San Ildefonso by the field party, one en route to Taos, and the other perhaps on their return. Regarding the first, Stevenson says, "But few specimens were obtained here. The people of this pueblo devote their time chiefly to agriculture and pastoral pursuits and have almost abandoned the manufacture of pottery, that in use by them at the present time being mostly obtained from neighboring tribes."[3]

Following this discouraging comment, however, in his accompanying list of the collections acquired at twelve of the Rio Grande pueblos, Stevenson again states for San Ildefonso, "The collections from this pueblo were the largest made during the year 1880."[4]

They comprised 88 specimens of pottery, of five distinct types, as follows:

1. Painted white ware, the white in all these being of a creamy color   35
2. Red ware with decorations in black   7
3. Red and brown ware without decorations   22
4. Black polished ware   21
5. Black ware not polished   3

Total   88

[6]

In two years the Smithsonian expedition acquired well over two thousand specimens of "articles of clay," including pottery, figurines, toys, and miscellaneous trinkets. Some 256 specimens were chosen for illustration, which resulted in excellent woodcuts and a few lithographs in full color. But unfortunately they are so unevenly apportioned that while 124 are devoted to the pottery of Zuñi Pueblo, only one is accredited to San Ildefonso.

Not until thirty years later, beginning with Saunders in 1910, did the pottery of San Ildefonso became better known and appreciated through the illustrated works of Spinden, 1911; Goddard, 1931; Wilson, 1920; Guthe, 1925; Kidder, 1924; Alexander, 1926; Bunzel, 1929; and Chapman, 1927, 1933.

Soon after 1920, with the improvement of their traditional pottery and the introduction of a new and popular type by a talented couple, Maria and Julian Martinez, there came a succession of somewhat less authoritative but notably enthusiastic accounts of the San Ildefonso potters and their wares. The resulting publicity has since brought their community into the limelight as the outstanding example of the revitalization of a pueblo through improvement of its arts and crafts.

TERMINOLOGY OF PUEBLO POTTERY FORMS

In prior publications on the ceramics of the Pueblo Indians, certain names have been given to pottery forms, some of which are not in accordance with accepted usage.

For instance, the term "bowl" has been applied to water jars, despite the English definition limiting the term to wide-mouthed vessels usually not quite hemispherical.

The Spanish term "olla" (ó-yah) has also been used mistakenly to designate water jars, though in Spain and throughout Latin America the term is applied only to plain, undecorated cooking pots, while the jar used exclusively for cooling and serving drinking water is rightly called "tinaja" (tee-nah'-ha). Although this distinction has not been observed by all the pueblos of the Rio Grande area, it is closely followed by the best-informed potters of San Ildefonso, who use also the Spanish term "tinajon" (tee-nah-hóne) for large storage jars.

One difficulty with the use of otherwise appropriate terms from the Tewa language is that they have seldom appeared in print. Even the most accomplished linguists have failed to give the layman a readily deciphered, phonetic spelling of Tewa ceramic terms.

In view of these complications, it seems best to adhere to better-understood English terms, more or less descriptive of the form and use of each vessel, as follows: food bowl; utility bowl; water jar; storage jar, including wide-mouthed and medium-sized; Ceremonial; miscellaneous forms and combinations, including

Traditional	*Modern*
Canteen	Pitcher
Bird-form	Two-handled, or lugged, water jar
Jar with lid	Bowl with arched handle

TECHNOLOGY

As already indicated, this study is devoted primarily to the decorative arts of San Ildefonso pottery. Accordingly, it has seemed best to include here only a brief account of the various materials and processes involved in its production. For those particularly interested in more details, there is available an authoritative work covering every phase of the craft in minute detail.[5]

Certain basic ingredients and techniques are used alike for the five successive types of decorative pottery produced at San Ildefonso during the past two centuries, but in the finishing of each, special materials and processes are required. Therefore, such details are reserved for further consideration in the several chapters devoted to each specialized ware.

CLAY AND TEMPER

The clay, light greyish-red in color, is obtained from pits near the Pueblo and, before use, is dried, ground, and sifted to the consistency of coarse meal. Mixed with it is a powdered tempering material of fine, light-weight, greyish volcanic tuff, in the proportion of about one part temper to two parts clay. The mixture is moistened and well kneaded into a mass of even texture, of the required consistency for modeling.

MODELING

Seated upon the floor, before a low box or stand, the potter places upon it a crude, shallow pottery tray, which serves as a movable base to support the new vessel. Into this the potter sifts a little sand to prevent the moist clay from adhering to its surface. First, a flat disk of clay is fashioned between the palms and then patted into the tray, to form the base of the vessel.

Next, rolls of clay are added, one above another, each pressed firmly onto the one underneath. This produces a thick-walled vessel which is then modeled and thinned by scraping inside and out with a spatula of gourd rind, dipped frequently into water, as the wall is steadied by pressure of the fingers or palm of the left hand. Meanwhile, with the left hand, the tray is given frequent slight turns, usually counterclockwise, to ensure even treatment from start to finish of the circuit.

The modeling of a simple bowl form with outflaring sides is a comparatively easy process, but if coils are added to provide for higher side walls and a somewhat restricted mouth, the potter must use the spatula on the outside, and steady the side wall from the inside while it is drawn upward and inward to the mouth.

To model a water jar, it is necessary to use a special form of tray, provided with a central boss, to give shape to the essential cupped base of the vessel. The building up of the coils and the modeling with spatula and hand proceeds as with bowls, but with the addition of several coils in extending the walls upward and inward in forming the neck of the jar.

A special process is required in the modeling of vessels larger than the standard-sized food bowls and water jars. These require the use of a larger tray, placed on a much stronger box or directly on the floor in a position that enables the potter by frequent shifting of her position to work at her modeling on all sides. The weight of the heavier coils necessitates more frequent intervals of sufficient drying to support the succeeding coils and the stress of modeling and scraping as the work progresses. Thus, the buildup of a large storage jar may not be completed in a day's work. In such case the structure is wrapped with wet cloths to prevent drying and cracking.

Special skills are also required for other forms, such as canteens, small-mouthed bottles, double-necked jars, and the adding of handles to such forms, but these have been made so seldom for use in the Pueblo that they are not included in this account.

As a final step in the modeling, both bowls and jars must be set aside until the upper part has dried enough to remain firm while the potter finishes the rim of each with the moistened tips of thumb and two fingers.

SCRAPING

Next, the exterior surface of the thoroughly dried vessel is moistened slightly with a wet cloth to permit scraping with the rib of a sheep or deer, the dull edge of a kitchen knife, or any other convenient implement. This further reduces the thickness of the wall and produces a more even surface.

MOPPING AND SLIPPING

Following the scraping, the entire exterior surface is then mopped with a wet cloth to further smooth the surface by redistributing the moist surface clay and thus removing any marks of the scraper.

The vessel is now ready for application by mopping of a semiliquid slip of clay of the desired color, on which decoration may or may not be applied with a brush. Since the techniques of slipping and painting vary with the type of ware to be produced, these stages are discussed in more detail in the sections devoted to each specific ware.

DECORATING

Throughout nearly two centuries of developments in San Ildefonso pottery styles, the major production has been that of wares with painted decoration, for which certain native pigments have always been used.

Among these, one indispensable material called "guaco" is derived from the sap of the Rocky Mountain bee plant (*Peritoma serrulatum*). Gauco is prepared by boiling the bee plant's succulent leafy stems, which are gathered in early summer. The resulting liquid is evaporated to the consistency of a thick, brown syrup which, when thoroughly dried, resembles the black of stick licorice.

For use, fragments of the dried pigment are softened in warm water to the consistency of a light, clear, brownish liquid that will flow readily from the brush. In firing, the carbon content burns to a more or less dense black, but is at its best only if applied on slips of adsorptive clays such as bentonite.

Brushes are easily prepared from the small blade-like leaves of yucca (*yucca glauca*), or from the larger leaves split into two or more strips, varying from 1/4 to 1/2 inch in width. An inch or more of one end is chewed until the loosened pulp can be scraped away, exposing the long, stiff, thread-like fibers which serve as bristles. If all the fibers are not needed, some are cut away at each side, leaving enough to make a brush of the desired width. It is used principally as a striping brush for painting lines varying from 1/16 to 1/18 inch in width.

In early times, a short-handled brush was used. This was held between the tips of the thumb and two fingers, with the little finger resting upon and gliding over the surface of the vessel at each stroke. With the pulling motion, the fibers lie closely parallel for over half their length, thus producing lines of even width. For filling in spaces outlined with the striping brush, others with greater width and shorter fibers are used.

But with the opening of a Government day school at San Ildefonso in the 1890s, the younger generation had learned to use pencils and pens, and preferred to develop their own skills with long-handled brushes. With elbow resting against waist, the potter has great freedom of forearm and wrist in pulling the brush sidewise or toward himself at each stroke, or in swinging it into graceful curves.

The technical quality of Pueblo pottery design depends largely upon careful preparation and use of both pigments and brushes. The fluid must be free from dust and lint, so that it will flow freely from the brush without spreading in accidental blotches; and the brush must be well made and kept in good condition so that it will produce smooth lines of uniform width.

FIRING

To ensure the best results, the firing is done in early morning, when there is least chance of strong winds.

No permanent kiln is used. Instead, a preliminary fire of dry wood is made on the level site reserved for firing. While the live coals still give off considerable heat, an improvised iron grid is placed a few inches above them. The larger vessels are then set, inverted, upon the grid so closely that they may even touch one another, and smaller pieces are nested between and upon them.

The resulting mound is then covered with odd pieces of sheet iron. Next, a brisk fire is made by thrusting dry juniper sticks underneath the grid, and, as it begins to warm the pottery, thoroughly dried cakes of dung are placed carefully around and over the sheet iron, so closely adjoining that they serve as both fuel and kiln, for their inner surfaces soon ignite and reflect their heat into the pottery from all sides. Occasional chinking of spaces between the upper dung cakes serves to prevent uneven firing at any point, while the interspaces below provide sufficient updraught for a satisfactory oxidizing atmosphere.

The highest temperature attained by such simple firing techniques seldom exceeds 750° C.; and the duration of firing may vary between 25 and 50 minutes, according to the number and size of the vessels.

On completion of firing, the vessels may be lifted from the ashes while still hot, and placed nearby until cool enough to handle. They are then wiped with a dry and later a slightly greasy cloth to remove all ashes.

The resulting wares are thicker and softer than the harder fired products of the more western pueblos, and also lack their resonance. But they wear well in domestic use, and the porous jars in particular serve well in cooling water by evaporation.

The foregoing description refers to the firing of the white- or red-slipped vessels.

The black wares differ in their firing process in that in the last stage the fire is smothered with straw or powdered dung, excluding the oxygen and producing a dense smoke. This penetrates throughout the porous vessel, producing the dark brown or black color. Experience has shown that these vessels must not reach the high temperatures of the other wares if the most beautiful metallic black luster is to be obtained. Consequently, the black wares are particularly soft and porous and will indeed tend to decompose on prolonged contact with water. Use of such vessels as vases must therefore be preceded by a waterproofing by the purchaser, or else a waterproof insert vessel must be employed.

POTTERY DECORATION

Next to mural painting, an ancient Pueblo art made known by archaeologists in recent years,[6] the decoration of pottery is most closely allied with the fine arts, in that the potter has great freedom in choice and application of designs to the otherwise finished vessels she has produced.

Only in the ancient Pueblo craft of ceremonial embroidery (practiced, until recently, exclusively by men) does the artist also have freedom to develop designs on the finished product, but the coarse texture of Pueblo weaving limits the embroidered designs to those produced in rectilinear style. In contrast, the decorative designs of basketry and weaving are an integral part of the very structure and must partake of the technical limitations of the crafts themselves.

Yet with freedom from technical restraints, the Pueblo potter until recent years has been bound by tradition to a somewhat limited repertoire of design motifs, which have become the set style in her community. However, the revival of an occasional motif from ancient wares is countenanced and may come into common use. Only in rare instances has an individual braved the displeasure and even ridicule of her contemporaries by experimenting with any radical innovations in design.

Certain features of design layout show especially well the conservatism that persists in the decoration of pottery. In general, the major painted decoration appears upon the upper exterior zones of bowls and jars.

Except on the black wares, the decorated zone of bowls is in every instance bordered above by two parallel black lines (immediately below the red rim stripe) and below by another pair placed immediately above the red underbody band. In the decoration of bowls the enclosed space is always treated as a single zone.

In the decoration of water jars, however, the slipped area is rarely considered as a unit. Instead, a pair of lines usually divides the space into a neck and a body zone. For convenience the outer lines of a band are termed "framing lines," and the inner, "banding lines." Thus, where two bands adjoin, each of the intervening paired lines serves as a framing line for one band and as a banding line for the other. This applies also to the large storage jars, but in a few instances the wide slipped zone is divided into three or more bands.

Concerning the designs themselves, it is of interest to trace something of the history of interpretation. The earliest notice of Pueblo pottery decoration is that in Stevenson's description of 1879-80[7] in which he names and identifies the design elements of a few of his San Ildefonso specimens in geometric terms, such as dots, zigzags, crosses, and triangles, and as serpents, vines and leaves, and the spiny leaves of cacti. His designation of crossed lines as stars, however, may have derived from the potters themselves. During the two or more decades following, only the most casual bits of information and terminology were picked up by travelers, Indian Service officials, and dealers in Indian curios, none of which had ever been recorded.

Finally, in 1909 and 1910, Spinden,[8] with some of the older San Ildefonso potters as informants, made the first study of the meanings of motifs used mainly in the decoration of Black-on-cream ware, which by then had been almost superseded by the rise of Black-on-red and Polychrome.

This was followed in 1925 by Guthe,[9] whose thorough account of all phases of pottery making at San Ildefonso includes interpretations of designs which he had watched and timed through every stage of their development, from the first brush stroke to the finish. At that date the production was mainly of Polychrome ware, with a smaller output of Black-on-red and a still smaller representation of the newly invented Matte-on-polished ware which within a few years was to become the outstanding product of the Pueblo.

The San Ildefonso section of the study made a few years later by Bunzel,[10] records the almost complete disappearance of the Black-on-red and Polychrome wares, and a mass production of Matte-on-polished for which certain modifications of the old motifs, but bearing the old names, had been developed to conform with the technical requirements of the new ware.

In addition to these important records, there are available my unpublished notes on the terminology of the designs given by numerous potters, beginning in 1920. While these as a whole show a basic agreement in the naming of the twenty or more motifs most frequently used, they reveal occasional instances of disagreements among the potters, and more rarely a discrepancy in the naming of a motif on two different occasions by the same potter.

The reader will notice the avoidance of the term "symbol" in descriptions of the many decorative devices used in San Ildefonso ceramic design. Various opinions have been expressed by anthropologists regarding the loose application of the term for this purpose. However, if we accept the basic requirement that a symbol must represent clearly an idea commonly understood by the culture in which it is used, there are at least two motifs in San Ildefonso design, the meaning of which would be understood throughout the entire pueblo area.

First among them would be the semicircular device called "cloud," whether used singly, in rows, or in banks of two or more rows. These, in Pueblo lore, express not merely the ever-changing aspects of clouds as features of a landscape, but denote entities of great ritual importance, as givers of rain in a semiarid land.

Second would be the stylistic forms of feathers, for though they are not easily recognizable as such, they denote the real feathers used in various ways to express concern of the people for favors from the sky powers which they say, in ancient times, was effected by use of birds themselves, liberated to bear their prayers aloft.

One other device, more abstract in nature, is the so-called line-break[11] which has survived through a thousand years of use in border bands of pottery decoration. But while it has been a concept of considerable importance in the past to the potters themselves, there was apparently no common agreement throughout the Southwest as to its significance. During the past fifty years the potters of most pueblos have made little use of the device; and at San Ildefonso particularly it is now disregarded.

During the preparation of this book, several problems arose in copying the designs of various vessel forms.

The exterior bands of bowls can be drawn without noticeable distortion at the upper and lower margins, but the interior designs of bowls with nearly upright sides must be expanded so as to include border lines and motifs which usually are placed only slightly below the rim.

In copying the neck and body bands of jars, there is little distortion, for the upper and lower margins are nearly equal in circumference. But shoulder bands cannot be represented in straight projections without considerable distortion, due to the great variance between circumference at the upper and lower margins. For these the most satisfactory solution is produced by making a tracing of the design, which when laid flat results in a collar-like projection. Such drawings, however, cannot be grouped closely, and therefore have been used only sparingly throughout this work.

No consistent scale of reduction could be maintained in preparing the drawings of uniform width, as used in most of the plates, for the vessels from which they were taken vary considerably in size. In addition, several drawings from specimens no longer available are copied from sketches made without notes as to size. In general, however, the drawings as reproduced may be considered to average between one-third and one-fifth natural size. Three repeats of identical units of design are used in most of the drawings, but where there is an alternation of motifs, for economy of space the combination is usually represented by one major between two minors.

Extremes of careless layouts, particularly of banding lines, encountered in some of the designs have been avoided, for they appear more exaggerated in a flat extended drawing than on the vessel itself, where they are minimized by their relation to the contours of the convex surface on which they are placed. It must be remembered, also, that the rightful place of Pueblo pottery in actual home use was often on the floor where any erratic layout of bands, from rim to base, is even more obscured.

SAN ILDEFONSO POTTERY COUNTS

To show something of the available material for study, I have included a census of San Ildefonso decorated pottery in museums and private collections, as of 1957.

	FOOD BOWLS	UTILITY BOWLS	WATER JARS	STORAGE JARS	CERE-MONIAL	MISCEL-LANEOUS	TOTAL
Black-on-cream	4	13	66	68	14	1	166
Black-on-red	30	4	118	10	3	4	169
Polychrome	101	19	285	36	40	29	510
Polished antique		1	2				3
Polished modern, plain	9		9				18
Polished matte, painted	12		14	2			28
carved:							
Intaglio	2						2
Cameos	5						5
Total	163	37	494	116	57	34	901

In no instance does the total for each pottery form indicate its relative abundance in domestic use. Thus, the disparity in the number of food bowls as compared with water jars of the first two wares, and particularly of the Black-on-cream, is no doubt due to lack of interest of early collectors in the simple forms of food bowls, with their scanty decoration confined to narrow bands, and to the fact that they were usually used until broken.

On the other hand, storage jars, despite their greater size and the difficulty of transportation, have been most favored by collectors, and are well represented in museums from coast to coast. In most cases their long survival was assured by protection in out-of-the-way back rooms.

One noticeable feature in the 1957 tabulation is the relatively small proportion of the late polished wares in museum collections as compared with that of the Black-on-cream, Black-on-red, and Polychrome wares. The poor representation is due, apparently, to the indifference of museums to acquiring more than a small representative group of contemporaneous wares that are still being produced in considerable quantities. However, with the addition of photographs and other data in the collection of the Indian Arts Fund, the total of the polished wares now available for design study is well over one hundred.

IDENTIFICATION OF SAN ILDEFONSO POTTERY MAKERS

The scanty records of San Ildefonso pottery acquired by most museums during the past fifty years or more give little or no information regarding the makers of the Black-on-cream, Black-on-red, and Polychrome wares.

In questioning the potters of the past generation regarding the early Black-on-cream ware, it was evident that they could not distinguish between the owners and the makers, even of those specimens once used by their grandmothers. Furthermore, in sifting information from several pages of notes on tests given in the 1930s at the Laboratory of Anthropology to the best-informed potters, individually and in groups, considerable variation was found even in their designation of the makers of the later Polychrome ware, though such pieces had been produced by contemporaries of their mothers.

In more recent years, studies of the hundreds of specimens of each type and period do reveal at least certain traits of form and decoration pointing to the work of individual potters, most of whom must remain unknown. Instances of such individual production are mentioned in certain of the plate descriptions. In a few cases, however, we have a clear record of the work of well-known and prolific potters who have not only created individual styles but have also signed their own wares.

In studying both ancient and recent pottery, we find indications of possible cooperation between Pueblo pottery maker and decorator. These may show, for example, excellent control of modeling and finishing, but bear decorations of the utmost crudity. And, less frequently, we find crudely modeled vessels decorated with admirable freedom and skill. Examples of each are cited in the following descriptions of the several wares of San Ildefonso.

CONDITION OF OLD POTTERY

It is difficult to explain the harmony produced by long use of Pueblo pottery by which even crudities of modeling and decoration, so apparent in new and unused pieces, are somehow softened by handling — often by many years of daily use.

The result is an unforeseen integrity — an added harmony of form, color, and finish impossible to achieve through the work of the potter herself — that appeals at first sight and handling not only to the antiquarian but to novices as well.

Familiarity with such venerable specimens is apt to engender a scornful appraisal of rare specimens of equal age that have not been subjected to daily use. Yet they are of particular value for comparison with unused specimens of more recent times.

Our knowledge of the older pottery of San Ildefonso would be even less complete than it is, were it not for the survival of numerous specimens, worn through at the base or fractured, that had been repaired and relegated to occasional use as receptacles for the storage of dry materials. Though it was difficult to repair a fracture or to fill in a break in a water jar so that there would be no seepage, several specimens show the successful use of piñon pitch for that purpose. A bowl or jar, if fractured, could be given further use as a container for dry materials by shrinking a band of rawhide around its rim or, if further reinforcement were needed, by applying a lacing of rawhide extending from rim to base. More than one specimen has a single sheet of rawhide completely enfolding its base and held in place by a lacing from above. In several instances the reinforcing material shows the wear of long use, thus appearing to have become almost an integral part of the vessel itself.

CHAPTER III

San Ildefonso Culinary Ware

OF ALL THE WARES produced at San Ildefonso, the culinary types, from earliest to late, have shown the least variation in form. With utility as the prime consideration, the cooking pots, bowls, and pitchers have been of simple contours best adapted for use over an open fire.

During the past fifty years the use of culinary wares has declined in all the pueblos. According to the Tewa potters, there are no distinguishing characteristics of materials, forms, and finish by which the work of each village can be identified, for there was frequent trading among themselves and also with the neighboring Tiwas and even the more distant Keres. Specimens in museum collections are labeled according to the pueblo where acquired, but none of those bought at San Ildefonso can be traced definitely to their makers.

Because of the emphasis in this book on the decorated wares, only a very brief account is presented of the relatively plain and utilitarian culinary vessels.

The proportions of tempers in the culinary ware of San Ildefonso have varied with their use by individual potters. At all times the material has been coarse sand or crushed rock, contrasting considerably with the micaceous clay used by the neighboring Tiwa pueblos of Taos and Picuris. In mimicry of the glittery effect achieved by these neighbors, however, the San Ildefonso potters gradually began to add a micaceous slip to their culinary wares, using imported material from the Tiwa pueblos. Rarely, the Tewa potters may actually have used imported Tiwa clay, giving a completely micaceous paste.

Modeling is as described in the previous chapter, but the base and walls of jars are made somewhat thinner than those of the decorated wares. This is done to produce more rapid and efficient heating of the contents, even though it renders the vessels more fragile. The surface is scraped (to remove irregularities in thickness) and is then given the usual mopping to further smooth the rough surface. If micaceous slip is applied, the glistening mica flakes float to the surface and are pressed flat against it.

The procedures of firing also are covered in the previous chapter. If great care is taken to prevent smudging, the finished vessels will retain the sparkling yellowish tone of the micaceous slip, but in most pieces contact with the fuel has produced smudge spots varying from light grey to dense black. Some potters purposely smudge their ware to provide an even, dark tone. But with continued use over open fires, even the vessels of the clearest yellow are soon blackened.

CHAPTER IV

San Ildefonso Black-on-Cream

TO THOSE UNFAMILIAR with more recent trends, it might seem as if a definite date could be assigned to the inception of San Ildefonso Black-on-cream (now known as Powhoge Polychrome). But very little information could be obtained. Although the oldest and best informed among the residents remember certain antique specimens as having been among the possessions of their grandmothers, they have not been able to tell when or by whom they were made. Thus, the information from such sources does not carry back much further than the 1850s.

Since no information regarding the period of this notable development in form and decoration could be had from the Tewa pueblos, the closest approximation is that derived from excavations at the more remote site of Pecos.[12] A once populous Pueblo, Pecos was gradually depleted and completely abandoned in 1838. While the major study was confined to earlier phases of the Pueblo's occupation, from A.D. 600 to 1600, exploratory excavations were also made in a portion of the site known to have housed the last of the population. These excavations revealed a considerable dependence upon pottery wares from the Tewa area, among which those from San Ildefonso were well represented. Thus, the existence of their well-established Black-on-cream ware before 1838 is now confirmed. Indeed, its origin may have been considerably earlier than the conservative date of 1800, as used in this study.

Of all the pottery forms produced in Black-on-cream times, the large storage jars, made solely for the hoarding of food, were the least subject to breakage. While the typical water jars were carried almost daily to and from the source of water, the larger jars remained undisturbed in seldom-used storage rooms or in little-used corners of living quarters where they were kept carefully covered. For this reason storage jars as a class are considerably more abundant than the smaller forms. It seems best, therefore, to base our study of the Black-on-cream ware on a detailed examination of the characteristics of the storage jars alone.

The place of origin of the large storage jars is unknown, for as yet no evidence can be had to fix their earliest use in any pueblo, but certainly they have had their greatest development and reached their maximum size among the pueblos of the Tewa and Keres groups in the Rio Grande area.

We have yet to learn just what economic factors led to the adoption of the large storage jars. While the more settled conditions and greater security of the 1800s may have prompted their spread, it is likely that the successful experiments of one inventive potter in molding increasingly larger forms may have served to set the fashion, which would soon have spread from pueblo to pueblo.

Whatever their origin, the storage jars of San Ildefonso grew in size with repeated experiments until the prevailing form reached a capacity of fifteen to twenty gallons. It is quite possible that only a few of the San Ildefonso potters took part at any time in the making of such large vessels; and that, having acquired a skill for such specialized work, they found no trouble in disposing of their product in their own or neighboring Tewa pueblos.

Whether the makers were many or few, their adherence to certain definitely localized concepts of form and design has served to distinguish the San Ildefonso product from that of the contemporary potters of Tesuque or of the Keres pueblos of Cochiti and Santo Domingo.

The forms of most storage jars are similar to those of the much smaller water jars, but with the omission of the cupped base which served no purpose in the larger vessels. Instead, the bottoms are heavily modeled to withstand the extra weight of the jar and its contents when filled. As with the water jars, there is considerable variation in the relative height and width and breadth of mouth and body of the storage jars.

Since the production of large storage vessels apparently was undertaken by only a few potters, the choice of motifs led to a design system unlike that of the smaller forms of food bowls and water jars. In adapting the familiar motifs to the much larger surfaces of storage jars, the potters were obliged to choose between two modes: either to enlarge the familiar motifs, or to use combinations of two or more repeated or unrelated motifs of ordinary size in place of one motif. In most instances they chose the latter. In the entire group there is only one outstanding example of the enlargement of the chosen motif.

The cream-slipped decorative zone is in every instance bordered by the paired banding and framing lines above and below. Not one specimen of Black-on-cream ware has been found in which detached motifs are placed freely on an unbordered zone. Even in bordered zones, detached motifs are rare. In a few instances, particularly in narrow neck or body bands, a repetition of free units provides the dominant or sole decoration of the band. More rarely a well-planned arrangement calls for the use of two or more free units in regular alternation. In some instances, also, a single minor motif is used to fill a gap left by careless planning of the major features. But altogether, in the 133 band designs in the first eight of the 174 plates in this book, only 11 percent have detached motifs in unpaneled bands, while in only 4 percent are they used in alternation with attached motifs.

Considering the ease with which decorative details of other pueblos might have been worked into the design system of San Ildefonso, there is but little evidence of such borrowing, even though there has been intermarriage and exchange of pottery as gifts with the neighboring Tewa pueblos and the Keres pueblos of Cochiti and Santo Domingo. A few such innovations are mentioned in the plate descriptions of the several San Ildefonso wares.

A common design feature of San Ildefonso Black-on-cream is the use of abstract geometric designs of unknown origin. (The term "abstract" is not intended to imply that geometric motifs were not given names by the ancient potters. Considering the interval of two centuries or more of their disuse, however, it is doubtful that any consistent terminology was handed down to the potters of the Black-on-cream period.) Several comparatively simple abstract-geometric motifs appear in the decoration of early prehistoric pottery wares from the western parts of the Anasazi region, and later a few such motifs were sparingly used in Santa Fe Black-on-white ware of the Tewa area. But with the decline of the Santa Fe type, the makers of four successive prehistoric wares, in turn, had developed distinctive decorative schemes in which such ancient geometric motifs were seldom included.

Thus, after a lapse of more than two centuries, it is difficult to account for the revival of the old geometric system in an early stage of Black-on-cream ware. And, to date, there is no positive evidence of its having been derived (as some believe) directly from any of the decorative arts of the Spanish invaders, whether in ceramics, metal, leather, textiles, or mural decorations of the early missions.

A variant of the typical storage jar is the large, wide-mouthed jar. While these are now considered to be more typical of Tesuque than of San Ildefonso, their description is quite pertinent to the discussion.

Only seven specimens of this type are known. All are comparatively low and squat in appearance, the average height being only 73 percent of the maximum diameter, as compared with 83 percent for the lowest of the normal form of storage jar.

Six specimens are fairly uniform in the proportionate width of mouth, approximately 70 percent of the maximum diameter, as compared with 46 percent for the normal, taller form of storage jar.

The one remaining specimen is unique in that its proportionate width of mouth is even much greater (76 percent) than in the average of the six above. In this respect it approaches nearly the proportions of the average large utility bowl, but its decorative scheme allies it more closely with the group of wide-mouthed jars.

A narrow neck band of simple design appears in the decoration of each of the seven specimens. The wide body band in every case is paneled, but three widely divergent ideas appear in the use of the device.

In three specimens, the band is divided into numerous panels, each housing a conventional group of feathers upon the apex of a triangle. In two, their arrangement is upright; in the third it is placed sidewise. The similarity of form and decorative treatment of this group mark them as the apparent production of one potter. In the fourth, the body band is divided into panels. The decorative treatment, repeated without variation in the panels, resembles in this respect that of the three just described.

Two other specimens are quite unlike the foregoing in the layout of the panels. They resemble each other in the use of only two paneling devices that divide the body band into elongate spaces, in which appear many of the motifs and arrangements common to the panels of the normal form of storage jars. In each specimen the treatment of the two panels is identical.

The decoration of the seventh specimen is quite unlike that of the preceding groups. Two narrow panels, on opposite sides of the jar, are flanked at right and left by D-forms bearing various decorative devices. Alternating with these arrangements are paired oblique paneling lines with separations similar to those used on jars of normal form.

It is not certain that any one of these remarkable wide-mouthed vessels is from San Ildefonso; all may have been made at Tesuque.

CHAPTER V

San Ildefonso Black-on-Red

DURING THE LONG PERIOD in which Black-on-cream ware was still the sole type of decorated pottery at San Ildefonso, experiments had been made by one or more of the potters with the use of a red slip in place of the usual cream. The exact date of the innovation cannot be determined. There is no evidence that the new ware reached Pecos in trade before the abandonment of the Pueblo in 1838,[13] and there is no mention of it in print prior to the visit of Stevenson to the Southwest in 1879-82.

In his report on pottery vessels collected at San Ildefonso in 1880, Stevenson lists seven specimens of "Red ware with decorations in black."[14] Not one of those is illustrated. But among nineteen pieces of various wares collected during the same season at Taos, he shows in figure 714 a San Ildefonso kiva bowl with black decorations inside and out. Regarding this specimen he says, "The outside is red but the inside is painted white; ornamentation in black."[15]

Since that period no additional information has been obtained regarding the advent of the new type, nor of the personnel involved. Therefore, in lack of a more definite chronology, it seems best to assign a tentative date of 1850 for the origin of San Ildefonso Black-on-red ware. That it was the product of potters familar with the modeling and decorating of the then standard Black-on-cream is confirmed by comparison of the forms and decorative motifs of the two wares which for perhaps a half-century were used side-by-side in the homes of San Ildefonso.

Only one new feature was involved with the production of Black-on-red, but this was more complex than the mere substitution of red slip for cream. Apparently the potters found that the surface of their red clay in its pure state, when compressed by stone polishing, became so glossy and repellent that it produced a poor bond between the slip and the black from guaco paint used in its decoration.

The difficulty was overcome by adding a small quantity of less dense cream slip to the pure red clay, together with an admixture of finely pulverized volcanic ash.[16] These two ingredients so counteracted the density of the red slip that, no matter how long and vigorously it was stone-rubbed, it retained a satiny semi-matte smoothness that absorbed and held the guaco paint well in the firing, thus usually producing black designs as dense as those on the best of Black-on-cream ware.

At most, the new ware seems to have comprised only a minor part of the total production of the early potters, but during later years there was apparently some individual specialization in the Black-on-red. At least one potter, Domingita Peña Martinez, was working exclusively with the new style and continued with a considerable production until the early 1920s. From then on, her daughter, Toñita Martinez Roybal, who had included a fair share of the new style in her own output, responded to the increasing demands of dealers and collectors and made Black-on-red her principal production for several years.

CHAPTER VI

San Ildefonso Polychrome

DEFINITION

THE TERM "POLYCHROME" as used in ceramics is generally understood to include all wares in which more than two colors appear, including slip, painted decoration, and even the color of a purposely exposed surface of the unslipped body clay.

To conform with this definition, the preceding Black-on-cream and Black-on-red wares rightly would be termed "polychrome" for they include the various tones of body clay, cream or red slip, dark red underbody band, red or black polished lip, and decoration in black. But for this study, based primarily upon painted pottery decoration, the term is reserved for only one San Ildefonso ware, upon which designs in both black and red are applied by brush.

ORIGIN

Apparently the originators of Polychrome ware had been familiar with use of the well-tested materials and techniques of the preceding Black-on-cream and Black-on-red wares. Also, mindful of the limitations of their clay, they had held to the comparatively low firing temperatures favored by their ancestors, for they were well aware of the injurious effects of overfiring.

The first experiments with the use of red with black may have begun as early as 1875. However, no examples were acquired by Stevenson in his collecting of 1879-80,[17] and no information on this point has been received from the descendants of the potters of that period. But certainly by the late 1880s Polychrome had begun to displace the long-lived Black-on-cream and by 1900 had become the dominant ware of San Ildefonso.

One great incentive for the production of attractive Polychrome pottery was the arrival of the railroad in 1882 and with it the sudden development of tourist travel to and from California. The newly developed tourist trade called for great quantities of pottery trinkets. But, if we may judge by the dearth of standard-sized pieces of that period in the collections of eastern museums, little encouragement was given the potters for increasing production of their best full-sized wares.

Between 1880 and 1900, with the development of San Ildefonso Polychrome, there was some increase in sales of larger and better-made pieces by the shops in Santa Fe, so that some of the San Ildefonso potters could make and sell more of this type of ware.

Often the Santa Fe dealers would make an offer for a wagonload of pots in exchange for merchandise; selecting the more salable pieces and then destroying the remainder.

Conditions improved somewhat by the turn of the century, but not until 1911 were a few of the San Ildefonso potters given an opportunity to demonstrate their craft at the Museum of New Mexico and to sell directly to residents and tourists who showed their appreciation of superior form and finish. Still later, with added experience gained at expositions, several of the potters were assured of a steady demand for their best products.

FORMS

The simple forms of Black-on-cream and Black-on-red were continued for some time in Polychrome ware, but with the rise of a younger generation of potters there came a tendency toward innovations, particularly noticeable in the proportions of water jars through elongation of the neck with a lowering and widening of the body. This graceful form was an adaptation of the style of nearly two centuries earlier, a form which had been perpetuated at nearby Santa Clara Pueblo.

FINISH

As with Black-on-cream ware the native cream slip also provided the background for early Polychrome decoration, despite the fact that it required vigorous polishing to render the surface fit for application of the designs. This fine finish continued until about 1905. At that time it was discovered that the slip of Cochiti and Santo Domingo required much less labor to finish, and much of this material, a bentonite-like clay, was acquired in trade from these Keres pueblos. It requires only a minimum of rubbing with a cotton cloth immediately after the last of several applications of the slip has been mopped onto the vessel. At San Ildefonso, Cochiti slip never was properly used, always looking grainy, streaked, and often dull grey. The dark red underbody band was retained. As a final touch, the lip of the vessel was finished with the usual polished red or, after about 1910, with black.

DECORATION

It is apparent that the use of red in painted decoration involved considerable experimenting before the potters reached some agreement regarding its relation with the design structure developed in black. From a study of the earliest examples available, it is evident that one or more potters had approached the problem by cautious applications of red in the form of dots, lines, and other minor, separate details. Others, perhaps with opportunities to see or hear of the Polychrome wares of the more western pueblos, had begun experiments with the use of red as a filler of spaces already outlined with black. The new technique required greater care than with the use of black alone, for considerable skill was required to paint such spaces without leaving gaps between red filler and black outlines, or without overlapping the lines.

DECORATIVE MOTIFS

The decorative motifs of the early phase are largely identical with those of late Black-on-cream, showing the inclination of the old potters to hold closely to their accustomed repertoire. But as time passed, in addition to a few new motifs there came modifications by the younger potters through new arrangements and more complex sequences within bands, made possible by the use of two colors: as, for instance, a regular repetition of motifs, but with an alternation of red and black in their details.

This marked complexity is shown clearly by the increased number of drawings required to include all the commonly used variations in early-to-late arrangements, as compared with those of the two preceding wares. Much more of the decorative styles is shown in detail in the drawings.

ROSTER OF POTTERS

True to the pre-literate custom of all peoples, and shared by the Tewa, the unwritten lore of San Ildefonso includes no mention of renowned warriors or traditional heroes, no famed philosophers, no wise counselors. Nothing is known of the ancient composers of ceremonial chants still in use. And, more to the point in a study of this nature, there are unfortunately no legends of outstanding artists and crafts workers, even though scattered examples of their work may have been treasured at the Pueblo.

Therefore, the only written accounts of the personnel of San Ildefonso for the past two centuries are those in the archives of the Catholic diocese of Santa Fe, recording births and christenings at the Pueblo. But even here, there is a confusion of family names because of the inclusion of several Spanish-American families who for a century or more have had rightful claims on land within the San Ildefonso grant. Thus, even the best informants of today would have some difficulty in determining which group may have welcomed as its own one such as "Luisa Montoya, baptized March 11th, 1823, six days after birth. Daughter of Juan Montoya and Carmelita Pino de Montoya."

Even so, some information regarding the potters and their wares of a hundred years ago might have been acquired as late as 1900. But since this study was not begun until 1920, the earliest of those then mentioned by name were born after 1850.

A list of the potters of that period whose work has been identified by the most reliable informants includes the following, recorded by birth dates:

Toñia Peña Vigil,* 1855; Martina Vigil Montoya* (Mrs. Florentino Montoya), 1856; Marianita, 1858; Domingita Peña Martinez (specialized in Black-on-red pottery), 1860; Nicolasa Peña* (Maria Martinez' aunt), 1863; Susana (Mrs. Ignacio Aguilar), 1868; Santana, 1873. [*Active potters until about 1915.]

Cipriana Martinez, 1881; Dolorita Vigil, 1883; Maximiliana Montoya Martinez** (wife of Crescencio Martinez), 1885; Ramona Sanchez Gonzales, 1886; Maria Montoya Martinez** (wife of Julian Martinez), 1887; Desideria Montoya Sanchez,** 1889; Toñita Martinez Roybal (daughter of Domingita Peña Martinez and wife of Juan Cruz Roybal), 1892. [**Sisters.]

The list should include also, among men, four gifted pottery decorators: Florentino Montoya, 1858; Crescencio Martinez, 1879; Julian Martinez, 1885; and Juan Cruz Roybal, about 1887.

It is pertinent to note here that no credit had been given to these early decorators of the Polychrome period, a condition that persisted until the ascendancy of the polished wares in the early 1920s.

It was then, at the author's suggestion, that these men were first given credit for their share in perfecting the wares of their wives, for this enabled the potters to concentrate on improving their modeling and finishing techniques. Thereafter, beginning with Maria and Julian, each couple signed their wares as a team.

As an example of the history of one husband-and-wife team, I have chosen the earliest for which data are available, Florentino and Martina Montoya. Their pottery was already well known prior to 1900 because of Martina's skill in modeling and, in later years, because of the growing importance of Florentino's work in decorating her wares.

Martina is said to have been unusually free to concentrate upon her craft, for though she bore many children, most of them died in infancy and only one, a son, reached maturity. Thus, as the demand for her pottery increased, she could devote more of her time particularly to perfecting her modeling and finishing. By then, Florentino had apparently taken over full responsibility for the decoration.

Florentino's interest and skill with ceramic decoration began with his occasional assistance in painting the pottery of Martina's mother, before Martina had developed her own craft. As his interest increased, he devised many variants of the old San Ildefonso motifs. In their later years an unusual circumstance led to a complete change in their base of operations. Martina was a daughter of Juan Arguero (later changed by parish priest to Vigil) of the Keres pueblo of Cochiti. He settled in San Ildefonso, married, and reared a family of four who, by Pueblo custom, learned in early childhood that they must divide their allegiance between the two pueblos.

Thus, on several occasions Martina and Florentino made visits to Cochiti. Florentino's prominence in the ceremonial life of San Ildefonso gave him entrée into the circle at Cochiti, and there he is known to have taken part in the winter ceremonies of the Hunt Society.

Eventually, between 1902 and 1905, Martina and Florentino were invited to make their home in Cochiti. There they continued their craft under circumstances that have long confused the ceramic experts. Martina was forced to adapt her techniques to Cochiti clay and slip and consequent polishing and firing methods. She retained her preference for her own San Ildefonso forms and finishes, however, and Florentino continued to apply his well-developed system of San Ildefonso decoration.

As a result, many specimens of their pottery of that period, acquired by collectors, now appear in museums, bearing the label "Cochiti." And who is to say they are not? Before their activities ended with the death of Martina in 1916, they had made many good-sized tinajóns, or storage jars, including a superb pair in Polychrome style now in the collection of the Indian Arts Fund. But unfortunately, Martina's firing technique was not adequate for such large containers. Several specimens found in use at Cochiti had developed cracks at rim and base. In such cases the usefulness of the jar had been prolonged only by lacing with rawhide.

In his stay of more than ten years at Cochiti, Florentino made no use of the decorative system of that Pueblo. At some time during that period, however, he adapted several minor design traits from the pottery of Zia Pueblo, which appeared as accessories of some of his best examples of pure San Ildefonso design. In only one instance, did Florentino adapt a complete Zia design for use on one of Martina's storage jars.

Just about the time of the Montoyas' stay at Cochiti, the San Ildefonso potters all began using Cochiti slip on their Polychrome vessels instead of the old stone-polished native slip.

Another of the pioneering men who decorated pottery is Crescencio Martinez. He was one of the first of a group of younger men who, as early as 1910, had found time and inclination to take part in the decoration of the pottery produced by members of their own families. Crescencio is said to have begun his work under the guidance of his mother, Domingita, who had specialized in production of Black-on-red ware. In later years he also gained further experience with design in decorating the pottery produced by his wife, Maximiliana Montoya, and also that of his sister, Toñita Martinez Roybal. Although Crescencio is mentioned by several potters as the leader in this participation of men in ceramic decoration, he seems never to have developed a distinctive style, such as that of Florentino Montoya. However, as the first among the young men of San Ildefonso to enter into the production of watercolor paintings of ceremonial dances, Crescencio's work had received much encouragement before his untimely death during the influenza epidemic of 1918.

The next active couple, Julian and Maria Martinez, are the most famous. Their activities have been discussed in a separate book, *María: The Potter of San Ildefonso*, and are not described here.

CHAPTER VII

Reminiscence: Development of San Ildefonso Polychrome

WITH THE ENTRY of the United States into World War I in 1917, tourist travel to the pueblos decreased and pottery sales went into a temporary decline. One favorable development, however, came about at this time through the arrival of Mme. Verra von Blumenthal and Miss Rose Dougan from Pasadena. Their purpose was to develop production of a better grade of ceramics at San Ildefonso that could be sold in greater quantity throughout the country. The two women built a summer home and quarters for workers at the foot of Tsankawi Mesa, some eight miles from the Pueblo, where they came each summer to supervise the production of two or more selected potters. (The ruins of their old home is now known as the Duchess's Castle, a local tourist attraction.)

Within three years the ladies found that their experiments of only two or three months each summer with only a few potters had made but little impression on production at San Ildefonso, and concluded that it would require more constant contacts and supervision than they could provide. Therefore, in 1919, at the close of a more extended stay, in conference with Dr. Edgar L. Hewett, Director of the School of American Research, they offered to turn over their work to the School and to provide an initial sum of $200 for a year's supervision of the project.

Dr. Hewett accepted the offer and appointed two members of the School's staff, Wesley Bradfield and myself, to work out the details of operation with the donors. The project, as developed by Mme. von Blumenthal, followed one carried on by her for many years in prewar Russia where she had developed a profitable business by reviving and improving the quality of lace work in village after village of Russian peasants. The requirements of the project were extremely simple. The proposed formula for the Pueblo potters was as follows:

1. Inviting the potters to submit their wares to us at the Museum before offering them for sale elsewhere.
2. Asking each potter to set her price, piece by piece.
3. Selecting a few outstanding pieces, if any, and explaining why they were chosen (for form, finish, decoration, etc.).
4. Adding at least 25 percent to the price named by the potter for those selected, and promising still higher prices for further improvements.
5. Explaining that selected pieces would be sold at the Museum at a markup sufficient only to repay the school for time devoted to the project by Bradfield and me.

We realized from the start that point 5 would be initiating a sales policy that might conflict with the interests of the dealers in Indian crafts who, as taxpayers, could rightly object to the program which required use of the facilities of the State Museum — a tax-supported institution.

As the program got under way, this situation did develop and eventually the sales feature of the project was abandoned. But in the meantime the project realized its main objective: the potters were in a position to demand more satisfactory prices from dealers for their attractive wares.

I have no record accounting for the expenditure of the initial and only appropriation of $200 for the work. But, as I recall, the greater part of the fund was used to purchase pottery during the early months of 1920, before the opening of the tourist season. Some of the pottery was disposed of at cost to visiting museum officials, but most of it was sold at some profit to summer tourists by Olive Wilson, then curator of the Art Museum, where the collection was stored.

As for field work, neither Bradfield nor I could have been spared from our duties at the Museum for lengthy absences, and even if that had been permitted, the difficulties of travel in mid-winter would have made such expeditions inconvenient and even hazardous. For that was before the era of improved roads and motor travel. True, there was daily train service on the Denver and Rio Grande narrow-gauge railroad to the north, but its nearest stops, marked only by signposts, were at least three miles from any of the Tewa pueblos. And train schedules were extremely haphazard, as I had learned a few years before.

I had had one mid-winter experience when, after an errand at San Ildefonso, I walked back to the railroad bridge and waited in mid-afternoon for a belated train to Santa Fe. With snow on the ground, I hovered over my little fire on the river bank until the train's welcome arrival at ten minutes before midnight! Naturally, I was not taking any further chances.

The potters from the Tewa pueblos were still using farm wagons and seldom made the trip to Santa Fe during the winter. At that time the Museum had not yet acquired its first Model T Ford. Everything considered, it seemed best to defer a tryout of our project until early summer. Bradfield and I gave it no further thought until a few weeks later when, to our surprise, Julian and Maria Martinez of San Ildefonso, appeared with a wagonload of their pottery.

Here was an unexpected problem. They were the last we would have picked for our experiment, for they were accomplished crafts workers who might resent our suggestions for improvement of their wares. However, we knew that they were forced to limit the time expended on each piece, for they had learned that the dealers would not pay higher prices for a more finished product. So, in hopes of finding one or more outstanding pieces in the lot, we decided to test our plan. It worked wonders!

We set aside four unusually well-formed and finished pieces and asked their prices. Then we commended the couple for the attractive qualities of their pottery and paid 25

percent more than they had asked. That concluded, we told them of our plan and prom-
ised even more for others in their next lot if they showed further improvement. Considerable time elapsed before we found an opportunity to extend our contacts. It so happened
that another San Ildefonso potter, Toñita Roybal, was the next to benefit by the project.

I met Toñita near the Museum as she was returning from a house-to-house tour of
several blocks, carrying two pieces of her pottery and discouraged over her inability to
sell them. One water jar showed promise; so after praising it, in Brad's absence I raised
her price by 50 percent and asked her to give even more time and thought to her next
lot. Toñita had inherited the Black-on-red style from her mother. I advised her to spe-
cialize with that. The result was that within a few months she was finding a ready sale
at three times the price of her former work.

That was enough to set things moving in San Ildefonso. The news soon reached every
potter in the Pueblo. Still, no facilities were afforded to Bradfield and myself to visit
the other Tewa pueblos. Only through chance meetings with potters from San Juan and
Tesuque was some slight improvement effected. As for the more distant Cochiti and Santo
Domingo pueblos, contacts with their potters, even in Santa Fe, were next to impossible.
Not until the first annual Santa Fe Indian Fair in 1923 did we find an opportunity to do
some further missionary work. The Indian Fair, by the way, was set in motion by a
generous initial contribution from Rose Dougan.

One incident of that first Annual Fair is worth mentioning here. Shortly before the
opening hour, Dr. Hewett, who had been giving the displays a hurried inspection, came
to me and said, "Chap, some of the pottery prices are getting out of hand. Toñita Roybal
has an ordinary size bowl priced at $12. You ought to do something about it!" I reminded
Dr. Hewett that the San Ildefonso potters had come a long way since he gave them their
first encouragement, and that they knew a lot more about selling than any of us. Then I
asked, "Do you know any better way for them to find what the buyers will pay?" He had
no ready answer.

I had admired the bowl, a little gem. Within a half hour after the doors were opened
I took the first chance to listen for comments on it, but was delighted to find that its
tag had already been marked "SOLD." That meant that the price, plus the Fair's 10 percent handling charge, came to a total of $13.20.

Shortly afterwards, with the improvement of highways and the building of a bridge
across the Rio Grande two miles from San Ildefonso, tourist traffic was directed toward
their Pueblo. From then on, the potters, particularly at San Ildefonso, were kept busy
supplying visitors who enjoyed the privilege of buying directly from the makers. So,
after a century or more as the most isolated of the Tewa pueblos, San Ildefonso finally
came into the limelight as the most progressive arts and crafts center among the Rio
Grande pueblos. By that time the watercolor paintings by their young men had also
gained national recognition.

During the 1930s, while I was devoting part time to field work as a consultant of the
U.S. Indian Service, Chester Faris, who was then Superintendent of the Northern Pueblos,

came to me with what, on the surface, seemed to be a most reasonable proposition. He was familiar with the success of Brad's and my initiative at San Ildefonso and so he began:

> You know the Rio Grande Pueblos as well and perhaps better than I do, and I am sure that you are aware particularly of the sad plight of Cochiti — away off on a side road, and dependent mostly on their farming. There are a few good potters there but their wares are made mostly for home use, for the nearest traders at Domingo find that it has little tourist appeal. Why can't you do for them what you have done for San Ildefonso?

I had never thought of listing the factors favoring that Pueblo in the order of their importance, but in our discussion I felt safe in saying that fully 75 percent of all purchases of Indian crafts were by women; and for Navajo and Pueblo silver jewelry, no doubt the figure would be more nearly 90 percent.

Most women who buy pottery are considering its use in their homes. Often I have heard a tourist say, particularly of Maria Martinez' polished, plain, or decorated black ware, "How lovely! It doesn't look too Indian. It might have been made almost anywhere. I like it because it will fit in well with my other things, for use, and for its lovely form and finish."

Considering this, I listed the following advantages of San Ildefonso, from a woman's point of view:

1. The pottery itself: more varied than that of any other pueblo (at that time Polychrome, Black-on-red, and three styles of red or black polished wares — plain, decorated, or carved).

2. The comparative ease with which tourists can visit the potters: 16 miles on a paved highway, and from there (at that time) 6 miles down a winding country road through Spanish-American farming villages to the Pueblo.

3. The picturesque setting of San Ildefonso: the background of the Rio Grande Valley, the mesas of the prehistoric cliff dwellers beyond, the attractive displays of pottery in the homes, and the potters in native dress.

4. A famous tea room, only two miles from the Pueblo: an added attraction for women as it helped fill in an afternoon's trip long to be remembered.

5. The favorable publicity: by the Chamber of Commerce, the hotels, and particularly the women of Santa Fe who treated their guests to the trip and recommended it to visitors.

In contrast, Cochiti in the 1930s was more distant, and a good part of the way was over an unpaved road, almost impassable at times after summer rains. I had several good friends there and had spent some time in the Pueblo since my first visit in 1901. In my museum work I had many occasions to recommend the Cochiti pottery as well made and the least influenced by Anglo notions. But, as Mr. Faris had said, except for trinkets, Cochiti had very little tourist appeal.

And as for the potters of nearby Santo Domingo, the men were opposed to any prying into their methods, as I was to learn some years later in study for my book on the pottery of Santo Domingo Pueblo. I had had a good friend there, one of the younger men in the Pueblo Council. He was in favor of my book, believed it would be a good thing for the Pueblo, and offered to get the approval of the Council. He came to me shortly afterwards and said he had gotten nowhere with the old men. "But," he added, "if you can wait a while I think I can help you." "How long would that take?" I asked. He thought a while and then said, "Well, I don't think I could do anything for maybe ten or fifteen years."

The high standards set by the San Ildefonso potters have been maintained through the past forty years despite the depression of the 1930s, World War II, the employment of many of the adults in nearby Los Alamos, and by unforeseen competition through the development of show-card painted trinkets at Tesuque and later in other pueblos, which catch the eye of the hordes of gullible tourists. With tourist traffic increasing by leaps and bounds, the friends of the Indians are led to wonder how long genuine Indian arts and crafts can survive.

CHAPTER VIII
Polished Black and Red Wares

HISTORY

AN UNUSUAL TRAIT in Tewa ceramics appeared early in the post-Spanish period, through the development of two types of lustrous, highly polished wares in two of the northernmost pueblos. These were the red, or red-brown, ware of San Juan and the smudged black ware of Santa Clara.

The art of smudging, in production of polished black ware, seems to have had a natural development in each of many worldwide areas, from ancient Egypt and China to the American Southwest in pre-Columbian times. For wherever ocherous clays have been used as slips, the potters have been plagued by the appearance of "smoke clouds" on their red slips, due to the falling of burning fragments of fuel against the upturned body of a vessel, which leaves a more or less dense black-smudged spot on the surface. With the knowledge of cause and effect of accidental smudging, the art of smudging must have been mastered in easy stages through experiments with the controlled smudging of entire vessels. But no precedent for the trait has been found in the excavation of numerous pre-Spanish pueblo sites of the Tewa and the adjoining areas.

However, in two or more remote regions in the Southwest, instances of far more ancient developments of similar, well-polished wares are now well known to archaeologists. In northern Chihuahua, Mexico, polished red ware predominated in one small area, and polished, smudged black in another.[18] Likewise, in a small area in southwestern New Mexico, the same smudging process was used to produce a lustrous black, usually on the polished interiors of bowls.[19]

Since production in both these regions is known to have terminated with their abandonment in the late fourteenth century, there is little chance that any knowledge of these ancient wares was acquired directly by the Tewa potters possibly as late as 1700. Therefore, it would seem that the development of the polished wares of San Juan and Santa Clara was due to a gradual familiarity with the use of red slip and the discovery that it was susceptible to a much higher polish than the traditional cream slip.

At San Ildefonso, the innovation made but little progress. Apparently the laborious process of stone polishing met with scant approval of the potters whose traditional Black-on-cream ware required only a cursory rubbing with the polishing stone before the painted decoration was applied by brush. At the turn of the century, even this slight production at San Ildefonso all but ceased. Only with the discovery of the black-on-black process, about 1919, was the interest in polished black and red revived.

TECHNOLOGY

Following the usual structural processes of molding, scraping, mopping, and drying, as described in Chapter II, the vessels are then ready for slipping and polishing. The slip is an exceedingly fine, smooth clay, reddish brown in tone,[20] from the Tewa and Keres areas. It is moistened in water to the consistency of cream and is applied evenly over the surface of the vessel by mopping with a soft pad of cotton cloth, folded flat, or, in earlier times, by a piece of rabbit fur. Next, while the surface is still damp, the potter uses a pebble, worn smooth by long use, to stroke the surface until by compression the entire vessel is highly polished.

As compared with modern polished wares, the early specimens are crudely formed and finished. Too great pressure was exerted in the initial strokes of the polishing stone, leaving minute depressed streaks that could not be obliterated by further rubbing. Furthermore, the lower third of the vessel is left unpolished, a trait apparently borrowed from San Juan. Yet, as with the well-worn specimens of other antique wares, there is a certain harmony of handiwork in all the free and easy techniques that is often lacking in much of the more expertly fashioned wares of today.

In firing polished red ware, the preliminary procedures are as described in Chapter II. The thoroughly dried pieces must be handled carefully and well placed to avoid scratching the glossy surface. In firing, the reddish slip turns slightly deeper in tone. Though the surface becomes hardened, yet the comparatively low temperature does not produce so durable a quality as that of commercial ceramics. If the potter prefers, the vessels can be smudged to a dense glossy black by a simple treatment at the close of the firing. While the pottery is still hot, a mass of straw or chaff, saved from threshing, or a quantity of well-dried and powdered dung is thrown over the heap. This produces a dense smoke which smothers the vessels for an hour or more so that no free oxygen reaches them. For the best black color, the firing must be cool. In fact, if the firing temperature exceeds about 650° c., although the ware is much harder and more durable, the resulting slight shrinkage of the slip produces a greyish gunmetal surface that is less attractive.

MATTE-ON-POLISHED POTTERY

The potters of today in San Ildefonso are fortunate in having inherited and developed their own types of pottery, made of native materials and finished by their own traditional processes without recourse to the use of nonceramic materials or techniques. This holds true even with the best known of their later types, the Matte-on-polished ware, which has held first place during the past forty years.

The invention of matte painting on a polished surface by Julian Martinez in 1919 was a true discovery, even though archaeological excavations in southwestern New Mexico during recent years have yielded numerous sherds bearing evidence of similar experiments.

In the early stages of his experiments, Julian used a solution of the red clay slip itself for painting the designs in matte. But having had difficulty in applying the improvised paint evenly to the polished surface, Julian made numerous tests of other materials. He finally found a shalelike substance that when rubbed on a hard stone slab could be reduced to a fine paste. After dilution the paste was applied by brush. It adhered smoothly and evenly to the polished surface.

In 1919 in his first experiments with matte painting on polished wares, Julian chose as the motif his own version of the *avanyu* (plumed serpent), which he had developed through occasional use in Polychrome decoration. With this he had his choice of painting the *avanyu* in solid matte on an unfired, polished vessel, or of producing a polished *avanyu* upon the matte surface of an unpolished vessel.

He chose the latter. He outlined the wavy form of an *avanyu* encircling the moistened body of a jar and then left the polishing to Maria. It was a difficult task. She could not use a free sweeping motion of the polishing stone. This left the edges uneven. Although they could be more sharply defined by retouching the edges of the surrounding matte surface with a brush, the combination was not satisfactory because of the comparatively great expanse of matte surface which was unattractive to the eye and harsh to the touch. The lack of sales appeal led the couple to abandon their initial experiments. Only a few specimens of this type were made, and rarely has one been preserved. But through further adjustments of the combination of polish and matte, the defects were eventually remedied in 1921 by first outlining with a brush an encircling zone on a well-polished jar and then outlining the *avanyu* within it.

The resulting spaces above and below the *avanyu* were then filled with the matte paint, thus producing the effect of a polished *avanyu* within a comparatively narrow background of matte, and leaving the greater part of the vessel with its attractive polished surface. By 1921 the *avanyu* design had also been enhanced by outlining a cloud cluster in each of the matte spaces above the downsweep of the *avanyu's* undulating body and by adding the pairs of finlike appendages below. These served further to reduce the areas of matte surface within the decorated zone. With this combination perfected, the essentials of the *avanyu* arrangement have since been maintained with only a few minor variations in details.

Meanwhile Julian continued his experiments with other motifs but found no other life forms in his San Ildefonso repertoire as suitable as the *avanyu* for use as polished motifs within a matte background. However, in his adaptation of a feather motif from ancient Mimbres pottery,[21] he made a wise choice in revising the combination of black and white by leaving the feathers in polished black and thus subordinating the minor areas used as a matte background.

CARVED WARES

Lending variety to the Matte-on-polished ware are two later types in which the decorating is produced by added techniques of incising, carving, and scraping.

The walls of carved ware are usually heavier than those of the three preceding types; their thickness varying from one-fourth to one-half inch, depending upon vessel size.

For both varieties of carved ware, Intaglio and Cameo, the carving is done before the slipping and polishing of the vessel. The outer surface of the side wall must be dampened to the proper texture for incising the outlines of the decorative motif by use of a knife blade to an average depth less than one-half the thickness of the wall.

For Intaglio, the motif is depressed by carving and scraping. For Cameo, it is the background of the motif that is depressed, thus leaving the motif in high relief.

INTAGLIO WARE

Very simple motifs are used for Intaglio, such as narrow crenelated, zigzag, or wavy bands. The motif is first outlined by incising; next, the intervening space is channeled by scraping. The only example of a more intricate, channeled motif is that of a triangular tipped-lightning motif.

CAMEO WARE

For the more prevalent Cameo style, the much larger motifs are also outlined by incising, as with Intaglio. Following this, the background is scraped away, leaving the motif in relief. In both styles, the depressed surfaces are then finished by brushing or mopping with a thin paste of slip. Finally, the uncarved portions of the vessel, whether of Intaglio or Cameo, are highly polished to produce the striking contrast with the matte surface of the depressed areas.

CHAPTER IX

History of Painted Tewa Pottery

by Francis H. Harlow

THE HISTORY OF TEWA POTTERY has recently become better known through the discovery of considerably more evidence than was available to Dr. Chapman. The details are discussed in several publications[22-26] so that only a summary is presented here, with emphasis on the San Ildefonso types and comparisons of them with the pottery at neighboring villages.

SANKAWI BLACK-ON-CREAM, SANKAWI POLYCHROME

Prehistoric ceramics in the Tewa area were never outstanding in quality and often were quite inferior, particularly in comparison with the fine pottery made by Pueblo Indians to the south and east. During the last prehistoric period, however, this began to change. Independent of influence from the early Spanish explorers, Tewa potters initiated improvements that were to bring them to the forefront of fine pottery making, eventually to the extent that other Pueblo areas began to copy Tewa ideas.

The first improvement was in form: instead of simple utilitarian globular shapes, jars were made taller and were sculptured with rim planing, with mid-body keels, and, most important, with a concave underbody for carrying on the head. The second improvement was in paste and surface finish: compared with the previous Biscuit wares, the paste was harder, so that vessel walls were both stronger and thinner, and the vessel surfaces were better compacted with the polishing stone. On surfaces that were to be painted, a slip was usually applied.

The center of this improved pottery-making was on the Pajarito Plateau, near the modern town of Los Alamos. The finest examples come from the ruins of Potsuwi'i, Sankawi, and especially Tsirege. They date in the period 1550-90 and are known by the type name, Sankawi Black-on-cream.

In the nearby Rio Grande Valley villages, however, the earlier Cuyamungue Black-on-tan continued as the principal pottery type until at least 1600. Most of the rare sherds of Sankawi Black-on-cream found at such villages as Nambe and Cuyamungue were probably imported or made by visitors from the Plateau. Cuyamungue Black-on-tan is easily distinguished from the improved pottery by its softer paste, poorer finish, heavier designs, and especially by differences in form. Jars are more squat and globular, and bowls retain a strong concave exterior flexure below the rim.

In the last period of Cuyamungue Black-on-tan there was some mimicry of the fine-line decoration of Sankawi Black-on-cream. This is especially noticeable at some of the northern villages such as Hungpobi (near Ojo Caliente). The northern variety has features of its own, however, that may eventually lead to a distinctive type name. At Hungpobi, for example, the vessels have a somewhat different paste, grittier in texture, containing abundant tiny micaceous flecks, and more grey-white than the beige paste to the south.

In some cases, the mimicry of Sankawi Black-on-cream by Valley villagers extended even to form. From Nambe, for example, there have come a few bowl sherds of Pajarito Plateau form. They are distinguished by their poor slip appearance, being streaked, flaked, and poorly polished. Similar examples from other nearby villages (notably Cuyamungue) have such a similar slip appearance that they might have been made by a single potter.

When the Valley potters finally did begin to master the new techniques, the style had advanced to the stage of Sakona Black-on-tan, which is distinguished by a keel structure on the bowls and by various features of design. (Sakona Black-on-tan and Sakona Polychrome are newly named pottery types.) This, however, was not until about 1600 and seems quite certainly to have been substantially assisted by the master potters of Tsirege, who had just abandoned their homes on the Plateau to move in with their neighbors in the Valley.

Vessels of Sankawi Black-on-cream also found their way to the Keresan villages to the south. Sherds have been found at Cochiti and near San Felipe. One jar was discovered in a cave near Tsirege. It was filled with cotton bolls that had been carried back from the Cochiti area in a jar originally made at Tsirege.

Thus, Sankawi Black-on-cream was made almost exclusively on the Pajarito Plateau, rarely found its way by trade to the south and east, influenced some design changes on ceramics to the east and to the north, and finally evolved into Sakona Black-on-tan at the time that the Pajarito villages were being abandoned and Oñate was arriving with the first Spanish settlers.

Brief mention should be made of a companion type, Sankawi Polychrome, of which a single well-preserved jar is the only known example. This vessel, in the Franklin Barnett collection at Prescott, Arizona, is known to me only from a photograph and a brief written description. Except for the addition of red to the designs, the jar appears to be completely typical of Sankawi Black-on-cream. No complete jars of Sakona Polychrome have come to light, so that detailed comparison of jar form with that type is not possible. Since Sakona Polychrome bowls are stylistically much advanced over those of Sankawi Black-on-cream, we also expect such a contrast for the jar.

SAKONA BLACK-ON-TAN, SAKONA POLYCHROME

The next stage in Tewa ceramics evolution was to a pair of types for which new names are here proposed: Sakona Black-on-tan and Sakona Polychrome named for Sakona village, near Pojoaque. (Examples of this pottery were made at several of the southern

Tewa villages, including San Ildefonso.) Both of these types are known almost exclusively from bowl specimens, which form the basis for the following description.

The earlier of the two types, Sakona Black-on-tan, differs from the ancestral Sankawi Black-on-cream principally in form and design. For the first time in the Tewa area, bowls

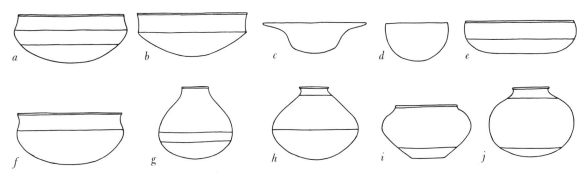

Figure 2. Vessel forms. The classic forms of the various pottery types described in this chapter are shown in the following drawings. Figure 2 illustrates some bowl and storage jar outlines, together with the placement of decorative bands.

a. A typical bowl of Sankawi Black-on-cream, with two design bands above and below the widest part.

b. The usual form for bowls of Sakona Polychrome, Tewa Polychrome, Ogapoge Polychrome, and Pojoaque Polychrome.

c. The soup-plate, a Spanish-influence form.

d. Hemispherical bowls were common during the eighteenth century, especially in sites near Santa Fe.

e. A variant form of Ogapoge Polychrome and Powhoge Polychrome.

f. The typical form for Powhoge Polychrome and Tesuque Polychrome.

g. A storage jar of Ogapoge Polychrome; the narrow design band is below the wide one.

h. An early storage jar of Powhoge Polychrome, with narrow design band above the wide one. The form is especially typical of San Ildefonso.

i. A wide-mouthed storage jar of Powhoge Polychrome, a form more typical of San Juan, Tesuque, and Cochiti than of San Ildefonso.

j. The typical form of late Powhoge Polychrome storage jars.

Figure 3. Type of Sakona Black-on-tan bowl.

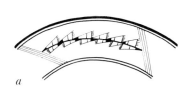  

Figure 4. Drawings.

have a keel sculpture, formed by an angular flexure around the exterior, somewhat below the rim (figure 2). The characteristic design features, illustrated in figure 3, are:

1. layout in an encircling band that leaves the center circle undecorated,
2. division of the band into panels, usually three or four,
3. occurrence of one or several diagonal lines in each panel,
4. use of elements like those from both late Sankawi Black-on-cream and early Tewa Polychrome.

These features show well on the type specimen, Museum of New Mexico #44862/11, illustrated in the accompanying photograph (figure 3). The drawings in figure 4 show this bowl again (b) in comparison with two other examples of the style. Example (a) is actually from a very late Sankawi Black-on-cream bowl, found on the Pajarito Plateau, and thus affording evidence regarding the origins of Sakona Black-on-tan. Example (c) is from a Sakona Polychrome bowl, which is distinguished by the addition of red slip to the bowl exterior below the keel.

The best estimate for date of manufacture of Sakona Black-on-tan is 1600-1700, with Sakona Polychrome dating about 1620-1700.

Tewa Polychrome, manufactured during 1650-1730, differs in having no designs on the bowl interiors; that surface being either red slipped or simply stone-stroked paste. Some of the variability of Sakona Polychrome is illustrated by thirty-five sherds from Cuyamungue dating prior to 1694, at which date the village was abandoned. Nine have a red exterior slip, while twenty-six have black on white above the keel. Eight of those with red exterior show that the red extends over the keel onto the underbody; on the interior, none of these has any design above the flexure corresponding to the exterior keel, but all have up to four concentric lines at that flexure. Of the twenty-six with exterior black on white designs, one has black on white underbody designs with red on the rim top only; the rest have red underbody slip that was polished before the white upper slip was applied. Three of the twenty-six have interior designs above the flexure, consisting of a simple running zigzag line or pair of lines; the other twenty-three are plain above the flexure. Twenty-four have red rim tops, two have white.

Sparse evidence indicates that jars of Sakona Polychrome are much like those of the succeeding, better-known Tewa Polychrome, differing mainly in the use of black on white designs on the upper body of Sakona Polychrome, in contrast to the overall red slipped upper body of Tewa Polychrome.

TEWA BLACK-ON-TAN, TEWA POLYCHROME

The trend to improvement of Tewa ceramics reached its climax in Tewa Polychrome. In many respects, the type resembles Sakona Polychrome. Bowls differ from those of the earlier type in that the old style of interior black on white design was discarded. At first this was replaced by red slip; later the interior was simply the unslipped stone-polished paste. Jars differ from those of Sakona Polychrome in that the earlier upperbody black on white design was replaced by a red slip, leaving only a mid-body design band of black on white.

A distinctive feature of Tewa Polychrome is that the red slip was always applied before the white slip, so that the latter overlaps the former along any line of contact. This feature, originating with Sakona Polychrome, persisted through Pojoaque Polychrome and Ogapoge Polychrome. On the succeeding Powhoge Polychrome, however, the process was reversed, the red being applied after the white.

The exuberant use of red that led to the formation of Tewa Polychrome from Sakona Polychrome apparently worked a hardship on the Indians, causing numerous trips to the red-slip clay beds. As supplies of the slip became harder to obtain, the slip was gradually omitted from bowl interiors, as already mentioned. Evidence from Cuyamungue shows, in fact, that the problem was recognized well before the abandonment of that village in 1694. At the same time, jar and bowl underbodies began to see progressively skimpier use of red slip. At first this meant that the basal resting place was left bare; soon the red was confined to a wide red band below the design area; but by about 1710, the red slip was applied in a band usually no more than one centimeter in width. By this time there were also significant changes in design and form, so that other type names, Ogapoge Polychrome and Pojoaque Polychrome, become appropriate.

Vessels of Tewa Polychrome are characterized by a number of features of excellence. The paste is so hard that vessel walls could be made thin, yet strong. The red and white slips are fine, clear, and well finished. (The hard, very finely striate white slip contrasts, for example, with the soft, stroke-marked white slip of Powhoge Polychrome.) Vessel forms were more elaborately sculptured than required just for utilitarian purposes. The sharp keels framing the design bands are particularly distinctive. Designs were fine, light, and delicate (though never so excellent as the best of the prehistoric pottery types from such groups as the Mimbres and Casas Grandes).

It has been suggested that many of the distinctive features of Tewa Polychrome were the direct result of Spanish influence, but the available evidence does not support this contention. The use of red slip is a direct influence from the nearby glaze-ware area to the south. The principal features of form were present (or nearly so) on Sankawi Black-on-cream before the arrival of the Spanish settlers. The use of curved-line design elements results as a simple modification of already existing features.

Spanish influence cannot be completely denied, however. The soup-plate form (figure 2c) and the little hemispherical bowls are examples of likely Spanish origin. Likewise, there are certain flowery curved-line designs on Tewa vessels that closely resemble those of imported Majolica wares. Furthermore, these innovative ideas are especially common on sherds from the Spanish villages, particularly Santa Fe. In most cases, the vessels appear to date after the 1680 Pueblo Revolt and are more appropriately classed as variants of Pojoaque Polychrome than of Tewa Polychrome.

Sherds of Tewa Polychrome can be found at all of the southern Tewa villages, as well as at Santa Fe and at Pecos. The Pecos and Cuyamungue collections have been especially useful for studying the type. At Pecos, all the vessels appear to have been imported, probably from Tewa potters at Tesuque, Nambe, Cuyamungue, Pojoaque, and Santa Fe.

Tewa Polychrome is also found at Cochiti and San Felipe, showing considerable trade with the Keres pueblos to the south.

Tewa Black-on-tan is the name that has been used to describe some sacred ceremonial jars that appear to have been made late in the period of Tewa Polychrome or early in the period of Pojoaque Polychrome. Rarity of material and lack of association with dating evidence make it difficult to present a detailed diagnosis. The vessels are small jars characterized by a sharp keel below mid-height, by a pair of vertical handles, and by black on tan fine-line designs in a wide upperbody band and a narrow lowerbody band. A more detailed description is given in "Tewa Indian Ceremonial Pottery."[24]

POJOAQUE POLYCHROME

Mera proposed this type name for jars having a mid-body band of black on white decoration and an upperbody that was slipped red in color. Later, Dr. Chapman discovered that Mera's fragmentary jar of Tewa Polychrome also had a red slipped upperbody, and the name Pojoaque Polychrome was dropped as a junior synonym. With the acquisition of considerably more data, however, it is now appropriate to revive Mera's name for bowls and jars that differ from Tewa Polychrome in several recognizable respects.

Vessels of Pojoaque Polychrome are distinguished by the confinement of underbody red slipping to a narrow band just below the black on white band of decoration. The designs, distinctive from earlier types, are characterized by somewhat different elements that employ more area of black. (See "Pueblo Indian Pottery Design."[25])

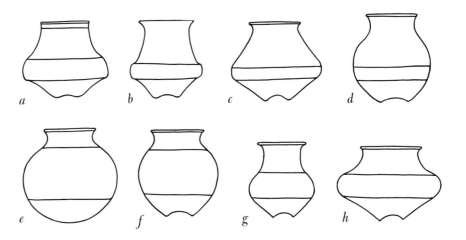

Figure 5. Evolution of water jars and placement of design bands.

    a. Sankawi Black-on-cream, with one mid-body design band and a narrow band near the rim.

    b. Tewa Polychrome, with but a single mid-body design band.

    c. Ogapoge Polychrome and Pojoaque Polychrome; a narrow mid-body design band is surmounted by red-slipped upperbody in Pojoaque Polychrome, but by a wide upperbody design area in Ogapoge Polychrome.

    d. Very late Ogapoge Polychrome, with narrow design band still below the wide one.

    e. Powhoge Polychrome from San Ildefonso, with convex support area.

    f. Powhoge Polychrome from Tesuque, also Tesuque Polychrome.

    g. San Ildefonso Polychrome, up to about 1910.

    h. A variant of San Ildefonso Polychrome, dating prior to about 1910.

Bowls of early Pojoaque Polychrome have the same form as those of Tewa Polychrome. Later examples show a loss of the angular keel, eventually intergrading with the rounded contours of Powhoge Polychrome bowls.

Jars of Pojoaque Polychrome are proportionately wider than those of Tewa Polychrome (figure 5c). This consistent feature, also seen in Ogapoge Polychrome jars, gives them quite a different appearance.

Thus, Pojoaque Polychrome is a recognizable transition type that is very distinctive in its mid-period, but which intergrades continuously with Tewa Polychrome at about 1710 and with Powhoge Polychrome at about 1760.

Sherds of Pojoaque Polychrome are quite rare, and available whole vessels number no more than about five or so. Even though this results in a rather scant diagnostic description, it now appears that recognition of the type is valuable as a time marker for the first half of the eighteenth century.

OGAPOGE POLYCHROME

Ogapoge Polychrome is a close cognate of Pojoaque Polychrome that is readily recognized because of the use of red in the designs. Both types show the same transitional features of form and red banding that occur between Tewa Polychrome and Powhoge Polychrome.

In addition to the use of red in the designs, Ogapoge Polychrome has one additional distinguishing feature: every specimen that is available for study shows the use of feather elements in the designs, suggesting that the vessels were made for ceremonial purposes only.

Jars of Ogapoge Polychrome are decorated on both upperbody and midbody. In this respect, they suggest jars of Sakona Polychrome, but differ from that type in the use of red in the designs, the invariable occurrence of feather elements, the broader shape, the confinement of underbody slipping to a red band, and the simple, unsculptured, flared rim that is not as strongly beveled as earlier.

As on Pojoaque Polychrome, many older features persist on Ogapoge Polychrome that disappear in the later Powhoge Polychrome. These are white over red slip intersection overlaps, fine white slip that is finely striate and crazed, and fine-line decoration, all features contributing to the appearance and excellence that is usual on these vessels.

In addition to bowls and jars of the water-jar size (about ten inches tall), Ogapoge Polychrome was also fashioned into little ceremonial jars with handles and into large storage jars. This last is represented by one fine large specimen, possibly from San Ildefonso, whose form heralds the globular Powhoge Polychrome jars to follow. This one specimen has the characteristic wide upper design band and a lower narrow geometric design band, with a narrow red band below this. The underbody is well-floated paste and is fully rounded at the base, both features in the style of the San Ildefonso Pueblo potters. The upperbody slopes gently (without a neck) to the relatively narrow mouth.

Thus, the form of this one available storage jar of Ogapoge Polychrome shows quite clearly the origin of the early Powhoge Polychrome storage jar form, which in turn was ancestral to the classic Powhoge Polychrome storage jar of the early nineteenth century.

Sherds of Ogapoge Polychrome are as rare as those of Pojoaque Polychrome, but preserved whole vessels are fortunately somewhat more common. Apparently these sacred vessels were treasured as heirlooms and more carefully handled than the everyday household pots.

POWHOGE POLYCHROME

By about 1760, the transition from Pojoaque Polychrome to Powhoge Polychrome was essentially complete. The result was a new pottery tradition that differed in many essential respects from the classical Tewa Polychrome of a century earlier.

The history of Powhoge Polychrome has been obscure for several reasons. The first is that, in contrast to earlier and later, there were no datable occurrences to which the phases of development of the type could be attached. Second, the type was not made after about 1850, whereas a closely related type, Kiua Polychrome, was made until recent times at Santo Domingo; the result being that many old Powhoge Polychrome vessels have been erroneously assigned a Santo Domingo origin. Third, neither Tesuque nor San Ildefonso has yielded very many sherds of Powhoge Polychrome during recent extensive searches of the areas around these villages. Finally, many of the vessels collected from these villages in the period around 1900 have essentially no data as to origin or recorded history. For all these reasons, and also because of his emphasis on the artistic features, Dr. Chapman continued to use the old name for Powhoge Polychrome: San Ildefonso Black-on-cream. His notes and text for this book show, however, that he recognized the necessity for a new name.

In spite of these difficulties, it has been possible to reconstruct most of the essential features concerning the evolution of Powhoge Polychrome. The primary data have come from sherd collections, especially those from Nambe Pueblo, from the excavations for the foundations of the Santa Fe Art Museum, from Pecos, and to a minor extent from San Ildefonso and Tesuque. Results of the analysis of these primary data could then be applied to a study of the numerous available storage jars of Powhoge Polychrome, to give a consistent picture of the design evolution of the type. The manner in which this sequence of analyses could be carried out will be seen from the discussion of the results.

First it should be emphasized that a weathered sherd of Powhoge Polychrome can have a considerably different appearance from that of a vessel that has been used and handled but never weathered. The latter often has a much darker, greasier, slicker, shinier appearance, in contrast to the clean, dry, light surface of a weathered potsherd. This must be kept in mind when comparisons are made. For example, a storage jar that saw nearly a century of usage and has been indoors all of its life looks very different from a sherd of the same pottery that has lain in the ground for a century. The difference has no significance to the taxonomic diagnosis and must be ignored.

It quickly becomes apparent to the investigator of Powhoge Polychrome that there are many variants of the type, both in time and among the villages where it was made. It is tempting to give names to these variants, but this will require much more extensive sherd collections from Tesuque and San Ildefonso. These contrasts will be emphasized in the following discussion, since they are of use in diagnosing the date and origin of any example that comes to hand.

PASTE

The paste of Powhoge Polychrome is basically the same as that of all the Tewa types. It is fine in texture, being minutely grainy or dusty in appearance, or sometimes matted-looking under a strong lens. It is tan near the surfaces, and often grey in the core. It never has the chunky texture of sherd-tempered paste nor the compact, glassy texture of early Hopi paste. The inclusion of large fragments or chunks is exceptional.

The variations, though slight, are important. At Nambe, which is located near the granitic Sangre de Cristo Mountains, sherds very often contain an abundance of micaceous glittering fragments. These are oriented parallel to the surfaces of the vessel wall, and accordingly are not apparent on a sharp cross break. They are most conspicuous on un-slipped surfaces such as the base of the vessel or the interior. It is tempting to use this as the basis for naming a separate type, in the way that Pantano Red-on-brown is distinguished from Tanque Verde Red-on-brown of the thirteenth century near Tucson, but the usefulness of such a distinction needs further proof before the proposal is made. Occasional sherds with micaceous glitter are also found at San Ildefonso and Tesuque, but usually the glittering fragments are very much finer than at Nambe. Sherds from various parts of Santa Fe also show the Nambe type of micaceous glitter, as would be expected from the proximity to the mountains and from the probability that either Nambe pots or potters, or both, were imported by the Spanish into the city.

A paste variant that is characteristic of Tesuque is the occasional inclusion of rather large chunks of pink crystalline material, often several millimeters in diameter. These are so rare that only one or two may be seen in a large sherd, but they appear to be restricted to Tesuque Pueblo, so that their occurrence is significant. Otherwise, Tesuque paste is usually quite free of visible inclusions and therefore especially homogeneous.

San Ildefonso paste also has a characteristic variation from those of the other Tewa pueblos. In this case the inclusions are small chunks (up to 1 mm in diameter) of a soft white material resembling pieces of laminated chalk. When present, they usually are fairly abundant, averaging from 3 mm to 10 mm for separation of neighboring chunks. However, this San Ildefonso variant does not become consistently present until the development of San Ildefonso Polychrome about 1880, occurring with progressively less frequency for earlier dates.

The Pojoaque sherds available for study show a very homogeneous paste, free of any inclusions except for rare tiny pebbles.

The Keres pueblos of Santo Domingo and Cochiti, which patterned their Kiua Polychrome after Powhoge Polychrome, use a paste that resembles somewhat the paste of their Tewa neighbors to the north. There are several distinct points of contrast, however, in that the Keresan paste usually is harder and more orange; but the most apparent and consistent difference is in the tempering material. At Cochiti and Santo Domingo, this invariably consists of an abundance of crushed crystalline mineral that is white or colorless. The contrast with Tewa paste is so great that even on this criterion alone, the sherds of Keresan pottery can be quickly separated from those of the Tewa area in any mixed sample. Only one confusing example is known to me, a storage jar with very typical Keresan paste but equally typical Tesuque slip and designs.

The surface finish of the unslipped paste gives another feature for which there is some contrast among the Tewa pueblos. San Ildefonso has the distinction of the most beautiful surface finish for the exterior unslipped areas below the red banding. The paste is actually floated, a process in which the finest particles are puddled to the surface and then polished by stone stroking. At Nambe and Tesuque, in contrast, the surfaces are simply coarsely stroked, leaving coarse graininess that cannot be called a polished surface. (On late examples of Tesuque Polychrome, however, the Tesuque potters proved they could outshine even San Ildefonso in the art of producing a floated paste surface with high polish.) Bowl interiors from all the pueblos were generally well smoothed, while jar interiors received variable treatment. Seldom, however, were the interiors floated to such a degree of perfection as that achieved by the best Cochiti potters of the nineteenth century.

SLIP

The old tradition of polishing the white slip with a smooth stone persists as a means of distinguishing the Tewa pots from those of adjacent pueblo areas. But there is considerable contrast in detail between the slip finish of Powhoge Polychrome and that of the preceding Tewa types.

The slip of Tewa Polychrome, for example, is hard, fine in texture, finely crazed, and polished in such a way that the stone strokes are scarcely visible. But the slip shows, under a lens, that the stones were always slightly rough, so that very fine scratches or striations are always present.

The slip of Powhoge Polychrome, while still fine in texture, is relatively soft, somewhat more coarsely crazed, generally shows well the individual strokes of the stone, and lacks the very fine striations of earlier ware. (Either the polishing stones were now smoother from decades of use, or else the striations always have eroded from this somewhat softer slip.)

Tesuque vessels often show a slightly dimpled or "hammered-looking" surface of white slip. This is produced by the bouncing of the polishing stone, much as bouncing tires form corrugations on a dirt road. The effect is enhanced on Tesuque pots because of the occasional large rock chunks that are in the paste. Seldom do the pots from the other Tewa pueblos have such an appearance on their white-slip surfaces.

Nambe and Tesuque pots sometimes have small rust-colored stain areas on the white slip that seem never to be present on San Ildefonso pots.

Red slip is used for red banding and for the rim top. It usually is dark red, only rarely orange. The finished surface is hard, slick, and well polished. No consistent variations among pueblos have been noted.

There is significant contrast, however, with both the white and red slips of the Keresan pueblos of Cochiti and Santo Domingo, a contrast which serves with that of the paste to distinguish very strongly between Powhoge Polychrome and Kiua Polychrome. The Keresan white slip is often filled with a tiny graininess. It is polished by an entirely different process, the smooth stone seldom being employed. Instead, the slip is polished by means of some soft material such as fabric or leather, leaving a very characteristic striate appearance under a lens. Even when the stone was used, the job was cursory, leaving many parts of the surface untouched by the strokes. Apparently "Cochiti slip," as the Tewas call it, did not need the compaction required by the "native slip" of the Tewas. This labor-saving feature was, in fact, envied by the Tewas, who eventually (after about 1905) used it almost exclusively on their pottery to avoid the laborious process of stone polishing. The white Cochiti slip contrasts with the native Tewa slip in yet another significant way. Tewa slip crazes in a series of very fine meandering cracks that end blindly. Cochiti slip crazes by scabbing: the cracks are formed because tiny scabs of slip turn up their edges slightly; the cracks, therefore, do not meander or end blindly. The Cochiti scabs, when rubbed, show a polished appearance on their peripheries while the centers remain dull. Such an appearance never occurs in the nonscabbing Tewa slip.

The red slip on Kiua Polychrome is also different from that of Powhoge Polychrome. The Keresan slip is softer, more orange, dustier in texture, takes a poorer polish, and flakes more easily. On Kiua Polychrome the red banding is usually at least twice as wide as on Powhoge Polychrome (several centimeters, compared with about one centimeter). After about 1800, red banding is the only use the Keresans have for red slip; the rim tops of Kiua Polychrome were consistently black or rarely white after that date.

PAINT

The black paint on Powhoge Polychrome fires to a sooty color. Occasionally it may vary to ash-grey in hue, but never does it have tinges of brown or tan unless it is so thin that the slip color shows through. The paint is guaco, apparently always having been made from the Rocky Mountain bee plant by boiling down the tender leaves and stems in the spring.

When the pot was painted, the solid black areas were outlined first, then filled in. Commonly the filled-in areas are more watery than the outlines.

The Keresan potters who made Kiua Polychrome also used guaco paint, a technique they learned from their Tewa neighbors at the same time that they were copying so many of the other features of Powhoge Polychrome. On Kiua Polychrome, however, the black is usually more dense, seldom showing a watery color for the filled-in area. It is likely that the difference can be attributed to the properties of the slip, for when Cochiti slip was used at San Ildefonso (after about 1910), the black paint became more dense and intense. Thus, the intensity of the black paint is useful as a minor distinguishing feature between Kiua Polychrome and Powhoge Polychrome, but exceptions can be found in which the Keresan paint is watery or the Tewa paint is densely black.

FORM AND DESIGN

In discussing the form and decoration of Powhoge Polychrome, we encounter most strikingly the fascinating variation that characterizes this pottery type. The sources of this variation come from three important factors:

1. Evolution through time: old styles were neglected and new ones introduced.
2. Differences among the pueblos: certain features became "trademarks" for particular villages.
3. Styles restricted to one potter: usually each major potter in a village developed her own distinctive features of style that differed in minor but noticeable ways from those of all the other potters.

These are the factors that tended to produce distinctive variations. At the same time, however, there were factors tending to produce homogeneity of style:

1. Old forms or designs sometimes returned to favor after a lapse of decades or more. This is especially true of Powhoge Polychrome because of the longevity of the abundant storage jars that served as venerable models for potters seeking inspiration for their designs.
2. It was very common for pots to be introduced to other villages through trade or as gifts. Even today, the Indians enjoy visiting neighboring pueblos for dances, fiestas, weddings, or other special occasions; and a gift of pottery, basketry, bread, or other items is considered very appropriate. Thus, a vessel or sherd collected at a particular village does not necessarily reflect the traditional style of that village, but may, however, have served as inspiration for a shift of style at its new home.
3. The individualistic styles of particular potters, if attractive and popular, soon were copied by friends and neighbors. This is how new pottery types usually were initiated through both the prehistoric and historic periods.

These factors contributing to individuality versus homogeneity of style must have been at work since the earliest times, but in the Tewa area the tendency to homogeneity was the stronger by far, prior to the sixteenth century. In the sixteenth century, there occurred the first real signs of individuality, leading to a division into two pottery areas. Gradually the individuality became progressively stronger, so that by 1700 each pottery type of the Tewa area occurred in no more than three or four villages. After 1800 the final stage was reached; the individual villages specialized to the extent that vessels made after about 1850 can be attributed with considerable certainty to the individual pueblo of origin.

This introduction to the subject of form and design in Powhoge Polychrome is meant to show why the type is at the same time fascinating and frustrating in its variability. It shows the origin of controversy that has arisen. For example, it has been stated by a prominent and knowledgeable resident of San Ildefonso that he believes no vessels of the Powhoge Polychrome type have ever been made at his village, every vessel having been imported from Tesuque. In contrast, it was thought by some early twentieth-century ethnologists that all such vessels had been made at San Ildefonso (which had developed a strong ceramic reputation by that time) and that any found at Tesuque were imported.

The truth lies between these extremes. (There is similar controversy about the nineteenth-century pottery of San Felipe Pueblo, and there the matter is still far from being resolved.)

Thus, while the following conclusions regarding space and time specializations of Powhoge Polychrome design and form are likely correct, they cannot be considered proved until much larger collections of sherds have been obtained from Tesuque and San Ildefonso.

Form: Vessels of Powhoge Polychrome were made in four different forms: bowls, water jars, ceremonial vessels, and storage jars. The first three are modified from the previous traditions of Tewa Polychrome and related types. The storage jars, however, were previously so rare as to be almost an innovation for Powhoge Polychrome. One storage vessel of Ogapoge Polychrome stands as the unique example, but by the early period of Powhoge Polychrome this large form had become so popular that many vessels have survived to recent times.

The principal modification in form leading from Pojoaque Polychrome to Powhoge Polychrome was the discarding of keels and other sculptural structures in favor of simple, rounded, globular contours. There are also other changes. On the exterior of a Pojoaque Polychrome bowl the black on white designs are confined to a band lying between the rim above and an angular keel below; below the keel there is a relatively narrow band of red slip. In the evolution of Powhoge Polychrome, the keel became progressively less sharp, but for a while the lower edge of the design band coincided with the position of greatest convex curvature. Eventually (probably by about 1800) most potters had widened the design band and/or narrowed the concave area below the rim to such an extent that the lowest framing line was well below the flexure point. Throughout the life of Powhoge Polychrome, however, the old idea of a narrow red band below the lowest framing line persisted on bowls (and on the water and storage jars, too).

The loss of the keel on bowls was coincident with a change in form of the underbody. Bowls of Tewa Polychrome are quite shallow below the keel, but those of Powhoge Polychrome are relatively much deeper. Thus, while the former requires a strong flexure, accomplished by an angular keel, the latter does not, and the keel was therefore dropped. The result is a more efficient vessel but less artistry of form.

The deeper underbody of bowls results in a more spherical shape that also was developed for water jars, reflecting a trend that occurred at most of the villages of the Pueblo Indians in the second half of the eighteenth century. As used here, "water jar" refers to any jar from about seven inches to ten inches tall. These were part of the standard complement of household utensils. They were made in abundance, since the average lifetime of service was likely to be no more than about ten years. Few have survived to the present day. The exceptions often are jars that were damaged too badly for further use but not badly enough to be thrown away. These were set into storeroom corners, to be discovered many years later by collectors who combed the pueblos for specimens.

Water jars had also been gracefully sculptured prior to the development of Powhoge Polychrome, but the new type lost these nonessential features. The resulting form was nearly spherical or elongate ellipsoidal, with a short outflared neck.

Bowl forms have not shown any consistent variation among the pueblos of origin, but there appear to be significant differences in jar forms. At Tesuque, the water jars were always supplied with a concave base for carrying on the head. At San Ildefonso this was often (perhaps always) neglected in favor of a uniformly convex, rounded base. Combined with the relative excellence of San Ildefonso underbody polish, this serves to give quite a different appearance from the jars of the two villages. One or two unusual jar forms from Nambe suggest some innovative experiments at that pueblo, but apparently the usual style was more like that at Tesuque.

Storage jars give the greatest wealth of material for comparative studies of form variation. More than fifty have been available for first-hand examination. Most examples have certain features in common: they have very little sculpture, they have a flat or rounded base, they have a short neck with flaring rim, they are quite gentle in their contours. Thus, any variations must be relatively subtle; they nevertheless are persistent.

The earliest examples have their greatest diameter somewhat below mid-height; above this they have a long and gentle slope up to the relatively small mouth. There is little differentiation of a separate neck, simply more or less flare at the rim.

By 1800, the greatest width was more nearly at mid-height, and the spherical upper part formed a rounded "shoulder" from which the short neck could be more clearly differentiated. The rim was still flared and the mouth remained small. As on water jars, there was a feature of differentiation between pueblos: at San Ildefonso the base was uniformly convex, while at Tesuque it generally was flattened to give more stable support.

As the century progressed, San Ildefonso gradually abandoned pottery making, reflecting the effect of a declining population. Storage jar forms apparently did not change appreciably during this period. At Tesuque, however, pottery making continued unabated, and an interesting form innovation was developed for storage jars (figure 2i). These vessels have a very large mouth, making them intermediate between jars and bowls. They are very similar to a style developed at Cochiti at the same time, illustrating yet another example of the close relationship between the ceramics of the southern Tewas and the northern Keresans.

In addition to bowls and two types of jars, there were many ceremonial vessels made of Powhoge Polychrome with a number of interesting forms that show differences both in time and among the various pueblos of origin. Included are rectangular bowls, terraced footed bowls, little jars with handles, and a variety of others. These have been discussed in some detail in "Tewa Indian Ceremonial Pottery." [24]

Design: In this category, there is little to add beyond the extensive drawings and discussions of them by Dr. Chapman in plates 1 through 59 which follow this chapter.

SAN ILDEFONSO POLYCHROME

The polychrome vessels made at San Ildefonso in the period after about 1880 fall into four quite distinct groups:

 1. A few pots were actually made for household use. These almost always continue many of the traditions of Powhoge Polychrome, being globular in form and dec-

orated in a style that continues the layout and elements of late Powhoge Polychrome. For these vessels, the only essential change was the addition of the red
paint. In particular, the slip was still the stone-polished native material and the
rim top was still painted red. These rare vessels were the last made at San Ildefonso for service at the Pueblo.

2. More common in 1880-1905 were the vases produced for sale to non-Indians,
    which also continued the older traditions of native slip and red rim top. They,
    however, were designed for beauty more than for service, and accordingly are
    softer fired (so as to avoid fire blemishes) and more brightly decorated in a host
    of innovative designs.

3. The third group is much like the second but differs in the use of Cochiti slip
    instead of the native slip. The surface is accordingly striate and grainy, rather
    than stone-stroked satiny. (At San Ildefonso, the use of Cochiti slip was never
    properly mastered; it always looks harsh and often grey, compared with the fine
    finish obtained at Cochiti and Santo Domingo.) Rim tops were usually painted
    black, as at the Keresan pueblos. This slip switch occurred about 1905, with the
    stone-stroked native slip never again to be employed. The Cochiti slip is very
    easily recognized, is profoundly different from the previous slip traditions, and
    has temporal significance. For these reasons the recognition of a separate type
    name may eventually be appropriate and useful.

4. Finally, in a progressive departure from the early styles, there arose a succession
    of new styles, still employing Cochiti slip. These were made from about 1920 to
    the present, but examples are quite rare. They usually can be recognized by the
    intense black of the black paint, by the departures from traditional form, and by
    the exquisite precision of the design.

Thus, while Dr. Chapman and many others have applied the name "San Ildefonso
Polychrome" to all the recent vessels with red in the designs, it is actually possible to dif-
ferentiate several variations in such a way as to emphasize the trends that were occurring.
The inception of the Polychrome design concept came just early enough to be employed
on the last of the San Ildefonso household pottery, stayed around long enough to get
the sales-oriented ceramics industry well started, then became nearly a "lost art" as new
techniques gained favor and the black-ware era dawned. But even though rare examples
of San Ildefonso Polychrome still are made, the last of the traditional Tewa white wares,
with stone-polished native slip, was constructed many years ago and the art surely will
never be revived.

NOTES

[1] John Greiner, "Journal," *Old Santa Fe* (July 1916), Vol. III, No. 11, p. 215.

[2] James Stevenson, "Illustrated Catalogue of the Collections Obtained from the Indians of New Mexico and Arizona in 1880," Second Annual Report, *Bureau of American Ethnology,* Smithsonian Institution, 1880-81, Washington, D.C. (U.S. Government Printing Office, 1883), pp. 429-65.

[3] *Ibid.,* pp. 432-33.

[4] *Ibid.,* p. 460.

[5] Carl E. Guthe, *Pueblo Pottery Making* (New Haven: Yale University Press, 1925).

[6] Watson Smith, "Kiva Mural Decorations at Awatovi and Kawaika-a," *Papers of the Peabody Museum of American Archaeology and Ethnology* (Cambridge: Harvard University, 1952), Vol. XXXVII.

[7] Stevenson, *op. cit.*

[8] Herbert J. Spinden, "The Making of Pottery at San Ildefonso," *The American Museum Journal* (October 1911), Vol. XI, No. 6, pp. 192-96.

[9] Guthe, *op. cit.*

[10] Ruth L. Bunzel, *The Pueblo Potter* (New York: Columbia University Press, 1929).

[11] Kenneth M. Chapman and Bruce T. Ellis, "The Line-Break, Problem Child of Pueblo Pottery," *El Palacio* (September 1951), Vol. 58, No. 9, pp. 251-90.

[12] Alfred V. Kidder and Charles A. Amsden, "The Pottery of Pecos," *Papers of the Southwestern Expedition* (New Haven: Yale University Press, 1931), Vol. I, No. 5.

[13] *Ibid.*

[14] Stevenson, *op. cit.,* p. 462.

[15] *Ibid.,* p. 465.

[16] Guthe, *op. cit.*

[17] Stevenson, *op. cit.*

[18] E. B. Sayles, "Some Southwestern Pottery Types, Series V," *Medallion Papers* No. 21 (Gila Pueblo, Globe, Arizona, May 1936).

[19] J. B. Rinaldo and E. A. Bluhm, "Late Mogollon Pottery Types of the Reserve Area," Chicago Natural History Museum, *Fieldiana: Anthro.* Vol. 36, No. 7 (1956).

[20] A. Maerz and M. Rea Paul, "A Dictionary of Color" (New York, 1930), Pl. 6, G-K, 8-12.

[21] J. W. Fewkes, "Designs on Prehistoric Pottery from the Mimbres Valley, New Mexico," *Smithsonian Miscellaneous Collections* (Washington, D.C., 1924), Vol. 76, No. 6, Fig. 120, p. 44; H. S. and C. B. Cosgrove, "The Swarts Ruin, a Typical Mimbres Site in Southwest New Mexico," *Peabody Museum Paper 15,* No. 1 (Cambridge: Harvard University, 1932), Fig. 153b, c, e, f.

[22] F. H. Harlow, "Northern Pueblo Matte-Paint Pottery of the Historic Period" (Santa Fe: Museum of New Mexico Press, in press).

[23] F. H. Harlow, "Historic Pueblo Indian Pottery" (Santa Fe: Museum of New Mexico Press, 1967).

[24] F. H. Harlow, "Tewa Indian Ceremonial Pottery," *El Palacio* (1965), Vol. 72, No. 4, p. 13.

[25] F. H. Harlow, "Pueblo Indian Pottery Design" (Santa Fe: Museum of New Mexico Press, in press).

[26] H. P. Mera, "Style Trends of Pueblo Pottery in the Rio Grande and Little Colorado Cultural Areas from the Sixteenth to the Nineteenth Century," Laboratory of Anthropology, Memoirs, Vol. III (Santa Fe, 1939).

Plates

BLACK-ON-CREAM WARE

Plate 1. Designs from exterior bands of bowls. Only a few specimens of Black-on-cream bowls were available for study. They provide but little information regarding the choice and application of decorative motifs in the exterior bands of the commonly used bowls, although literally thousands of them must have been made during the century or more when Black-on-cream ware was the dominant type. In the group of only ten available designs, four are from food bowls ranging from 11 to 13 inches in diameter. The other six are from larger utility bowls.

Static arrangements appear in five designs (*c-e, g,* and *i*), and dynamic in *a, b, f,* and *h*. Only one (*j*) combines static features with dynamic. Arranged in order, from simple to complex, the free, unattached units of *a* are followed by attached units in *b*, alternate free and attached in *c,* repeated in panels of *d,* and spanning the band in *e*. Both attached and detached motifs appear in *f* and *g*, and paneled divisions in *i* and *j*.

The more meticulously designed, complex attached units in *h* are from a large utility bowl of a comparatively late period when the potters had begun to borrow occasionally from the motifs of the more attractive Polychrome ware.

Plates 2 through 6. Neck designs of water and storage jars. Because of the general similarity of neck designs of water and storage jars, the two groups have been mingled for convenience on plates 2 through 6. These represent a selection from approximately 70 percent of all specimens examined.

Of the total of ninety designs used, only thirty-five are from water jars, as compared with fifty-five from the combined groups of large and medium storage and wide-mouthed jars The disparity between the two totals is explained in part by the greater frequency of use of certain favored motifs on water jars, as many as six duplications of one design having been noted.

Throughout the entire series, the difference in size between the necks of the various types of jars seems to have had little effect on the nature or complexity of the designs themselves. The number of repeats of design units in the circuit of all neck bands varies from two to twenty-two, and though the majority range between four and nine repeats, there is no evidence of preference for the otherwise ceremonially important number, six.

The neck designs of plates 2 through 6 fall into two distinct classes, static and dynamic, and also into a third class in which the two types are used in combination in each design. Of the ninety designs, thirty-eight are static, thirty-eight dynamic, and fourteen are combinations of the two.

In the construction of design motifs, three distinct types appear: rectilinear, curvilinear, and combinations of the two. These variants are considered in the description of each plate.

Plate 2. Static designs from necks of water and storage jars. Of the static designs of plate 2, four are rectilinear (*b, e, g,* and *q*); nine are curvilinear (*a, c, d, f, j, m-o,* and *r*); and five (*h, i, k, l,* and *p*) are combinations of the two.

The designs are arranged where convenient, in sequence from simple to complex, as follows:
Motifs free, repeated (*a* and *b*).
Motifs attached to one banding line (*c-i*).
Motifs attached to both banding lines (*l-r*).
Combinations of free and attached (*j* and *k*).
The only identifiable graphic motif is that of leaf clusters in *a,* with their contrasting black, and dotted surfaces.

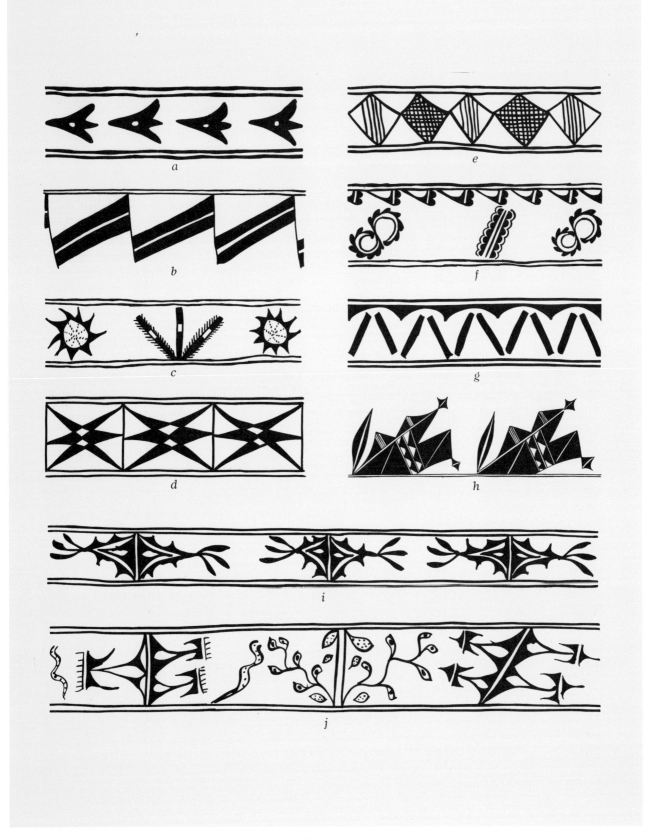

a

b

c

d

e

f

g

h

i

j

PLATE 1

In *j*, the wavy double lines may be interpreted as snakes or running water. Among other abstract forms bearing names, the semicircular clouds predominate, followed in number by rain-far-off, and the rain lines of *k* and *l*. They are the only examples found, in which the lines are not attached to cloud forms. In *q*, the stepped forms may be interpreted as clouds or terraces of mesas or mountains. The open spaces within the upper rain-far-off units of *p* are unusual in Black-on-cream design, though they appear frequently in the later designs of Polychrome ware. The open breaks in the lower band are quite unusual.

In *h* and *i*, the simple combinations of roughly semicircular units crossed by a straight line produce two recognizable forms in alternation: clouds above and rain-far-off below the line.

Plate 3. Static designs from necks of water and storage jars. The twenty designs of plate 3 are attached to the banding lines above and below. They comprise mainly motifs repeated in uninterrupted sequences from *a-o*.

In *d*, black leaves or feathers distract from the zigzag arrangement of dot-filled bars. In *p*, the black leaves between clouds touch the upper banding line, dividing the band into panel-like spaces. The next four designs (*q-t*) are developed on paired-paneling lines. The panel arrangement is complicated in *t* by an unusual crisscrossing of diagonal lines across the paired verticals.

The zigzag in *e* extends across the entire band, unlike plate 2*e* and *g*. It is the only rectilinear design in the group, in contrast with the recticurvilinear forms (*a* and *f-h*), and the purely curvilinear forms in *i-n*. In *j*, the outlined semicircular cloud spaces produce intervening rain-far-off forms in black, a pleasing combination in Pueblo symbolism. The cloud spaces in opposed arrangement, in *k-n*, produce other intervening black motifs. The layout of *o* is unique in Black-on-cream design.

Graphic elements appear in only three designs, leaves in *c* and *p* and leaves or feathers in *d*. The remaining seventeen designs are mainly abstract geometric, though the group includes many repetitions of commonly used forms for which names are given, such as clouds, rain, etc., as noted in the previous plates.

Plate 4. Dynamic designs from necks of water and storage jars. In contrast with the static groups in plates 2 and 3, the eighteen dynamic designs of plate 4 do not include one example of exclusively rectilinear construction, even the repeated motifs in *c*, being modified by slightly curved outlines.

Ten of the designs are entirely curvilinear (*a, d, f-l,* and *n*). In *m* and *o-r*, the vertical lines serve to divide the bands into panels, though the effect of paneling is not as apparent as in the use of paired lines such as in *q-t* in the static designs of plate 3. The design in *r* is unusual in that the verticals cross the intervening space between the upper and lower bands.

The free units in *a* and *b* are repeated in detached arrangement. In the four following they are adjoined. More or less graphic units are used in *a, b,* and *e*. In *a*, the motifs have been interpreted as either leaf clusters or seedpods. Leaves appear in *b* and upon the stem of *e*. The wavy line of *f* suggests a vine, but the attached motifs are unrealistic. In *g*, the only design with repeated motifs attached to one banding line, only a few realistic forms of leaf appear among the crudely drawn units.

In the remaining figures *h-r*, abstract motifs prevail though as noted on plates 2 and 3, names are given to some details, such as cloud spaces and rain-far-off. A most unusual figure appears in *n*, the graceful units only lacking heads to appear as realistic swallows in flight. The motifs in *i* resemble adjoined pairs of units such as those in *f*.

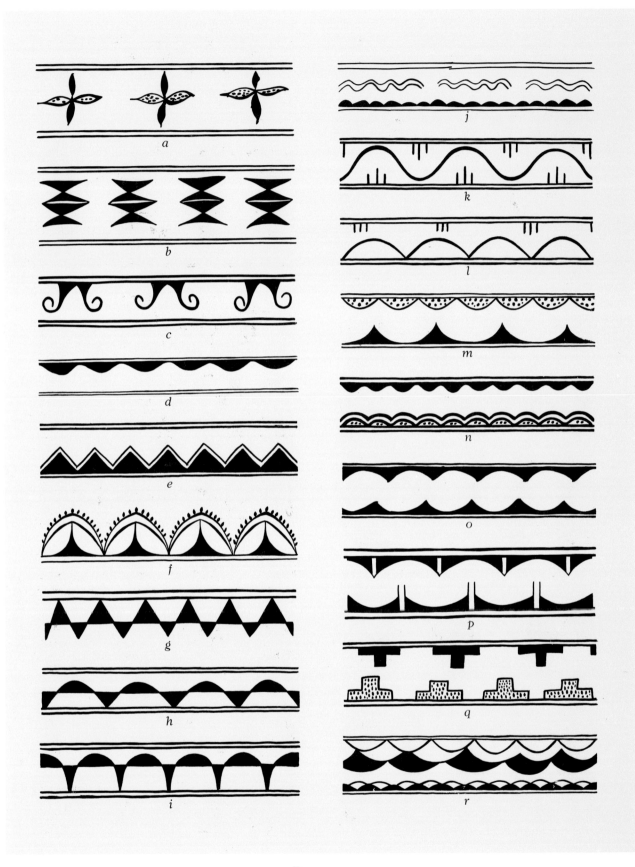

PLATE 2

57

a

b

c

d

e

f

g

h

i

j

k

l

m

n

o

p

q

r

s

t

PLATE 3

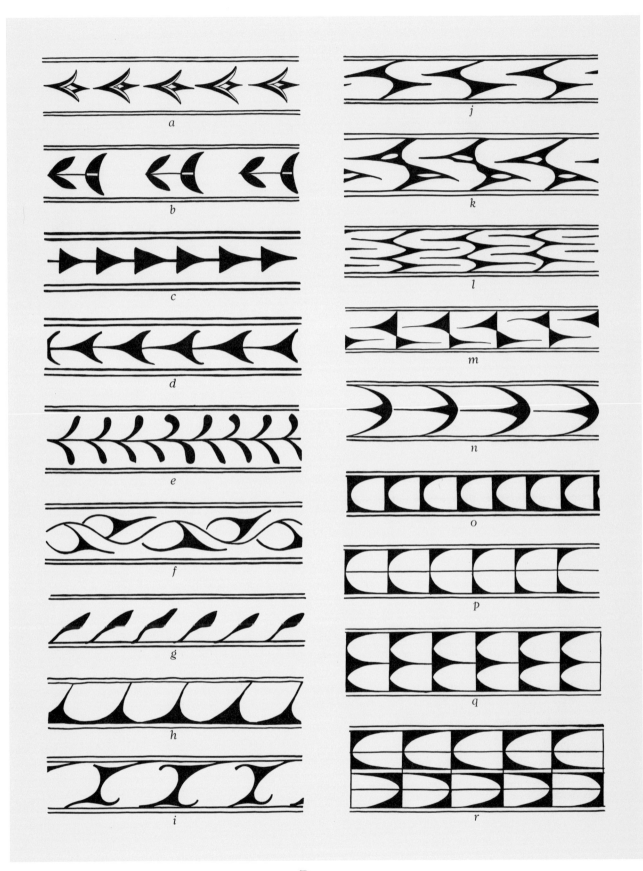

PLATE 4

59

Plate 5. Dynamic designs from necks of water and storage jars. The paneled arrangements of the preceding plate are continued through eleven of the designs of plate 5 (*a-j* and *r*), single lines being used to divide the bands into panels.

The seven other designs (*k-q*) are developed on paired oblique lines separating the bands into rhomboid spaces. In *q*, a zigzag effect is produced by joining two of the long oblique arrangements with a shorter motif spanning the band.

Two of the paneled designs (*i* and *r*) consist of double bands without the usual intervening space, such as that in plate *4r*.

In the group are four designs of the rectilinear type (*b, d, e,* and *h*), the others containing both rectilinear and curvilinear details. Of the rectilinear group, *b, e,* and *h* are direct copies of motifs handed down from prehistoric ceramic decoration.

A curvilinear modification of *b* appears in *c*. In this, the vertical and oblique lines are first drawn as in *b*, but the horizontal middle line is replaced by curved segments in each panel, giving a wavy effect to the middle of the band.

The arrangement in *e*, commonly called "beads," is clearly the source of the two following figures, *f* and *g*, with curvilinear treatment of the oblique lines.

While the motifs in *a, i,* and *l-r* resemble the vertically placed rain-far-off symbols shown in the plates 1 through 4, there is less agreement as to their meaning, and particularly when they are attached in rows as in *a, i,* and *r*.

Plate 6. Mixed designs from necks of water and storage jars. Single bands. Single-band designs are continued in the upper portion of plate 6. Of these, true paneling with double lines appears in *a-c*. Though paneling is only a structural device, the effect is so pronounced that it affects somewhat the dynamic effect of the motifs within panels. Thus all the arrangements in the single-band group of paneled and nonpaneled designs (*a-e* and *i-m*) may be classed as combination static and dynamic.

The arrangements in *a-c* illustrate the tendency to group the decorative motifs on the paneling lines. Though barely perceptible in *d*, the static form of the ovals is in contrast with the off-balance placement of their elongate appendages.

In three other single-band designs (*e, i, k*) commonly used static border motifs of clouds and rain-far-off are opposed to dynamic, free or attached motifs. The otherwise completely static arrangement in *l* is modified by the oblique open bands in the clouds which give almost as lively an effect as that in the oblique stripes in *m*. In the latter, the repeated motifs at the base are among the earliest examples of the "butterfly" arrangement which continued into the Polychrome period. In this, as in later examples, the middle and side elements are interpreted as leaves. The alternating serpents and plant forms in *j* lend variety to the group.

Double bands. Of the six examples of double bands (*f-h* and *n-p*) four are combined static and dynamic (*f, g, n,* and *o*); one (*h*) is static only; and another (*p*) is dynamic though the effect of the paneled structure in the upper band detracts somewhat from the dynamic placement of the rain-far-off motifs. The group contains only one graphic motif, that in the lower band of *o*, interpreted as either leaf or feather.

Plate 7. Static designs from bodies of water jars. The fifteen static designs of plate 7 are from the bodies of water jars only; a representative group from storage jars appearing in plates 2 through 6. Free units in repetition are shown in *a*, alternating in *h*, between attached motifs in *i*

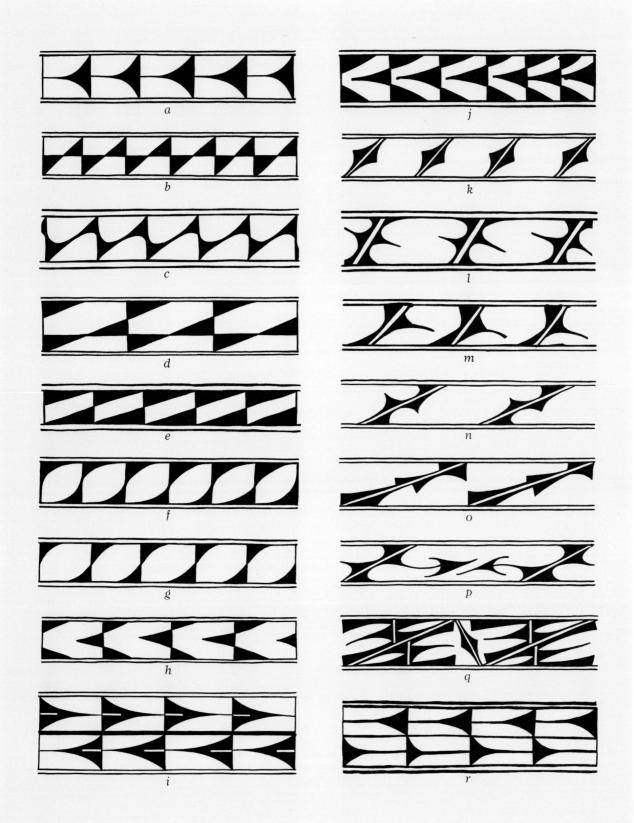

PLATE 5

61

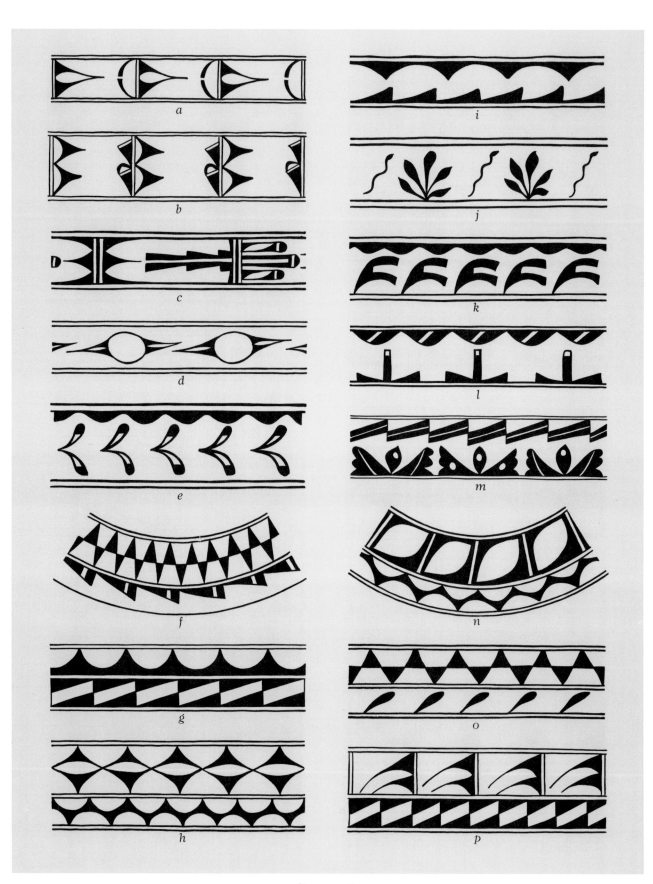

PLATE 6

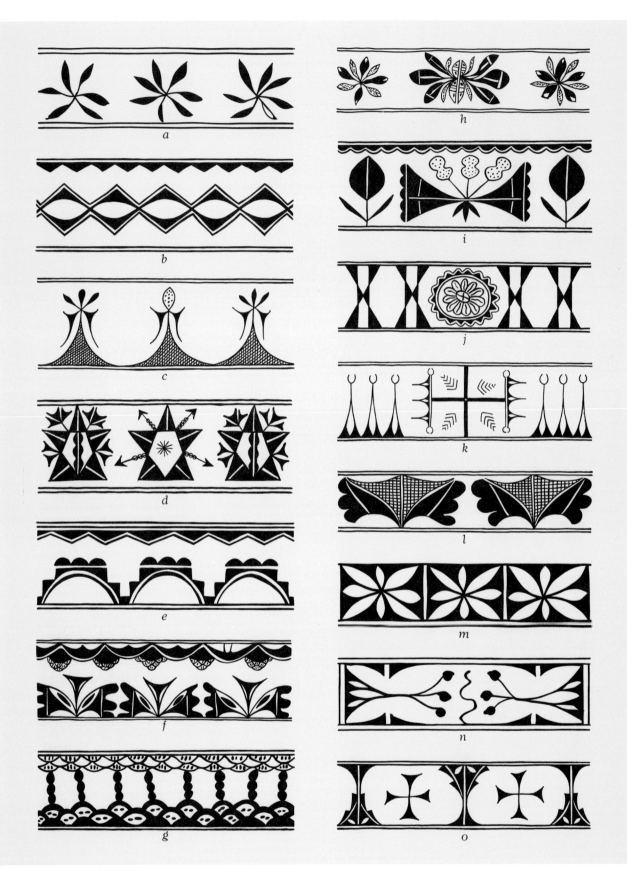

PLATE 7

and *j*, and singly in *o*. The free, continuous band in *b*, based on the crisscross zigzag, is similar to the attached forms used in neck designs (plate 3).

Repeated units attached to one border only are shown in *c* and *d*. In *e* and *f*, decoration is applied to both upper and lower bands. In *g*, the upper and lower bands were united apparently as an afterthought by use of the straight unusual uprights in heavy black. In *k*, the middle unit, attached above and below, alternates with the triple units attached to the base only.

Following these are four paneled designs (*l-o*) with varied details. In *l*, one whole panel is shown, together with a half-panel at each end. The paired-paneling lines are all but hidden by the massive details of the two balanced motifs. Three complete panels appear in *m*. But in *n*, because of its elongate form, only one panel is used. In addition to the two panels used in *o*, sufficient space has been added to complete the two motifs at left and right for comparison with the inverted position of the same motif at the middle. This alternate reversal of paneling units is fairly common, as shown in plate 8*d* and *f*, and in numerous designs from storage jars (plates 2-6).

Among the graphic details, leaves are most numerous. These vary from recognizable forms in *a*, *c*, *h*, and *i* to others less realistic but so identified, such as *d* and *f*, the black portions in *l*, and also the open space forms in *m*. Seedpods appear in *c*, *h*, and possibly in *i* and *n*, a flower in *j*, a medallion in *j*; and rain drops are used in the clouds of the upper bands of *f* and *g*. In the latter, the pairs of dots in the heavier lower band are said to represent the eyes in masks of the mythical "cloud people."

Plate 8. Mixed designs from bodies of water jars. Dynamic (a-j). Dynamic arrangements appear in ten body designs (*a-j*). These comprise a smaller group than the static forms in plate 6. In *a-c*, the upper and lower rows of motifs do not adjoin. In *b*, the three minor static details of rain-far-off serve only to fill unusually wide spaces between the leaf clusters. They do not appear on the opposite side of the jar. In *c*, the upper and lower motifs come within a hairbreadth of joining.

Double-paneling lines are used in five of the designs (*d-h*), but their static effect is minimized by the more lively arrangement of the various motifs applied. Rectilinear details appear in the upright blocks of *d* and *f* and in the zigzags of *k*. They are also used but less consistently within the triangles of *g*. In *i*, the oblique middle motif was added apparently to fill the unusually wide space between two of only three repeats of the major motif.

Graphic details are numerous; leaf forms appear in five designs (*b-d, h*, and *i*). The whirling clusters in *d* are the only free units in the group. Presumably the pairs of graceful forms in *e* are intended as feathers.

Combinations (k-n). Combinations of static and dynamic details are more commonly used as shown in designs *k-n* and throughout the entire series of plate 8. Free motifs include the more or less static leaf clusters in *k*, the birds, and the middle clusters of problematic units in *n*. In *l*, the lively device of leaves on a wavy stem contrasts with the static effect of the two end motifs. Because of the extreme length of the panel, the latter could not be shown as halves of balanced pairs, such as those in plate 7*l*. In *m* and *n*, only the birds in side view disturb the balance of the other motifs.

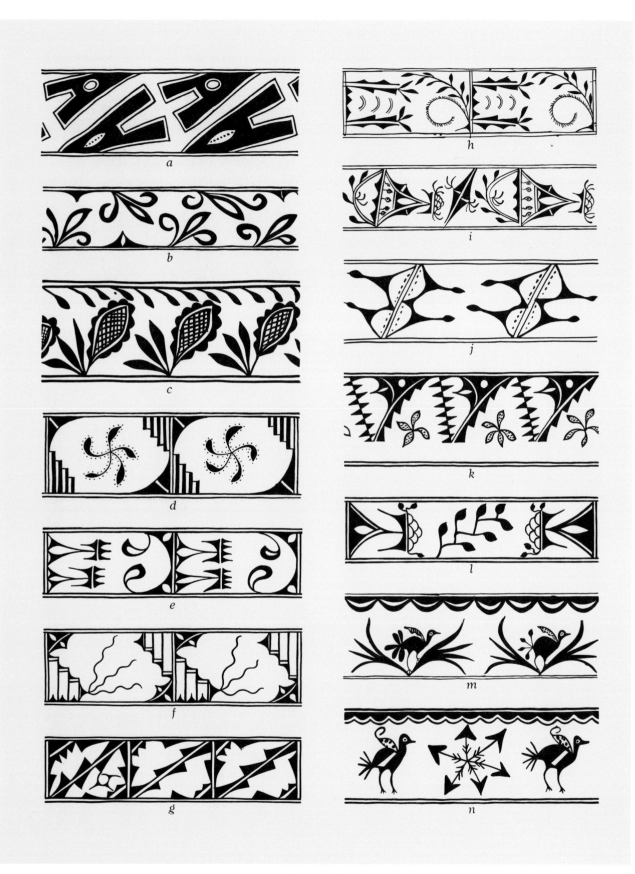

a

b

c

d

e

f

g

h

i

j

k

l

m

n

PLATE 8

Plate 9. Combinations of static and dynamic designs from bodies of water jars. Combinations of static and dynamic elements are used in each of the fourteen designs of plate 9. Free units appear in various combinations. A single static feathered disk appears in *i*, and others in *b* and *h* alternate with free dynamic motifs. The spiral motif in *h*, attached to an otherwise static device, throws it off balance. Other free units of dynamic type appear in *e, f*, and *l*.

Throughout the entire plate scarcely one element can be found, however abstract in appearance, that has gone unnamed by the potters of the Black-on-cream period. Of the clearly graphic motifs, the birds in *a, c,* and *e* are unusual. In the jar from which *a* was taken, four birds facing right were used, widely spaced, around the body band. In the view shown, the space proved too narrow to accommodate a fifth bird of normal size. Normally, in such a case the potter would have substituted a narrower motif as a filler. Instead, by caprice, she solved the problem by telescoping the bodies of two birds.

In *c*, the unattached, highly stylized bird with only one leg is one of two of that style alternating with birds of normal form. Still more stylized are the tiny birds in *e*, used in spread-eagle fashion.

The plant forms graphically shown in *e* are quite unusual. Leaves also appear in three other designs (*g, m,* and *n*).

Only two of the designs (*f* and *g*) show motifs attached to both upper and lower banding lines. Paneled arrangements are used in four figures (*j-m*). In *j*, there is an alternation of unlike motifs. In *k*, only two half-panels are shown; *l* includes one whole panel and parts of two adjoining. In *m*, reading from left to right, a panel of major width is followed by a narrower one at the right, and this alternation is repeated on the opposite side of the jar. In effect, however, the basic structure of paneling is subordinated to the major motif at the left, alternating with the minor one, bearing the barbed leaves.

PLATE 9

67

Plate 10. Designs from bodies of storage jars. The designs in plates 10 to 17, inclusive, are from three distinct types of storage vessels, each having its own more or less specialized uses. Of the group, four plates are from storage jars, one from medium jars, and one from wide-mouthed jars.

Body designs alone are shown, the accompanying neck designs having been included with those from water jars, in plates 2 through 6.

Two distinct methods have been used in representing the designs: one in extended bands as in plate 10*a*, and one in lunettes as in *c*.

Unpaneled layouts are comparatively rare. The four in plates 10*a*, 11*a*, 15*b*, and 17*a* best represent the type. With these few exceptions paneling is the accepted mode of band layouts in the group.

In *c*, the two elongate panels cover the entire circuit of a huge jar. The exceedingly complex and confusing design is built on four distinct structural devices: paneling bands, triangles, one volute, and overlapping curvilinear devices at each end resembling the more regular D-shaped spaces of *f*. Within each complex is an open-space leaf, two of which contain wavy lines. A third wavy line, possibly a mere space filler, appears at the lower left of the middle paneling band.

In addition to the structural devices named, fourteen familiar details are used in filling spaces, or as appendages; principal among these are feathers, leaf spaces, rain-far-off, and narrow cloud bands. Minor appendages from two other jars are shown in *d* and *e*.

In *f*, only one of two fairly identical panels is shown. This obscures somewhat the close relation of the two unlike figures at left and right, such as appears in similar figures from water jars. In comparison with *c*, the arrangement in *f* is quite simple with more sparing use of details. Conspicuous among them are the six volute appendages of triangles in varied positions.

Designs from bodies of storage jars. In figure *a*, only three repeats of the rectangular units are shown, the fourth having been defaced by erosion which has also made necessary the restoration of the lower parts of the three units, as shown by light outlines. However, enough remains of the fourth figure to indicate that it had matched the middle one in size and complexity. Thus the four units were placed in the commonly used A-B A-B, succession. Apparently all four figures were attached lightly to the banding lines.

Each arm of the middle rectangle supports an upright band composed of three pointed feathers and bearing a triple-feather cluster at each end. The triple open-space figures in the arms are also interpreted as feathers. The unnamed motifs placed diagonally in each of the rectangles and the accompanying serrate details are the only deviations from an otherwise well-balanced static arrangement.

The static motif in *b* is one of two large units comprising the complete decoration of a large jar. Its middle pedestal, supporting a cloud cluster, is quite unusual. Open-space forms of cloud, leaf, and eye are used within the crude rectangle. The long drooping points of the triangular figures resemble somewhat the points of feathers in *a*.

a

b

c

d

e

f

PLATE 10

Plate 11. Designs from bodies of storage jars. The design in *a* includes three or four motifs comprising the circuit of a body band, the fourth (a tip of which shows at the extreme right) being similar to the extended middle D-shaped figure, except that it adjoins the otherwise detached figure at the left. Three of the motifs are kept free from the banding lines, but the medallion at the right is purposely attached above and below.

Figures *b* and *c*, when adjoined, cover the entire body band of a huge storage jar. The confused layout in *b* minimizes the skillful drawing of its details, which are used with better effect in the well-planned layout of *c*.

The static arrangement in *d* is quite unusual, the basic checkered, paneling bands being obscured, particularly at the left and middle, by the appendages on both sides.

Outstanding in the group are the elaborate seedpods of *b* and *c*, resting on equally complex triangles, and the equally ornate two-lobed figures. Used on or near them are the usual details of feather, rain-far-off, cloud bands and clusters. In *a* also, the delicate effect of cloud clusters on long stems is quite unusual.

In their detached use, the clusters of three, four, and five angular units in *d* may have no significance as leaves, feathers, or flowers, though the attached cluster at the upper right might be given one of such names.

Plate 12. Designs from bodies of storage jars. Considerable variety is shown in the eight figures of plate 12, varying from small details to others covering one half or more of the circuit of a jar.

One half of the complete band appears in each of the designs *a* and *b*, the bilaterally symmetrical arrangement in *a* contrasting with the unbalanced use of varied details on either side of the banding lines. The upright zigzags (*c* and *e*) are placed at the middle of two panels, thus helping to divide a band into four spaces. In *d*, the crude medallion contains a flowerlike arrangement with petals so shaped that they give a whirling effect. One half of a complete band is shown in *f*, and another in *h*. Between them, in *g*, the two panels complete the circuit of a jar.

Some interesting developments of familiar motifs are found in several of the bands. The feathers at the left end of *b*, with open-leaf spaces placed diagonally, are more elaborately drawn in *f*; and particularly with the horizontally placed group at the left terminating in pointed appendages, in which an eye is placed. In *g*, the elaborate seedpod motifs are given greater freedom of space than those noted in plate 11*b* and *c*. The checkered terraces in *h* are unique. Four distinct uses of clouds appear in *b*, *f*, and *h*. Vegetal details are also used in *f*, *g*, and *h*.

Plate 13. Designs from bodies of storage jars. Two motifs (*a* and *b*) attached to paneling lines are shown free from their banding lines as exceptionally well-designed and executed figures. In contrast are the crudely painted, heavy black details in each of the three panels of *d*. Though there is an apparent attempt at bilateral symmetry in the layout of the two end panels, there is considerable variance in the treatment of leaf forms.

One of two long panels of a large jar is figured in *f*. Bilateral symmetry is fairly maintained in the use of a D and a feather group at each end, facing the two heavy black rosettes at the middle. Open-spaced white clouds appear in the bodies of the feathers and also in the pointed tips. Rain drops appear in two at the left, and rain lines in all four at the right. Rain drops are also placed in the two rosettes.

Bilateral symmetry is dominant in one of two long panels, shown in *g*, though it is broken at the middle by a jagged device running slantwise from upper right to lower left.

a

b

c

d

PLATE 11

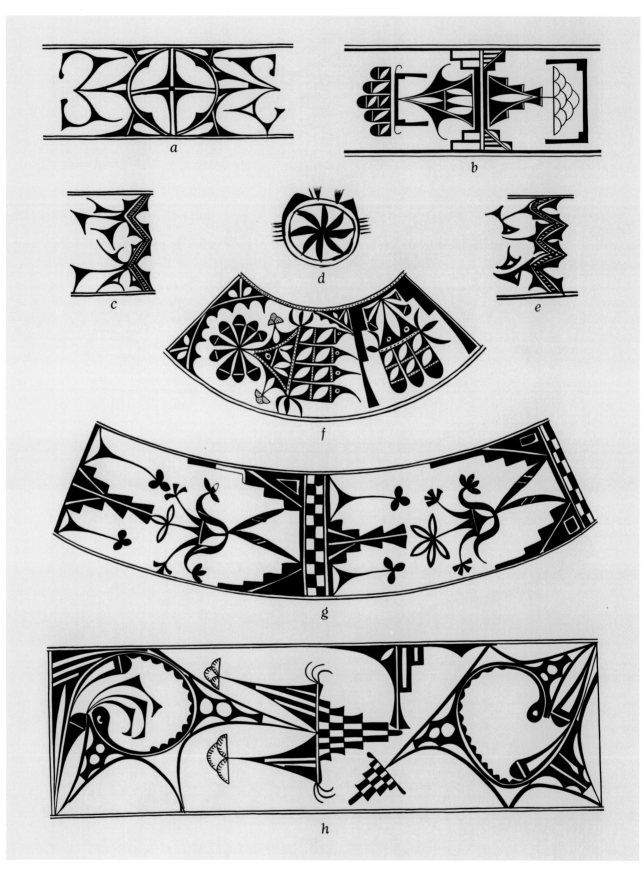

a

b

c

d

e

f

g

h

PLATE 12

PLATE 13

73

Plate 14. Designs from bodies of medium jars. The layouts of plate 14 include three static, two dynamic, and three combinations of the two — all from medium-size jars.

In *a,* two panels of the body design appearing in the developmental series are shown. It is repeated here as an example of irregularities in the size and form of the checker spaces and also as an added illustration of the common use of a dynamic neck design with the static body motif.

Two of six repeats of a body motif in *b* show no uniformity as free or attached units. The C-shaped figures are rarely used and are as yet unnamed.

The two panels in *c,* varying somewhat in proportions, show use of a detached static motif, as repeated in eight panels. Use of a vertically placed rain-far-off device as a pedestal in *d* is quite unusual. Surmounting this, and also a similar figure in *f,* are clusters, apparently of vegetal details.

The two panels in *f* and *g* are from two separate jars. Though varying in their orientation and in certain details, they are obviously the creations of one skilled potter. In both, the dotted stripes within the wide panel bands, the heavy black stripe between the upper corners of *f,* and the left-hand corners of *g,* are telltale marks of the same brush.

A layout somewhat like that of *f* appears in the static middle panel of the heavy and crude pattern of *h.* The end panels might pass also at first glance as static; instead, the three triangular figures of each surround a volute attached to the banding line at the lower right.

Plate 15. Designs from bodies of storage jars. The four designs in plate 15 are all from large wide-mouthed jars. In *a,* an unusually long panel makes up half of the entire band, the obliquely placed complex middle unit was obviously designed to interlock with the two major end units at the lower left and upper right. Viewed from any point, the entire two-paneled design appears to be dynamic throughout.

In *b,* a well-organized static layout gives almost the effect of paneling, the alternating motifs being separated by uprights which fall short of the upper banding line.

The combination of a narrow and a wide panel in *c* represents one half of the complete band. Certain features of the irregular layout suggest a relationship with that in plate 3; in both *b* and *c* we find the rare use of a small band of black clouds with rain lines attached. The crude layout of the smaller panel mars what otherwise might have been a most effective static arrangement.

Familiar details of leaf, feather, cloud cluster, and rain-far-off appear in approximately equal numbers throughout the groups. The two disks at the middle of *d* add a new note; the upper with its border of lazy feather and the lower with five points of rain-far-off.

Plate 16. Paneled designs from storage jars. Through use of the lunette form throughout the series of ten designs in plate 16, a comparison can be made of the various modes of layout within panels that may be classed as static, dynamic, and combinations of the two.

Static layouts appear in the crude panels of *a* and *b,* though confused somewhat in *a* by the addition of minor details. Although the major motifs in *c* are essentially static, a sense of motion is created by their reversal in alternate panels. The jagged border in the left-hand panel also affects the regularity of the paneling bands at middle and left. In the remaining designs (*d-j*), the paneling is effected by use of obliquely drawn borders, their inclination varying from slight in *h* to extreme in *d* and others.

In such dynamic layouts, the best effects are produced by use of major details in the resulting acute angles, as in *f, g,* and *j,* but without use of a detached middle motif as in *i.* In

a

b

c

d

e

f

g

h

PLATE 14

a

b

c

d

PLATE 15

76

PLATE 16

77

contrast with such single layouts, the off-balance middle motif of *d* and the well-designed static device in *e* detract from concentration of design on the oblique border lines.

Usually the paneling motifs are identical throughout the many repeats in a band, as in *g*, *i*, and *j*. Only one example (*f*) has been recorded of the use of two unlike motifs, repeated consistently in panel after panel, so that like motifs appear paired on the oblique paneling lines. One additional arrangement on oblique panel lines appears in plate 18*d*.

Among the decorative details of the group are several unusual items. In the panels of *b*, a device resembling the D figure is used pendant from the upper banding line. In *f*, the volute and seedpod are well composed, and in *i*, the lively rosette is outstanding. Also the use of stars, as in *h*, has not been noted elsewhere in storage jar design. Otherwise the usual leaf, feather, and checker play their part in many of the designs.

Plate 17. Designs from bodies of storage jars. The four designs are from specimens made available after the preceding plates were assembled.

In *a*, the well-balanced arrangement of major static and minor dynamic motifs represents one half of the completed band. The middle medallion provides another example of complex, abstract geometric design. The two end designs are similar in construction though varying in minor details, rain lines being used in the horizontal arms in one in place of cloud clusters in the other. The four whirling leaf clusters liven the otherwise static group.

The extended arrangement in *b* also occupies one half of a band. As in *a*, the middle medallion also encloses an abstract geometric motif with twelve irregular points instead of the usual eight. The two large volutes outweigh the medallion, giving a dynamic character to the combination. Their dotted crosses are unique. Minor details include rain-far-off, lazy feather, cloud cluster, and many-pointed star.

The portion of a body band used in *c* covers approximately two-thirds of a complete A-B A-B layout, the tips of the other B unit barely appearing at the ends of the drawing. The solid and well-balanced middle motif is the largest and most massive device found thus far on a storage jar. With its pair of feathers at each end, it seems to fit in with the later developments of combined geometric and more realistic concepts. The entire band shows a consistent alternation of the large static motif in contrast with the smaller, lightly designed diamond motifs and their leaf appendages accenting the effect of movement.

The entire design of another jar is used in *d*. In concept the layout is essentially static, with minor irregularities in form and orientation of the four detached devices placed at the lower edge of the band. One consistent dynamic detail is that of the upper border with its crooks pointing to the right. The obliquely placed diamond figures are unnamed, and their appendages seem to represent, alternately, leaf and feather. Other minor details are the well-designed lazy feathers, and tiny open-space clouds under the arms of the uprights.

a

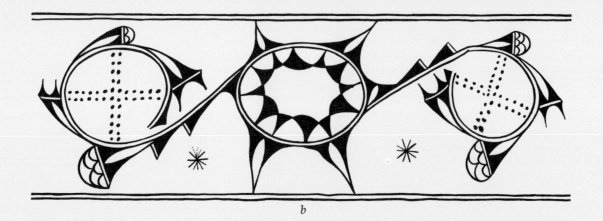

b

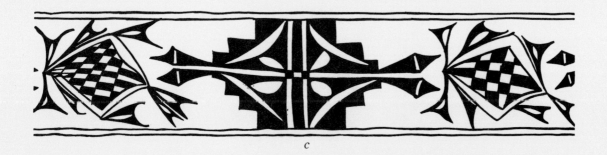

c

d

PLATE 17

Plate 18. Designs from bowls, water and storage jars. Supplementary. The fourteen designs were made available only after the original plates, 1 through 16, were assembled. Some of the designs shown on this plate are similar to the designs shown on the preceding plates.

First in order are the crudely drawn geometric details in *e* and *f*. Several other designs with crude brush work are worthy of inclusion because of their unique character and contents. In *a*, three of five bodyless birds appear, inverted, in the neck band of a water jar. Two easily identifiable hummingbirds in *j* are designed in typical Black-on-cream style.

Rain lines appear on the tiny crescent clouds and rainbow of *b* and also in *n*. Used with the checkered leaves of *h* are two other vegetal details not yet identified. In frequency of use, the familiar leaf and rain-far-off outnumber all the other commonly used details.

Only one segment of an oblique paneled band appears in the lunette arrangements of *d*. Here, unlike the arrangments in plate 16, the design extends bilaterally from the middle of the slanting panel lines.

Plates 19 through 31. Abstract geometric motifs. The term "abstract" is used with the realization that potters of centuries past may have attached specific names to many of the designs of this group and that the makers of early Black-on-cream ware may have inherited a trace of such lore. However, because of lack of consistent terminology, it has seemed best to designate the group in terms of the simplest names available.

Plate 19. The earliest datable examples of Black-on-cream decoration are those recovered in the excavations at Pecos. Therefore, since they are mainly of the abstract geometric type, it seems best to give priority to them, even though a few examples of the latest developments are included in the collection.

The simplest decorative treatment, dots and dashes, is derived from Anasazi ceramics through nearly a thousand years of early-to-late developments. Such ornamentation, applied mainly to structural lines, was continued, but with diminishing favor, through the post-Spanish Tewa series and even more rarely into the design system of Black-on-cream. Of the four uses of dots shown, only a few examples are known, the rarest being those in *a* and *b*. Somewhat more in evidence are the free dots in *c* and spanning in *d*. These, however, are used particularly between paired, upright paneling lines. The continuous fringe of pendant dashes in *e* is rare. But a more frequent and specific use of both dots and dashes is apparent as accessories of the important series of rain symbols used in the decoration of special vessel forms for ceremonial use. These are considered under the head of Ceremonial pottery.

Plate 20. There is not a single example of a free, detached unit of abstract geometric design that has been found in use as a major motif in band decoration. However, a starlike device shown in plate *7d* is so lightly attached to the upper banding line that at first glance it might pass as a free unit. The basic geometric construction of the motif, obscured by over-ornamentation, is more readily understood by reference to this plate.

PLATE 18

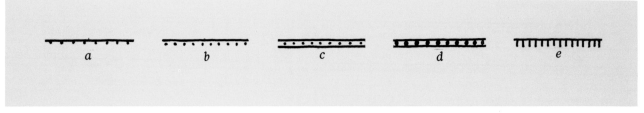

PLATE 19

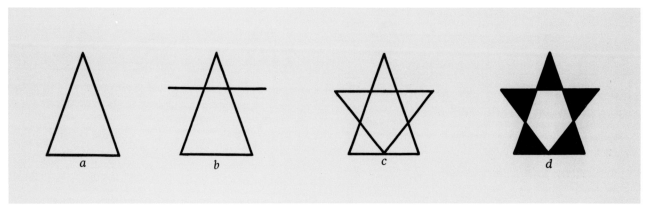

PLATE 20

PLATE 21

83

Plate 21. In the twelve designs in plate 21, the formalized development of two groups is shown; those at the left (*a* and *b*) use straight lines throughout. In *a*, the layout begins with the diagonal crossing of two lines. In the next stage a horizontal line is added; and in the third, a horizontal and two vertical lines are used to enclose three triangular spaces which in the final stage are filled with black.

In the second stage of *b*, two of the X-figures are adjoined. Next, four horizontal lines are added. Apparently the paired middle lines were used to break up the comparatively large middle space. By so doing the result is a pair of semiattached hourglass-like figures as shown in black in the final design.

Two distinct uses of a curvilinear astroid motif are shown in the development of *k* and *l*. In *k*, the combination of astroid and enclosed circle produces the four triangular spaces which in the final stage are filled with black.

In *l*, the same astroid provides the basis for superimposing an identical figure with its points diagonally placed. By filling only the resulting triangular spaces, an octagonal, open-space, central figure is produced.

Bilateral symmetry is apparent in all four figures as viewed in the upright position, and in *j*, *k*, and *l* when viewed sidewise. This is true also for the first two stages of *a* but the addition of vertical and horizontal lines in the third stage produces symmetry only in the upright position.

Plate 22. The prevailing informal treatment of geometric motifs is evident in many of these designs, as may be seen by comparison of *b* and *c* with their formalized counterparts used in the developmental series of *d* and *h* in plate 21.

In *a*, the four elongate points of an astroid are symmetrically placed about a circular open space. In contrast, the large circles of *d* and *e* are bordered with five points less even in form. The whirling effect of the points in *e* is quite unusual. In *m*, the elongate figure is in effect a distortion of *a*.

The detached designs in *f* through *j* show a decided preference for medallionlike structures bordered by radiating points and other details. Two similar figures (*k* and *o*) are semidetached. In *k*, the bordering fringe is confined to the free spaces above and below the band.

The more symmetrical rectilinear devices in *g* and *i* are detached units of motifs more commonly used within panels of band designs. Irregularity in spacing of the radiating black points of *h* and of the details within the disks of *f*, *h*, and *j* are characteristic of the freedom used by the potters of the later period when rosette arrangements came into use, in which such extreme examples as *l* and *n* are not uncommon.

Plate 23. Eight abstract geometric designs are shown in successive stages of development from the barest essentials to the completion of one or more units in solid black. Several examples of each are found in the narrow neck bands of water and storage jars, where they provide a marked contrast with the much wider and more elaborately decorated body bands.

The first four rectilinear forms (*a-d*) are of particular interest for they had been in constant use on Anasazi Black-on-white wares for well over a thousand years. Yet they had been ignored in the Tewa area for at least two centuries before their reappearance in San Ildefonso. The only modification is that in *b*, the ancient version of which was never bordered by banding lines.

The second group includes two rectilinear crisscross motifs (*e* and *f*) and two of a later period with combinations of rectilinear and curvilinear details.

The eight designs are evenly divided between static and dynamic. Of the static group (*a*, *e*, *f*, and *h*), only one (*a*) is of ancient origin. Its simple zigzag motif is quite unlike the complex,

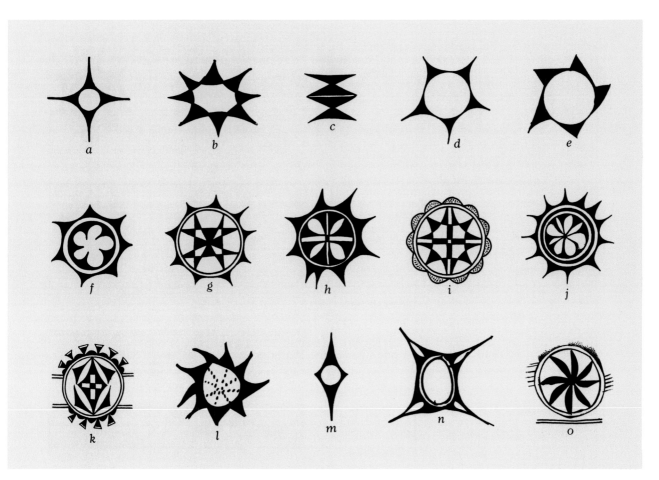

PLATE 22

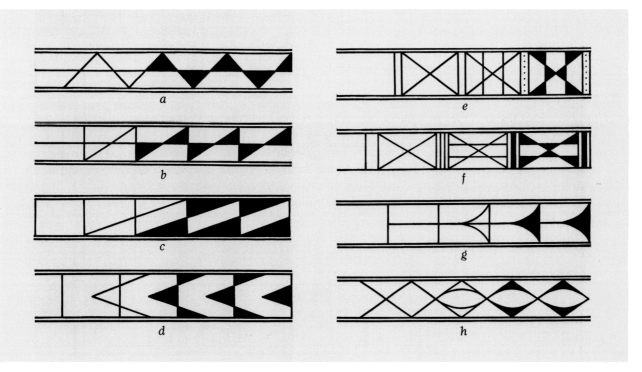

PLATE 23

paneled, crisscross units of *e* and *f*. In contrast with the static group, the four dynamic motifs (*b-d* and *g*) depend on paneling produced by single lines only.

As in *a,* the horizontal line in *b* divides the band into two spaces. When crossed by the vertical lines, the resulting panels are further divided by a single diagonal. This leaves two pairs of unlike spaces; either might be filled with black and the more effective is that produced with the triangles.

The median horizontal line is absent in *c* and *d.* In *c,* each oblique line extends diagonally across two panels. This divides each panel into three angular spaces, thus providing two modes of filling with black. In every instance, however, the triangular spaces are chosen.

The numerous examples of *d* show a wide variation in construction based partly on the relative width of the panels and also on the length of the pair of oblique lines. In this specimen the oblique lines start from the banding lines above and below, at a point half way across each panel, and converge at the center of the adjoining panel. In others, the device is more elongate. Rarely do the oblique lines begin from the upper and lower righthand corners of one panel and extend through to the left side of the adjoining one, thus producing five instead of the four spaces in each panel. In every instance the artists have chosen to fill the adjoined triangles with black rather than the intervening V-shaped open spaces.

The median horizontal line appears again in *g* and provides a convenient guide for the two curved lines, converging about midway in each panel. In all four of the dynamic designs (*b, c, d,* and *g*) the effect of motion toward either left or right is optional, there being no evidence of a marked preference for either in the available specimens. Last in the series is *h,* a frequently used static device that combines the straight lines of two crossing zigzags with the curved lines to produce open leaf-shaped spaces and that contrasts with the triangular spaces above and below.

Plate 24. Average and extreme examples of erratic layout of abstract goemetric designs. Plate 24*a* is average. Two panels from the same vessel, extremely erratic layouts, are shown in *b* and *c.*

Plate 25. In addition to the usual free and easy treatment of design with its resulting minor aberrations, still others arise from lack of system in laying out the repeats of an entire band.

In most examples of Black-on-cream decoration it is quite apparent that no preliminary measurements are made to assure the artist that the design as it encircles the vessel will reach the point of beginning without a break in the rhythm of details and spaces, as the two ends of the band are joined.

Also the length of the original unit may be gradually expanded or contracted, so that the spacing of the final repeat is at considerable variance with that of its opposite, as they meet. Some of the results of such haphazard joining are shown.

In *a* and *b,* the regular motifs are used throughout the bands, but in *a,* the abrupt variance between the narrowly and widely spaced units betrays the start and finish of the band. In *b,* the gradual variance in width of panels leads by degrees from one extreme to the other.

In *c* and *d,* the erratic joining is effected by use of added elements.

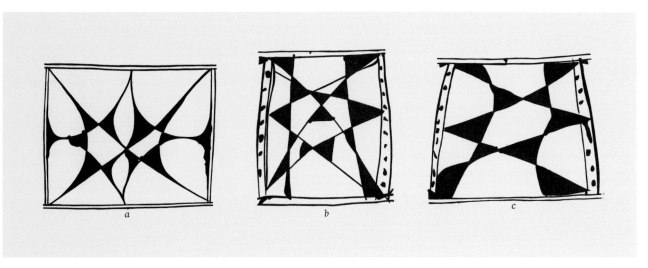

PLATE 24

PLATE 25

Plate 26. The series of twenty-four designs shown in plate 26 begins with *a*, in which the unpaneled overall arrangement consists of a repetition of crisscross lines in pairs that provide elongate spaces for filling with black. In *b*, single lines divide the bands into panels in each of which a four-line diagonal crisscross provides spaces for a more intricate use of black than that in *a*. The more commonly used paired lines of *c* provide panels in which the simple line crisscrossing of two laterally placed Vs is further complicated by the addition of two vertical lines, thus providing ten triangular spaces for filling with black. The use of dots seems to accent the panel dividers.

A more complex device appears in the panels of *d*, in which the sixteen rectangles of each are crisscrossed by diagonals, producing four triangular spaces within each square. By using an A-B A-B alternation both horizontally and vertically in the placement of black in the adjoining rectangles, the construction lines disappear. This, the only known example of the device in the post-Spanish ceramics of the entire Southwest, is matched also by only one sherd recovered in the excavation of a Pueblo site.

(Although the motif appears in early Islamic art, there is no evidence of its diffusion to the American Southwest through Spanish contacts.)

Plate 27. The group in plate 27 includes four of a series of fourteen paneled designs, the constant feature of which is a crisscross of single, double, or multiple lines. In *a*, four slightly curved lines supplement the crisscross, each extending from a corner of the panel to the middle of the opposite side. This produces a symmetrical figure of eight spaces, six of which are filled with black. An astroid is added in *b-d*, as shown most clearly in the second panel of *b* and the first of *d*. In *b*, the astroid is crossed by an arc, above and below. In the lateral parts of the astroid, additional arcs provide leaf spaces; the combination produces fourteen spaces, ten of which are filled with black. The paired-paneling lines of *c* and *d* give greater emphasis than the single lines of *a* and *b*. In *c*, the corner-to-corner arcs used in *b* are missing, but with the use of two vertical straight lines a more complex figure is produced. In the process, the pair of leaf spaces is placed vertically. The combination gives eighteen spaces, fourteen of which are filled with black. In *d*, the basic arrangement is identical with that of *b*, except for the systematic A-B A-B alternation, panel by panel, of the position of the arcs and leaf spaces, as shown by the third panel, in contrast with the second and fourth.

Plate 28. One additional combination, that of a single-line crisscross and an astroid, appears in *a*. It is of special interest for it comes from the excavations at Pecos and is therefore the only design in the group of twenty-four that can be dated definitely as pre-1839. It is also unique in that the side points of the astroid merge into triangular forms attached to the paneling lines.

Paired lines are used in the crisscross of *b* and *c*, and multiple in *d*. In *c*, the sparing use of black, in only a portion of the crisscross and in the many angles within and about the astroid, gives a lacy effect, quite unlike that in the preceding designs. In *c*, the arcs of the astroid are widened to match the crisscross, thus producing a more simple but very effective arrangement. The more intricate design of *d*, done with unusual precision, is an outstanding example of the possibilities of the familiar combination of crisscross and astroid in the hands of a capable artist. It is notable also for the use of four corner-to-corner arcs, instead of the two in *a* and the preceding group (plate 27). But the four are so widely separated by the multiple-line crisscross that they form only sections of a corner-to-corner astroid, shown most clearly as outlined in the third panel.

a

b

c

d

PLATE 26

a

b

c

d

PLATE 27

a

b

c

d

PLATE 28

Plate 29. In this group, more or less complex paneling devices and attached motifs tend to distract from the central figures within the panels.

The design in *a* is from the exterior bands of a huge bowl in which nine panels are used. In this the usual crisscross is missing. The arcs in the panel corners match those forming the astroid, thus enclosing four petaloid or leaf spaces in each panel. These compete with the astroids, particularly when viewed in groups of four and centered on the middle of the paired-paneling lines. There is a regular alternation of the checkered astroid as in the third panel, with the finer grid of the fourth. In *b*, the basic paired-line crisscross is used in each panel, but in alternate panels the astroid is replaced by an intricate arrangement surrounding the inner rectangle. The intricate paneling in *c* tends to minimize the simple, effective arrangement of black within the panels.

An unusually intricate arrangement appears in the body design of a storage jar, where by superimposing a six-pointed curvilinear device on a more simple elongate group, a twelve-point arrangement is produced. The designer must have found the experiment most confusing, as is shown by numerous mistakes made in reproducing it in panel after panel. A similar lack of planning is apparent also in the neck band of the same jar, shown formalized in plate *22b*.

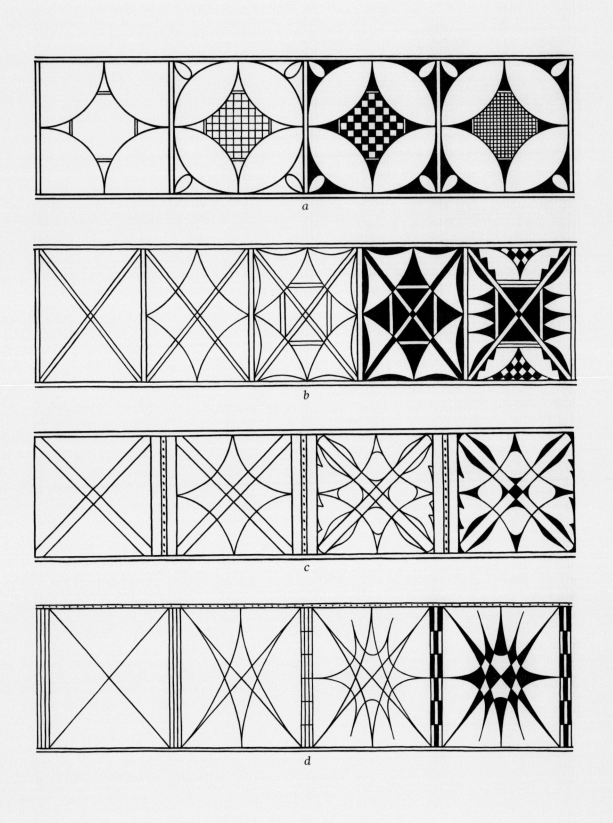

a

b

c

d

PLATE 29

93

Plate 30. Additional developments in complex panel divisions are shown in plate 30. The diagonal crisscross series ends with *a* in which the stepped motif is built on the paired diagonals. In *b* and *c*, the crisscross is placed upright. The corner leaf spaces in *b* and the feather motifs in *c* indicate a somewhat late period in Black-on-cream design, when such obvious touches of realism were coming into use. No vestige of the crisscross or astroid remains in *d* where the upright, terraced motif is attached only at the top. The jagged borders of the multiple-paneling lines are unusual.

Plate 31. The tendency toward use of conventionalized motifs of realistic significance, as noted in plate 30, is more pronounced in *a-c* of this plate.

In *a*, the single-line crisscross forces the petaloid motifs into upright and horizontal positions, the former in open space, and the latter in black. The paired-paneling lines of *b* are carefully maintained, uncrossed; that feature alone distinguishes them from the crossed, paired lines within each panel. As in *b*, the eight petaloids of *c* are left as open spaces; the intervening black areas are confined to moderate size by the eight bordering scallops. The final design (*d*) might well have been grouped with the similar motifs of plate 27. But since it is obviously an experiment in use of the motif from a paneled band, for use in unpaneled repeats, it deserves special mention. Apparently in joining the crisscross and lateral arcs of adjacent units, the artist had not foreseen the necessity of overlapping their lateral points, thus throwing the motifs off balance.

Plate 32. Motifs emanating from the abstract geometric series and persisting throughout the later, more free decorative system. Several distinct geometric motifs appear which include, first, the terraced group (*d, e,* and *g*). Although usually placed pendant or upright on banding lines, they may also appear attached laterally to panel dividers or other vertical lines or bars. There are two types: solid as in *e* and *g*, or bipartite as in *d*. Rarely, only one-half of a bipartite form is used as in *f*.

Second are the simple forms of cove (*b*) and bracket (*c*) used in corners of panels, as shown in *a*. Third are the many variants of stepped groups of elongate vertical bars, also used as corner devices of panels, as shown in *a* and *f*.

In nearly every instance the interpretation of all such motifs has been that of "steps," or, more specifically, Kiva steps, though occasionally the stepped forms of *d, e,* and *g,* may be termed "mountains." (The same forms are often called "clouds" by the Hopi potters.)

A more varied group of such corner devices, from storage jars, appears in plate 42.

Plate 33. Rosette arrangements of plant details from water jars. Free, unattached vegetal motifs, mostly in rosette arrangements, are used in most instances as minor space fillers between major motifs. With the exception of the plain black leaf forms in *a* and *g*, the others vary from four mere lines in *e* to ornate dotted forms in *b-d* and *h*. The cluster of detached units in *f* might be intended as either leaves or petals.

The ornate stems in *i* suggest a vegetal intent, but the points may be intended as points of lightning, arrows, or tongues of *avanyus.*

Plate 34. Leaf forms from water jars. Lanceolate forms predominate, varying from extremely narrow (*c*) to wide (*l-n*) and from mere outlines to solid black with the intermediate use of dots as in *d* and *e* and open spaces within the black forms of *j-n* and *p*. The truncate form in *h* is known as either leaf or feather, according to the association.

The apparent leaf within a leaf in *f* and the oaklike form in *g* are unusual. More common is the truncate form of *h*, which may mean either leaf or feather, according to its association with other details.

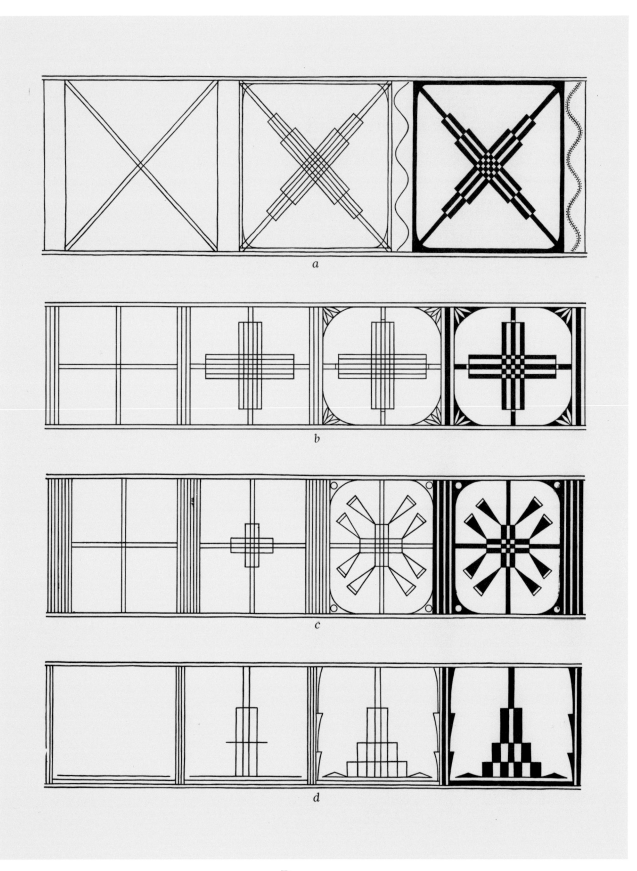

a

b

c

d

PLATE 30

PLATE 31

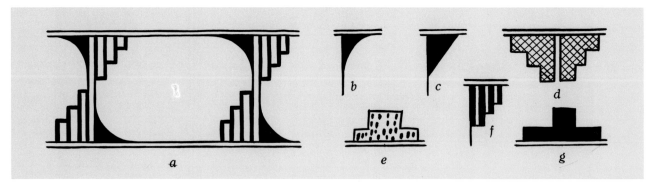

PLATE 32

96

PLATE 33

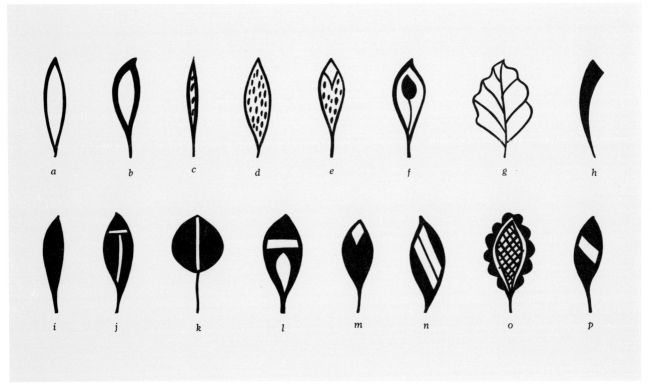

PLATE 34

Plate 35. Lazy leaf forms from water jars. Each of the group of eight leaf forms in plate 35 has a distinct upsweep to the right. Included are a triple cluster of fairly realistic forms in *a*, a group of four elongate forms in *f* (the lowest of which does not actually touch the banding line), and a formalized bifurcated unit in *e*. In the one pendant design (*b*), the bifurcated black units may have been intended as leaves, and the intervening dotted lanceolate forms might also have been intended as such.

In the remaining four designs, the stylized forms commonly called leaves either touch the banding line lightly as in *g*, or lie flat against it as in *c, d,* and *h*. These are prototypes of even more stylized forms developed in the later Black-on-red and Polychrome wares.

Plate 36. Miscellaneous vegetal details from water jars. The fourteen details in plate 36 are mainly finials from the stems of branches of plant forms. They range from fairly realistic representations such as the flower in *l*, the trefoil in *h*, and the buds or seedpods in *n*. The combination in *a* is purely fanciful, as is the combination of triple clouds with leaves in *k*.

Plate 37. Forms of feathers from water jars. The eight forms of feathers represent those most commonly used during the Black-on-cream period. Of these, the rounded variety in *a-c* and the more elongate in *g* and *h* are reasonably realistic. The more abstract forms in *d* and *e*, with scalloped tips, are less recognizable. In *f*, however, the white truncate tip identifies it as the turkey's tail feather, prized for certain ceremonial use.

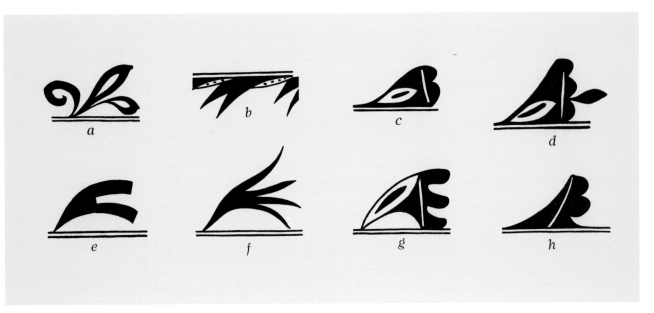

PLATE 35

PLATE 36

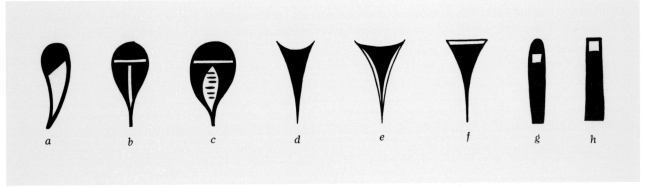

PLATE 37

Plate 38. Cloud arrangements from water jars. Of the sixteen variants in the use of cloud motifs shown in plate 38, nine show the unvarying use of the semicircular cloud repeated in single rows pendant from banding lines as shown in *a-j;* while only one (*j*) includes a secondary row in outline. In *k* and *l,* the cloud units are staggered in a triple row. The greatest variation is in the treatment of the cloud spaces: outline only in *a,* solid black in *f,* use of various details of rain dots and rain lines, and bordering bands (or lines) of *c, d,* and *i.* In *o,* a single unit of an outlined pendant cluster is repeated at intervals. The two arrangements in *m* and *p* are derived directly from similar motifs placed upright. Here they appear as minor details, at the tips of longer, horizontally extended motifs.

Plate 39. Birds from water jars. Two fairly distinct types of birds are included, namely primitive forms in *a-c, e, g,* and *i;* and three of a later period in *d, f,* and *h.* These early forms are in outline, with fillers of dots, crosshatch, and clouds. Four of these are without feet and two (*e* and *g*) with feet showing. The representation of wings in *e* and *i* is not commonly used. If detached, they might serve better as leafy stems of plants. The layout of *b* is quite unusual, only the wings and tiny head giving a birdlike character to the otherwise abstract form.

Of the later period, the two birds of more realistic form in solid black (*d* and *f*), form the same body band and are dwarfed in their setting of leaf motifs. The perching birds (*h*), also of solid black, are part of an informally extended group.

Plate 40. Plant forms from water jars. Vegetal motifs, combining two or more details such as roots, stems, leaves, flowers, or seedpods, are rare in Black-on-cream decoration. Despite the importance of corn, it does not appear in recognizable form on domestic pottery. The nearest approach is that in *c* in which the plant is placed horizontally. The sinuous outlines of some of the leaves in *e* and *g* suggest scrub oak, and the finials in *g* are possibly intended as acorns. None of the other forms is identifiable, the purpose of their use being apparently to express concern for vegetation as such.

Plate 41. Elaboration of vertical panel borders. The tendency toward use of a more complex grouping of motifs in decoration of large storage vessels, also extended to elaboration of structural details, is shown in the somewhat formalized drawings of sixteen variants of upright panel borders in plate 41, and particularly in the use of the heavy black stripes in *h.* These are made by first outlining, as in *a,* and then filling the intervening space with black. The same outlining is used for the checkered group (*i-m*) and also for the combined recticurvilinear group (*n-p*).

Plate 42. Elaboration of corner devices within panels. As with the paneling bands in plate 41, the increased space of large storage vessels led to the use of larger and more ornate corner devices. Of the twenty-four shown in plate 42, only six are rectilinear in all details: *k, l, p, u, w,* and *x.* The others vary between the simple curvilinear form in *a* and the ornate combinations of rectilinear and curvilinear details in those between *n* and *t,* among which are open-space leaf and cloud forms. The latter, in *r* and *t,* are produced by use of rain-far-off motifs in solid black.

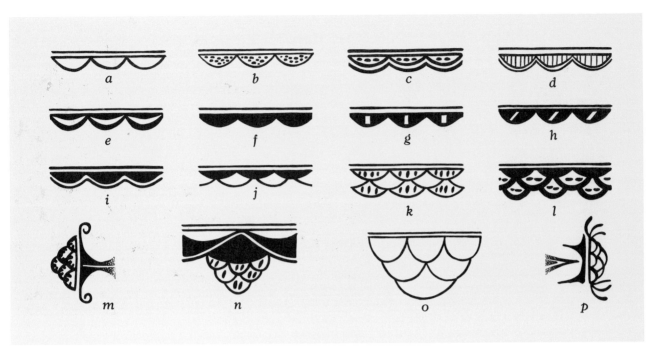

PLATE 38

PLATE 39

PLATE 40

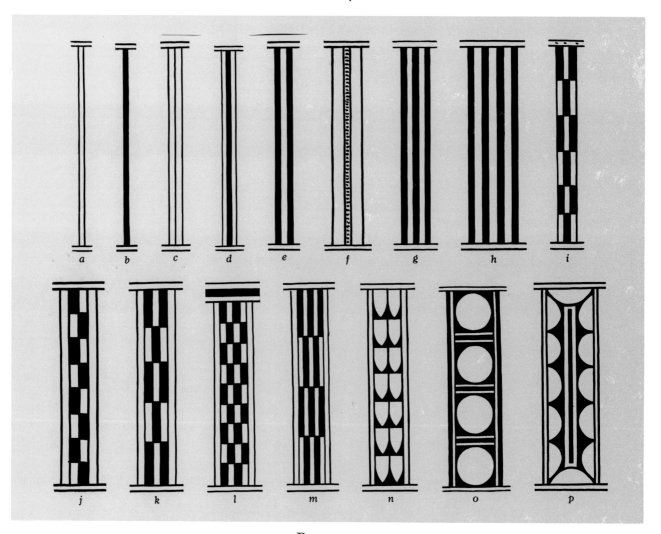

PLATE 41

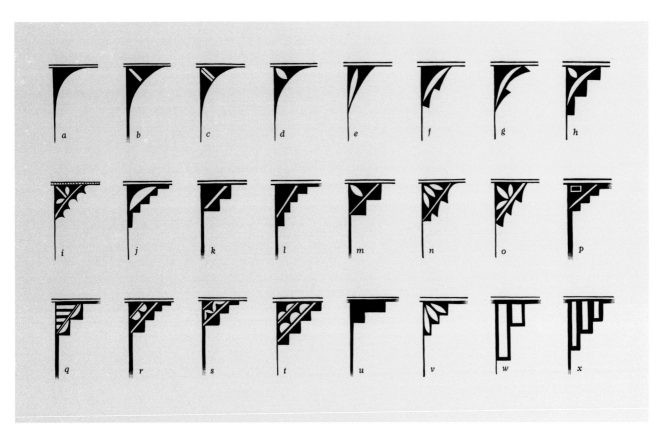

PLATE 42

Plate 43. Decoration developed within triangles. Because of their comparatively large size the majority of triangular forms commonly used in the decoration of storage vessels are classed as "major," thus leaving the term "minor" for a considerable secondary group of smaller triangular forms often attached to the majors.

The group of nine in plate 43 is shown divested of secondary border lines and other exterior ornament in order to stress the varied modes of decoration within the triangular spaces. Five distinct motifs are used in the group: bands, triangles, checkers, and open-space leaves and clouds.

Plate 44. Additional decoration developed within triangles. Among the nine triangular forms of plate 44 are two unusually elongate forms (*a* and *h*); two bounded by compound curves (*d* and *g*); and one (*c*) with considerable distortion. The single rain-far-off units in *e* and *h* produce unusual open-space forms.

Plate 45. Minor triangles, usually attached to volutes. Unlike the major triangular forms in plates 43 and 44, the major group of seventeen in plate 45 consists of relatively small devices attached smoothly to volutes, medallions, or other curvilinear forms, as is best shown in *b, i, j, o,* and *p.* They are not bordered by secondary outlines or by still smaller attached details, but in their embellishment they resemble quite closely some of the major forms.

Plate 46. Feathers from storage vessels. Despite the complete absence of birds as decorative motifs for storage vessels, considerable use is made of a greater variety of feathers than those used on such smaller domestic utensils as food bowls and water jars. Though the basic forms of the twenty-four in plate 46 are no more varied than those from water jars, as shown in plate 37, yet their greater size seems to have led to a remarkable diversity of decorative details, most of which tend to stray even farther from realism than the stylized forms themselves. The forms fall into two distinct groups, described in botanical terms as cuneiform (*a-o*) and linear (*q-x*). In both classes, the rounded tips give at least a semblance of feather forms.

This leaves only one (*p*) with no class resemblances to any natural object — a fanciful combination of cloud spaces above the transverse band and rain-far-off below.

Plate 47. Flat-tipped feather forms. The flat-tipped feather forms of plate 47 are identified as the white-tipped tail feathers of the wild turkey. Two distinct uses of the form are shown, classed as lazy (*a-e*) and erect (*f-h*). The lazy group includes feathers attached to straight lines of border bands, and others warped by use on curved lines. The erect forms are used as minor decorative units on bands or on major arrangements as in *g.*

Plate 48. Miscellaneous feather forms. Many of the forms in plate 48, classed as feathers, are so stylized that they bear no resemblance to real feathers. But since they are used in feather clusters as in *c* and are so called by some informants, they are here included under that term.

Despite the ritualistic importance of the white, black-tipped tail feathers of the golden eagle, they are not used on domestic pottery; the closest approach is the two round-tipped forms in *c*, with black instead of white for the bodies. White-tipped turkey feathers appear in *c, f,* and *l.* The remaining forms vary from the three linear types (*j, m,* and *n*) with long pointed tips to the extremely stylized group. When used singly or in clusters they lend variety to arrangements.

Plate 49. Vegetal forms. A considerable variety in vegetal forms is shown in plate 49. One notices at once the complete absence of designs using the corn motif, which during the Black-on-cream period seems to have been restricted to use on Ceremonial pottery. The lazy leaf form as used on water jars (plate 35) is also missing. Fairly realistic arrangements appear in the vine of *d,* the upright panel of *i,* and the clusters of *e, j,* and *k.*

PLATE 43

105

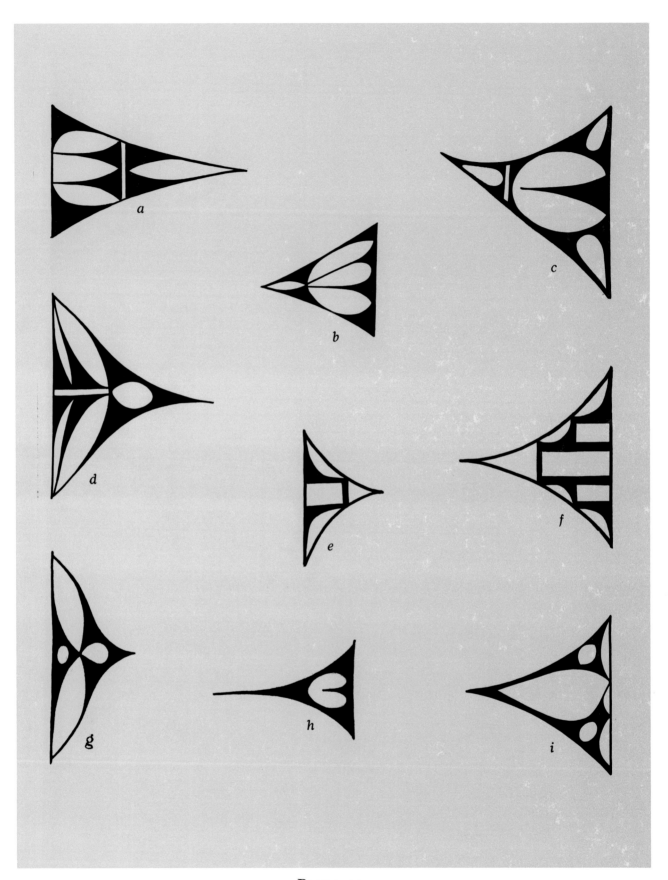

PLATE 44

106

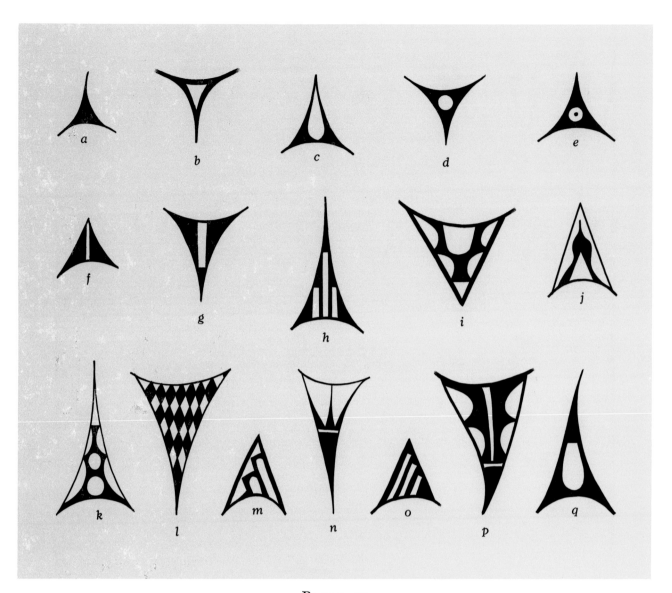

PLATE 45

107

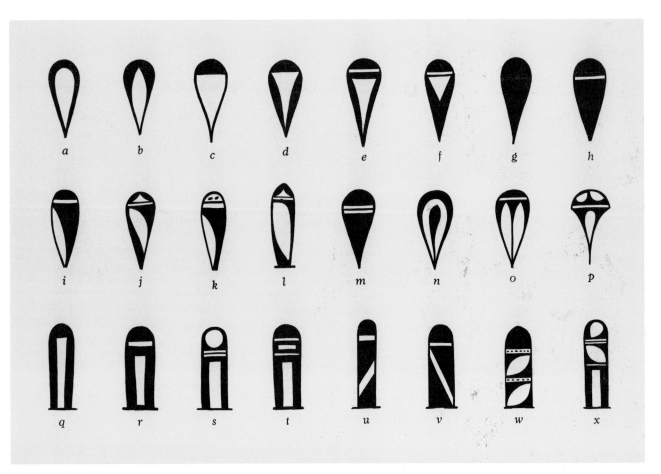

PLATE 46

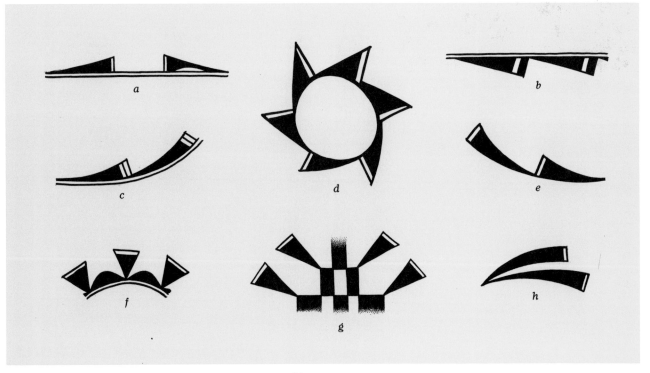

PLATE 47

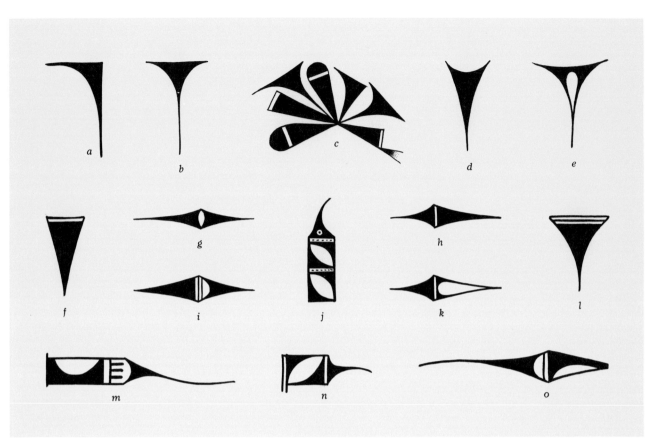

PLATE 48

PLATE 49

109

Plate 50. Leaf forms. The basic forms of most of the leaves in plate 50 resemble those from water jars shown in plate 34; those in *k, l,* and *o* show the greatest variance. The form in *k* suggests a feather instead of a leaf, though its use on the upright stem of plate 49*l* would rather indicate leaves.

Plate 51. Seedpod motifs. One outstanding trait in the decoration of storage vessels is the use of comparatively large variants of the so-called seedpod motif, as shown in the nine examples of plate 51. With the exception of *e,* all the forms have been grouped upright for comparison. The seedpod, appearing in smaller and simplified form, is frequently used by potters of Cochiti Pueblo on food bowls and water jars, but at San Ildefonso it has not been found in use on such small vessels. The typical, more or less rotund body form prevails in all but one example (*d*) where it is replaced by a hexagon. The greater size of most of the nine examples has led to considerable elaboration.

A single spike, such as that used at Cochiti, is represented in four examples (*a, d, f,* and in the lower unit of *e*). Double spikes occur in *b* and *g* and in the upper units of *c* but are replaced apparently by the pair of nubbins of *h.* Three spikes are used in *c,* each bearing a trefoil; and in *i* they are replaced by a bar, connecting the seedpod by another motif. Another added feature is the leaf cluster within the hexagon of *d.* The elongate appendages at the base of *a, b,* and *g* are apparently intended as leaves, but the white tips of those in *f, h,* and *i* might pass as turkey feathers.

Plate 52. Variations of rain-far-off. (The text explaining the details of plate 52 was not available. Since Dr. Chapman knew exactly what he wanted to say in presenting these designs, an explanation by another would be presumptive.)

Plate 53. Volutes and related forms. The group of miscellaneous minor details in plate 53 includes several in which the involute is an important feature and varies in range between those with less than one complete circuit, as in *a* and *j,* and the more involved forms of *d* and *h.* Two motifs (*a* and *j*) resemble somewhat the single-spiked seedpods of plate 51. No names are assigned to the bilaterally symmetrical forms of *b, c, f,* and *h.*

Plate 54. Cloud forms. The use of clouds in rows as border bands was not favored in the decorative scheme of storage vessels. Only one example (*l*) appears in plate 54 in which a cluster of three clouds alternates with vegetal forms. In *c,* however, a triple cluster is appended to alternate rain-far-off symbols on a border band. The triple arrangement appears in eight of the designs attached to various motifs; the others vary in number from six to fourteen. A rainbow appears above the two upper clouds of *m.*

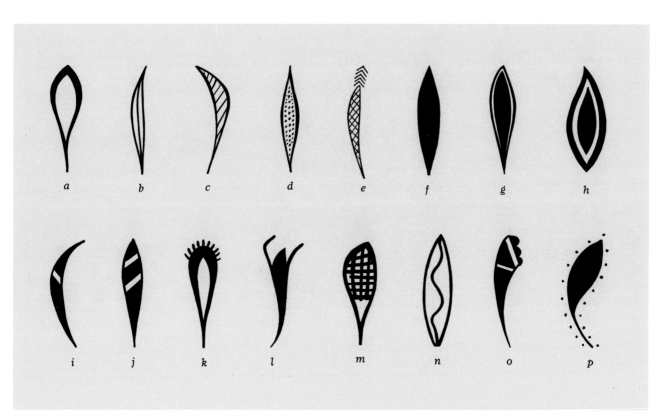

PLATE 50

111

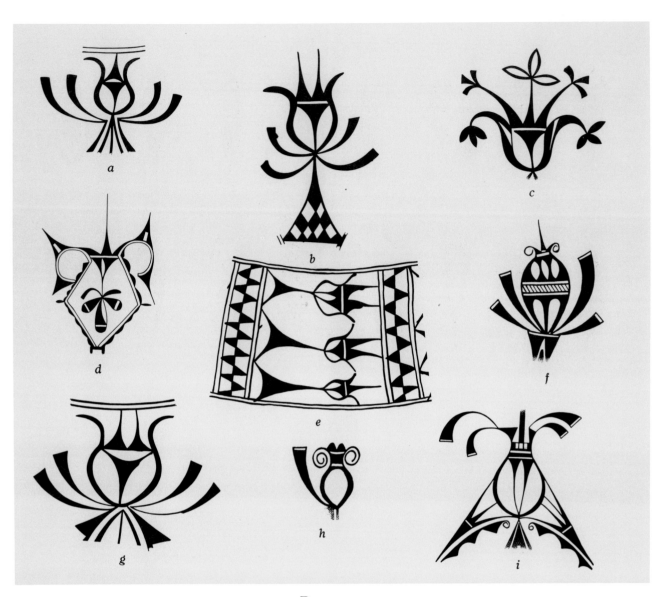

PLATE 51

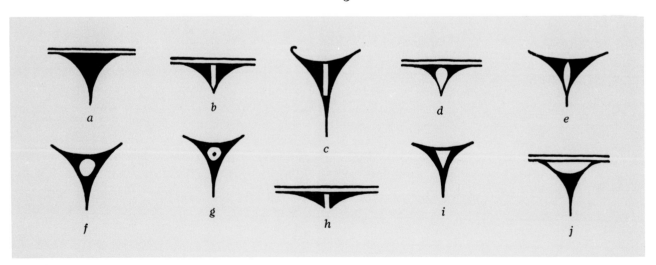

PLATE 52

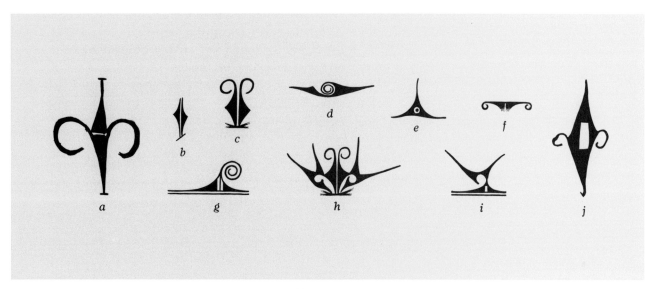

PLATE 53

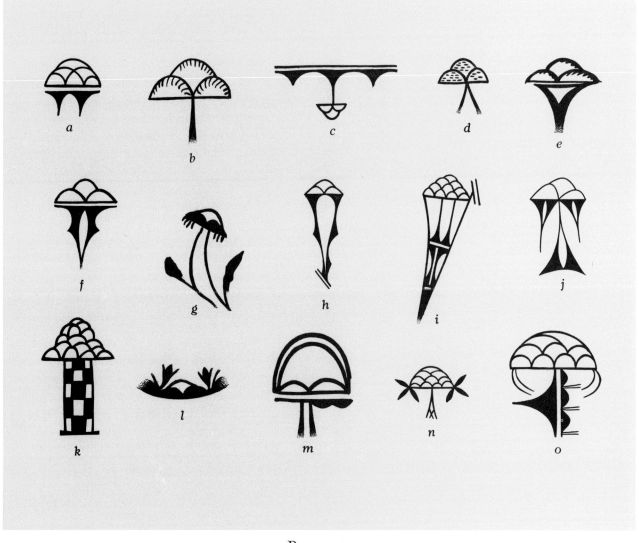

PLATE 54

Plate 55. Designs from Ceremonial vessels. The group of eleven motifs in plate 55 includes seven which might be considered at first glance to have no special significance but which are important in pueblo rituals. Of these, two terraced figures (*d* and *f*) appearing on the border bands and the unattached pair in *g* are usually known as "mountains"; but occasionally the interpretation is "clouds," a concept more commonly recognized by the potters of the Hopi pueblos. The terrace appears also in the border band of *i* and in the major, free arrangement of *e* where it supports two unusually realistic corn plants. Within the terrace are crisscross lines of rain blown by the wind. Below, on the usual bar with rain lines, are two U-shaped motifs resembling the body structure of ornate seedpods, such as appear in plate 51. The astroid form of morning star appears in *j* surrounded by crosses indicating lesser stars. Rain-far-off appears pendant in *a* and upright in *c*. The detached quatrefoil in *b*, the bordered cloud band in *k*, and the unusual arrangement in *h* of trefoil with the two pendant rain-far-off symbols complete the group.

Plate 56. Cloud motifs from Ceremonial vessels. With only a few exceptions the twenty-two cloud arrangements of plate 56 show the inexpert brush work of men in charge of rituals who could not entrust the painting of Ceremonial vessels to uninitiated artists. Yet most of the essentials are easily identified when compared with the best of those from domestic pottery (plate 54). Shown out of context, the least identifiable rendition of clouds is the bank in *n* spotted with huge rain drops. An innovation in cloud forms is that of the double-lined crescent units in *q*, which are repeated more crudely in *h* and *p*. The importance of rain for vegetation is shown in *d*, *f*, *l*, and *v*.

Plate 57. Variations in heads of avanyus. A considerable diversity of opinion regarding the appearance of *avanyu*, the Tewa version of the mythical horned or plumed serpent, is evident, particularly in the crude representations of its head, as shown in plate 57. Of the sixteen variants, a single horn appears in eight; a pair in *p*, and, possibly, in *d*. There is some variance also in representation of the eyes. They are not shown in three (*f*, *k*, and *m*); but they appear singly in ten and in pairs in three (*a*, *d*, and *o*). Teeth are shown in the mouths of five; and in all but four, lightning as a symbol of rain is used in place of a tongue.

Plate 58. Decoration of the bodies of avanyus. Decorative devices used with the bodies of *avanyus* are varied, as is evident in plate 58 where sections are shown from twelve specimens. These vary from plain black to more ornate; some of them are derived from early post-Spanish examples, principal among which are those including open-space bars. Rectilinear outlines are rare; only two (*j* and *i*) have been found. Two others (*k* and *l*) show cloud banks on each upswing of the curvilinear body forms — giving added evidence of the association of *avanyu* with rain in Tewa belief and ritual.

Plate 59. Human figures from Ceremonial vessels. Human figures appear in six of the eight items of plate 59, supplemented by two details of heads only. Done in the same crude fashion noted in plates 55 through 58, the majority indicate male characters known as "Chifoneti," who participate in certain Ceremonial dances of the Tewa. They are identified by their striped bodies and a coiffure of two braids of hair held erect by wrappings of corn husks, as in *h*, or by use of a bifurcated buckskin cap. The two crudely drawn heads (*e* and *g*) are from the same Ceremonial vessel: *a* depicts the cap, but in *e* the head is apparently adorned with feathers. The two quaint figures in *f* are not identified.

PLATE 55

115

PLATE 56

116

PLATE 57

117

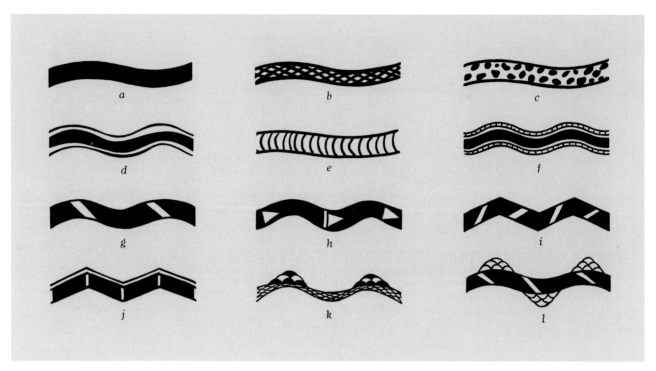

PLATE 58

118

a b c

d e f g h

PLATE 59

BLACK-ON-RED WARE

Plates 60 through 71. Conforming with the sequence of plates in the Black-on-cream section, the designs in plates 60 through 71 of Black-on-red ware are arranged in like order: first by their origin from (1) the interior and (2) the exterior of bowls, and next from (3) the necks and (4) the bodies of jars. Then, within each of those four groups, the designs also follow the structural sequence set up for the Black-on-cream ware.

Since this original group of twelve plates was mounted many years ago, the acquirement of new and desirable material has warranted the inclusion of five more (plates 72-76). The added material, however, contains many neck designs from the later tall-necked jars, comparable in proportions and design treatment with the body designs. Therefore it has seemed best to disregard the sources of this new material and to place them in sequence based solely upon design structure.

Plate 60. Decoration of bowl exteriors. Since no free, unattached design units are to be found on the exteriors of bowls, the series of plate 60 begins with six static arrangements (*a-f*), pendant from the upper banding lines. These vary from the widely spaced cloud clusters of *a* to use of attached, repeated, and alternating units of cloud, rain-far-off, and vegetal motifs. Wavy bands appear under the pendants of *d* and *f*, the former attached, and the latter free. In *f*, the oblique open spaces in the pendant band give a dynamic effect to the otherwise static motif. The two remaining (*g* and *h*) lend greater variety to the static group. In *g*, a major motif attached below alternates with minor motifs attached both above and below; in *h*, the extended motif, a simulated zigzag, fills the band.

Following the static group are five designs of combined static and dynamic motifs. The minor wavy motif in *j* is classed as static, for it has no apparent effect of movement to right or left, such as appears in the upper and lower motifs. In *k* and *l*, the pendant bands are static in contrast with the decided dynamic quality of the major motifs.

Beginning with *m* is a group of six dynamic arrangements. The motifs in *m-o* are attached either above or below; in *p* and *q*, paneled arrangements are used. In *r*, apparently the oblique paneling lines were added after the border motifs were drawn, for they do not connect with the lower banding line.

Of the three most commonly used motifs, rain-far-off appears in eleven designs, vegetal details in six, and clouds in five. Unusual motifs appear in *i* and *q*, the latter being derived from pre-Spanish wares.

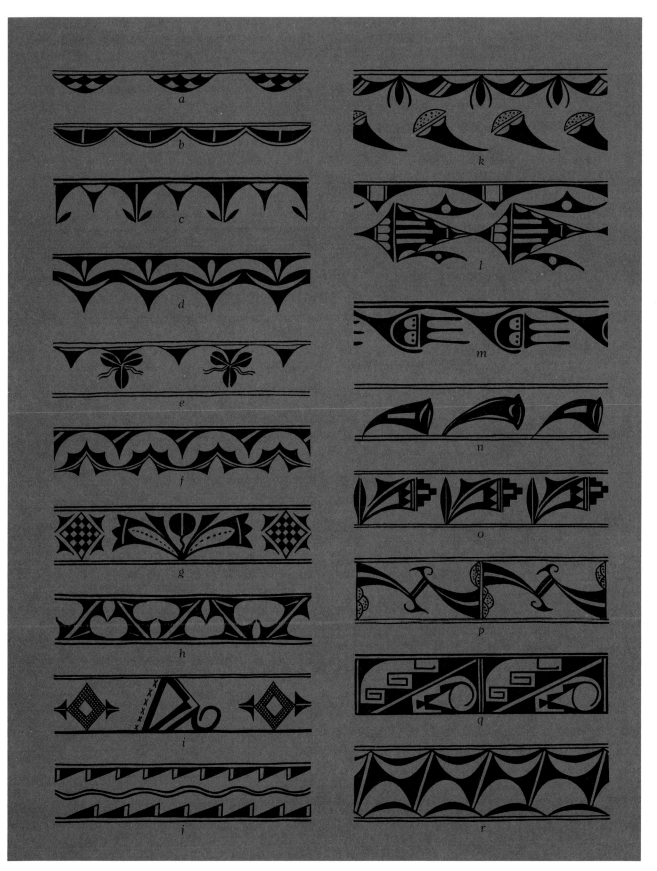

PLATE 60

121

Plate 61. Static designs from interiors of bowls. One additional static design from the exterior of a Black-on-red bowl is used, full width, in plate 61. With this exception the group includes four static arrangements from the interiors of bowls.

Since interior decoration was not a trait in the bowls of the preceding Black-on-cream ware, the Black-on-red artists were not bound by tradition in planning new arrangements of their familiar motifs for use within circles. A preference for detached motifs is apparent in the four static layouts of plate 61, rotational symmetry being chosen for the detached motifs of *a* and *b*. In *d*, bilateral symmetry is used alike on the horizontal and vertical axes. The crude layout of *e*, with unlike motifs in the details above and below the central rectangle, limits the symmetry to that on the vertical axis. Also, with the rectangle somewhat off center, the artist has spanned the narrow space completely by attaching the motif to the banding line.

Familiar details derived from Black-on-cream ware such as cloud bands and banks, quatrefoils, terraces, rain-far-off, crosses, and volutes appear here and also in the many plates that follow. In addition, the two crisscross devices in the center rectangles of *b* and *e* are related to those shown in the development series.

Plate 62. Static and dynamic designs from interiors of bowls. One additional example of static designs from the interiors of bowls is that in *d*, a bilaterally symmetrical arrangement of a double bird in combination with volutes and motifs suggesting elaborate seedpods.

The four other designs include both static and dynamic details in various combinations. In *a*, a dynamic border houses a static arrangement of detached motifs. In *b*, the major dynamic zone surrounds the minor static motif at the center. In *c*, a narrow space separates the static rim band from what was intended as a static layout in the major disk. However, the misshapen volute in the lower left throws that side off balance. Besides the dynamic rim band in *e*, the four lively birds also give a dynamic quality to the well-conceived but faulty drawing of the otherwise static major arrangement. In this, the center rectangle with its crisscross lends further variety to the two in plate 61.

Plate 63. Decoration of necks of water jars. Static arrangements are used in all the basic layouts of the seventeen designs in plate 63.

As in the preceding plate, the use of free, unattached elements or motifs in the neck bands of ollas is exceedingly rare. Only three examples from more recently acquired specimens appear in plate 77. Thus the only free motifs in plate 63 are the continuous arrangements in *a* and *b*.

Following these are *c-i*, in which static motifs are attached to either the upper or lower banding line. In *c*, the motifs are widely separated; in *d*, *e*, and *g*, they adjoin. The single continuous motif in *f* is constructed on a single horizontal line. Alternation of major and minor details adds variety in *h* and *i*.

In *j-n*, the motifs are attached to both upper and lower banding lines. The only widely separated motifs are those pendant in *j*. In the three remaining (*o-q*), the motifs span the bands; they are separated in *o*, adjoined in *p*, and constructed on a median line in *q*.

Of the more prevalent motifs in the group, the frequency in order of use is as follows: rain-far-off, leaf, and cloud. The terrace appears in *g* and *n*, and an unusual form of feather in *c*. Perhaps because of the wish to preserve the identity of the leaf in *l* and the rain-far-off in *m*, the artists used care in leaving the narrow spaces between upper and lower motifs.

a

b

c

d

e

PLATE 61

a b c d e

PLATE 62

124

a

b

c

d

e

f

g

h

i

j

k

l

m

n

o

p

q

PLATE 63

Plate 64. Decoration of necks of water jars. Continuing from plate 63, five static designs are shown in *a* and *e*. In basic construction three (*a-c*) are continuous, though there is a minor effect of paneling in *c*. More positive paneling is used in *d* and *e*.

Combined static and dynamic details appear in *f-n*. The alternating units of *f* are attached to the bottom banding line, yet the dynamic figures are purposely separated from the upper banding line by barely perceptible open spaces.

In *g-k*, pendant static units are opposed to dynamic devices placed on the lower banding lines. The combination of a free wavy band, with the serrate lower border of *m* is apparently from the same brush as that in plate 60*j*. The obliquely placed spanning device alternates with static figures which, as in *f*, are actually kept from merging with the upper banding line. Repeated, free dynamic units in *o-q* vary from the extreme of informality to repetitions of a well-constructed unit. Of the entire group of seventeen designs, only three are abstract geometric; a fourth (*b*) is modified by the addition of leaf units. Rain-far-off appears in seven figures, clouds in five, and leaves in five.

Plate 65. Decoration of necks of water jars. The dynamic group beginning with *o* of plate 64 is continued throughout plate 65. One additional free, continuous arrangement appears in *a*. Following this is a group of nine arrangements (*b-j*) with repeated units attached to the upper or lower banding line. In *k* and *l*, the repeated pendant units are opposed by similar arrangements placed on the lower banding line. These are followed by five arrangements (*m-q*) of repeated devices spanning the bands.

Abstract geometric units appear in *i* and *m-q*. A familiar device from Black-on-cream ware is used in *p*. Of the identifiable elements, the leaf prevails with free forms in *a, c, g,* and *j,* and lazy forms in *f, j,* and *l*. The cloud is used only in *a*. The upper units in *a* and also in *k* may be intended as rain-far-off. Both upper and lower crooks in *k* have been called "rain blown by the wind."

Quite unlike the designs of Black-on-cream ware, the arrangements of *b* and *h* point to an interesting development of such arrangements in the more spacious body bands of water jars that appear in some of the following plates.

Plate 66. Decoration of necks of water jars. Greater variety appears in the fourteen dynamic designs of plate 66; even the three abstract geometric arrangements of *e, g,* and *i* are quite distinct from those in the geometric bands of Black-on-cream ware. Several, particularly *b-d, j, m,* and *n,* show the influence of more ample space for elaboration afforded by the tall necks of the later period. Throughout the entire group there is a repetition of like units spanning the bands.

Single-line paneling is noticeable in *f* but less apparent in *h*. In constructing the simulated double-line panels of *g,* the outlining of the diagonal open spaces preceded the laying in of the verticals, the inner lines of which do not span the band. True double-line paneling is used in *j,* an elaboration of the more simple motif from Black-on-cream ware.

Only a few of the familiar, named motifs appear, such as rain-far-off adjoining sidewise in *a,* lazy leaf in *b* and *n,* seedpods in *l,* and clouds in *m*. The bird motif in *c* is an excellent example of the later combinations of realism with abstract design. In the elaborate, obliquely placed motifs of *d,* the rain lines suggest a possible intent of cloud in the elongate structure ending in three feathers. The hooked devices at the sides are apparently a survival from Black-on-cream design.

PLATE 64

127

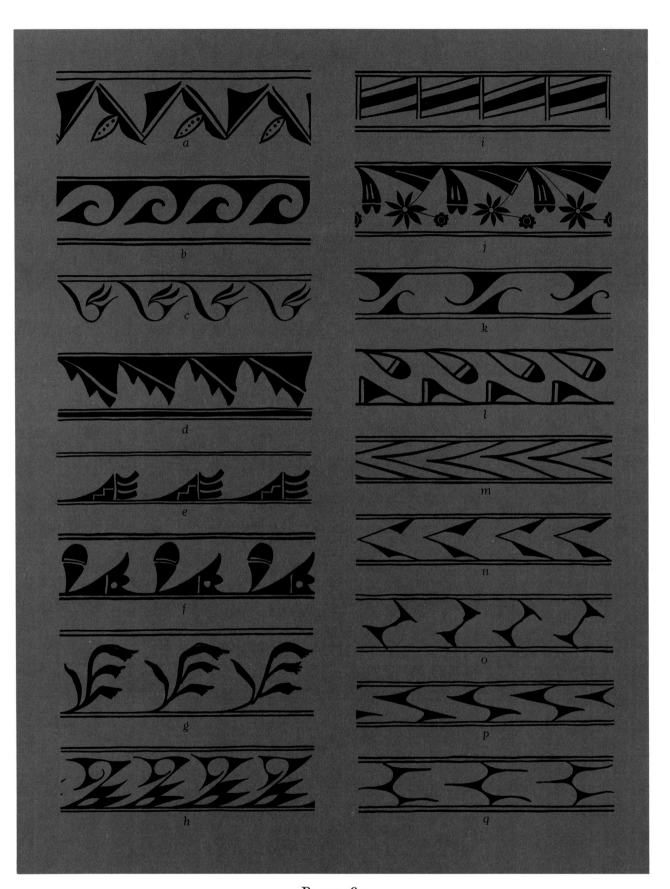

PLATE 65

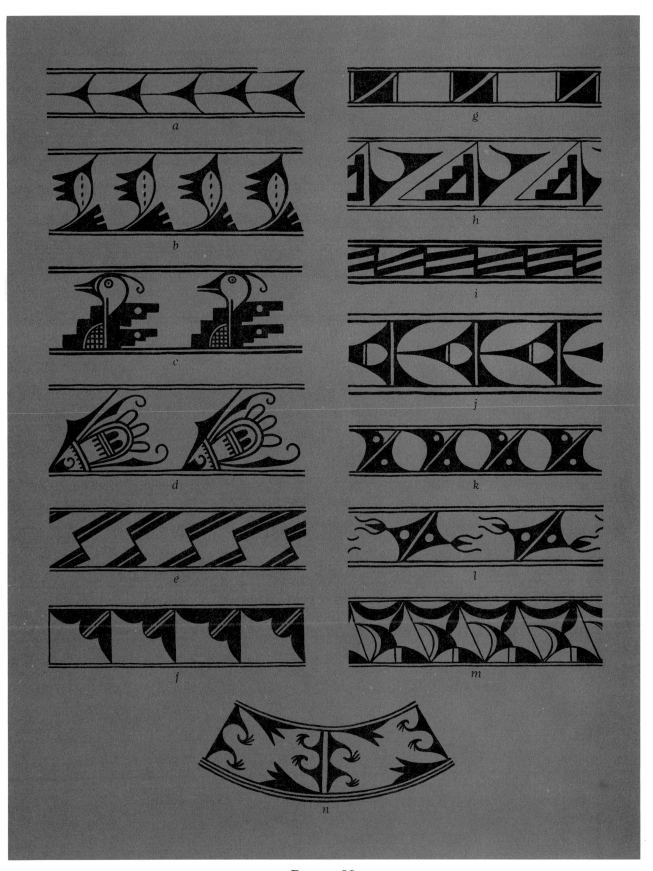

PLATE 66

Plate 67. Decoration of necks of water jars. The seven designs in plate 67 give the reader a clear view of the relation of the more confined upper or inner portion of the designs to the wider expanse below. Those from the upper portions of the jars are a pleasing compromise between the distortions of either the vertical or horizontal views as adopted for most of the drawings in this book.

The group is assembled without regard for the sequence adopted for the plates of extended bands. Five figures (*a-d* and *f*) are from the necks of jars, and *e* and *g* include both neck and body bands. The one static layout in *b* is in contrast with the combined static and dynamic in *c*, *e*, and *g* and with the dynamic only in *a* and *d*.

Familiar abstract geometric details appear in *c* and *e* and in the elaborate device at the left in *g*. The more commonly used, named devices are apparent in the others, including in order of frequency: leaf, cloud, rain-far-off, seedpod, and the minute clusters of lightning in *a*. Figure *g* is an outstanding example of a bold massive treatment of five or more elements assembled in arrangements peculiar to Black-on-red alone.

Plate 68. Decoration of bodies of water jars. The fourteen static designs in plate 68 range from free, repeated units in *a* and *b* to more complex arrangements such as those in *f*, *g*, and *n*. The free motifs are repeated in *a*. In *b*, the major motif alternates with minor motifs. Only one abstract geometric design appears in *c*. The free zigzag resembles those used in Black-on-cream design. The free motifs in *d* adjoined by curved lines are purposely separated by narrow spaces from the banding lines. Only one minor dynamic detail appears in the whole static group; the obliquely placed open spaces in the pendant leaves of *d*.

In *e-h*, the designs are pendant from the upper banding line. In *e*, they are more widely spaced, but in each of the others, there is a merging of three or more elements.

In *i*, the bilaterally symmetrical plant forms spring appropriately from the lower banding line, as do the less realistic motifs in *j*. The repeated major motifs in *k* are purposely kept free from the pendant upper border and the lower banding line. But the three following designs (*l-n*) are alike in that opposed, repeated design units are attached to both upper and lower banding lines.

The group contains a profusion of favorite decorative details; among which are seven examples of cloud, six of leaf, followed by rain-far-off, seedpod, flower, terrace, and the checkered device interpreted as fields. Five of such details are used in the "butterfly" arrangement of *b*.

Plate 69. Decoration of bodies of water jars. The fourteen designs in plate 69 are evenly divided between static and dynamic. Continuing the group of arrangements with motifs attached to banding lines, above and below, as shown in plate 68, are four designs (*a-d*), the latter with an added median band.

Next are *e-g*, in which the repeated units span the bands. The effect of the paneling produced by the paired lines of *e* is all but concealed by the checkered spaces on both sides, while the paneling of *f* is not consistent as shown by the abnormal arrangement at the left. In *h-n*, the combination of static and dynamic units produces an unusual variety of arrangements. In three (*h-j*), dynamic free major units alternate with minor free statics. In *j*, perhaps through careless placement, the crudely drawn oval units are attached below. The lower banding and framing lines were omitted in *k*. In *l-n*, a free space separates the upper pendant bands from the motifs

a

d

b

e

c

f

g

PLATE 67

131

PLATE 68

PLATE 69

133

attached below. The addition of an informal vine in *n* gives a dynamic contrast with the static borders above and below.

Even though the patterns in *e* may be classed as abstract geometric, yet the checkered arrangements are known as "fields." Of the more familiar and named units, the leaf predominates but is closely followed by cloud and rain-far-off. Less frequently used are the rainbows and faces of "cloud people" in *c*, the medallions in *h*, and the floral units in *i*.

Plate 70. Decoration of bodies of water jars. Continuing with the combinations of static and dynamic motifs of plate 69*h-n* are five figures in plate 70*a-e* showing various arrangements. The free unattached motifs appear only in *a*, the dynamic units being placed between static details of the upper and lower borders. In *b*, *d*, and *e*, the static motifs alternate with the dynamic. In *c*, the static effect is broken only by the use of obliquely placed leaf forms beside the lower motifs.

Beginning with *f*, the nine remaining figures are dynamic; in *i*, the otherwise static motifs of the lower band are made dynamic by the addition of minor volutes. One extended unattached arrangement appears in *f*; and in *h* and *i*, the upper and lower motifs are separated. The graceful free-flowing units of *g* are attached above but kept purposely separated from each other without reaching the lower banding line. In *j-n*, the bands are spanned by designs varying from the simple layouts in *j* and *k* to such lively, well-planned, and executed motifs as those in *l* and *n*.

Included among the named motifs are five examples of rain-far-off, five spirals (volutes), four of leaves, three of clouds, two of terrace, and one each of lazy leaf, seedpod, and circle. Open-leaf spaces also appear in *d*, *e*, and *k*.

Plate 71. The four designs of plate 71 include two (*a* and *c*) which show the normal freedom of technique found in the decoration of most Black-on-red ware. The design in *a*, from the terraced end of a Kiva bowl, is somewhat more elaborate than the average of bowls of that type.

The complex terrace arrangement is quite unusual, as are the two vegetal forms placed on the outermost cloud banks. Lightning is represented by the two pointed motifs within the terrace, and also by the two used to fill the wide space at the right. Dots and rain lines give variety to the four cloud banks.

The otherwise bilateral symmetry of the middle figure in *c* is marred by variations in the lateral appendages. The astroid at the left, however, is unusually well designed.

In contrast with *a* and *c* are two remarkably well-designed and executed bands (*b* and *d*), showing minor variations in the use of similar symmetrical motifs developed during the 1920s by Toñita and Juan Roybal.

Plate 72. The five designs of plate 72 lend considerable variety to those designs thus far shown. The unusually extended design in *a* covers one-half of the circumference of a water jar. A wide brush was used throughout to produce the heavily outlined figures and the details within. The pendant cloud band and the cloud banks beneath them give a pleasing contrast to the intervening motifs flanking the median line. The forms themselves have been interpreted as rain clouds, and the diagonal crosshatching is known as "rain blown by the wind." Rain dots are also shown within the disks.

The quartrefoil motifs attached to the cloud banks, intended as either flowers or leaf clusters, contain lines and dots so arranged that they suggest the features of a human face. Other vegetal details are attached to the cloud banks.

In *b* and *c* are two unusual representations of birds; the regular repeats of identical forms in

PLATE 70

135

a

b

c

d

PLATE 71

PLATE 72

137

b contrasting with the varying details of both birds and appendages in *c*. Further irregularity is shown in the attachment of one figure to the lower banding line.

The characteristic freedom of Black-on-red design is apparent in *d* in the alternation of major and minor symmetrical units in each of which vegetal details are used. The four flower motifs of the major figure contain cloud clusters, in three of them rain drops appear.

Regularly repeated diagonal bands within the panels of *e* provide triangular spaces in which corn plants and birds are placed with the utmost freedom. In the order of their use, clouds appear in four of the designs, vegetation in four, and birds in three.

Plate 73. Supplementing the group of neck designs of water jars in plates 63 through 67 and the body designs in plates 68 through 76, the sixteen designs in plate 73 include both static and dynamic arrangements of free repeated units and of units attached either to the upper or lower banding lines. Complete spanning of bands is barely indicated in *l*, but well planned in the body band of *p*. A consistent alternation of major and minor motifs appears in the arrangements of static and dynamic motifs in *f* and *g*.

Plate 74. (The text explaining the details of plate 74 was not available. Since Dr. Chapman knew exactly what he wanted to say in presenting these designs, an explanation by another would be presumptive.)

Plate 75. The twelve designs in plate 75 use a variety of arrangements, including one free (*g*), one attached below (*e*), six attached above and below (*a, b, d, f, h, i*), and four spanning the bands of *e* and *j-l*. The excellent drawing in *b, d, f, i,* and *k* contrasts greatly with the inept handling of the otherwise effective layout in *l*. The lone, detached motif in *g* is unidentified.

Plate 76. The fifteen designs in plate 76 include eight arrangements of spanning bands, *a-d* and *h-k*. In the remaining seven (*e-g* and *l-o*), the motifs are placed above and below the paired banding lines between neck and body. In several, such as *f* and *m*, the variation between the relative spacing of the units of the upper and lower bands is barely apparent, but is more noticeable in the bold trefoil units of *g*. In contrast, the combination in *e* is well controlled; and in *l* there appears an outstanding example of the use of the upper and lower motifs to produce a series of well-designed static units. The dynamic layout in *o* also shows due regard for the relative spacing of the triangular motifs above and below.

Plate 77. Paneling is used in all but one of the fourteen designs of plate 77, the lively arrangement in *h* hardly qualifying as such. Some exception might be taken also with respect to such arrangements as those in *e* and *f*, and more particularly in the oblique group (*j-l*) in which the primary purpose of the paired-paneling lines is obscured by the massing of heavy black details upon them. Paired lines are used throughout with one exception, that of *d*, in which an open space is used on both sides of a heavy black, vertical band.

The crude design in *b* shows an alternation of wide and narrow motifs, either of which may have been intended as panel dividers. The slight tilt of the narrow motifs makes it impossible to determine whether they are meant to be upright or oblique.

Among the motifs used are six examples each of leaf and rain-far-off, three of seedpod, and two of turkey feather (that in *g* being of the lazy form). Unusual arrangements of clouds, rain drops, and rain lines appear in *c*.

PLATE 73

139

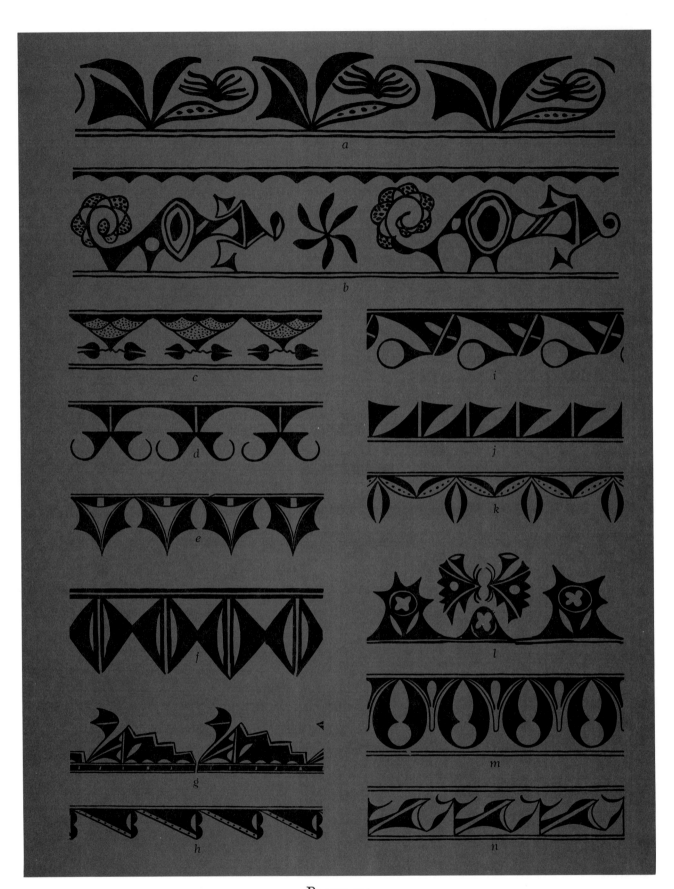

PLATE 74

140

PLATE 75

141

a

b

c

d

e

f

g

h

i

j

k

l

m

n

o

PLATE 76

PLATE 77

143

Plate 78. The miscellaneous group in plate 78 contains a few detached figures of life forms done in early style (*e, f,* and *h*), others of later origin such as the form in geometric style (*i-l*), and the crude representation of some ceremony in *m.*

Presumably, seedpods are represented in *a-c.* If so, the arrangement in *b* seems to indicate a sudden direct fruition from roots to seeds, without an assist from stalk and leaves.

Of the four band designs, those of *n* and *q* seem aimless as compared with the average of those in preceding plates. The simple arrangement in *p,* possibly representing the black tips of eagle feathers, is unique, as is also the more labored production in *o.*

Plate 79. Abstract geometric motifs. The rarity of abstract geometric motifs in Black-on-red ware may be taken as at least negative evidence that the ware came into use in mid-Black-on-cream times. Those in plate 79 are mainly in the form of bilaterally symmetrical, stepped terraces; the six forms including *c, d,* and *f-i.* Three other forms include the nondescript arrangement in *a,* the inclined, stepped form in *b,* and the corner bracket in *e.*

Plate 80. Vegetal motifs. Naturalistic representations of plant forms were rarely used in Black-on-red decoration, the somewhat stylized arrangement in *l,* and the more crude layout in *p* representing extremes in their use. The formal grouping of leaves in *a, e, i,* and *n* and the use of symmetrical leaf motifs in several other designs show a preference for balanced forms, as distinguished from those in *g, j,* and *k.*

Plate 81. Leaf forms from Black-on-red pottery. The rarity of plant motifs permitted little use of leaves in their proper setting. Instead, they appear as separate entities, attached to banding lines or to motifs within bands, where in number and variety they exceed those from Black-on-cream ware. The majority of the twenty-four in plate 81 are lanceolate in form, and many of them are bilaterally symmetrical. But even more favored are those with a more or less graceful twist from stem to tip. A few in the group (*p-w*) are given unrealistic contours similar to some of the forms in the Black-on-cream series; dots and eyes also add to their variation.

Plate 82. Lazy leaves from Black-on-red ware. The group of twenty lazy leaf motifs in plate 82 shows considerable variety not only in form but also in the degree of their attachment to banding lines or to other motifs. In *a-j,* the attachment is only at the stem. In *k-t,* attachment varies from the mere touching of stem and tip in *k* to complete contact as in *l-o* and *q-t.* In *p,* attachment is at only three points.

A few fanciful forms appear, including that of the leaf in *e* with its involute arm enfolding two tiny lines.

PLATE 78

145

PLATE 79

PLATE 80

146

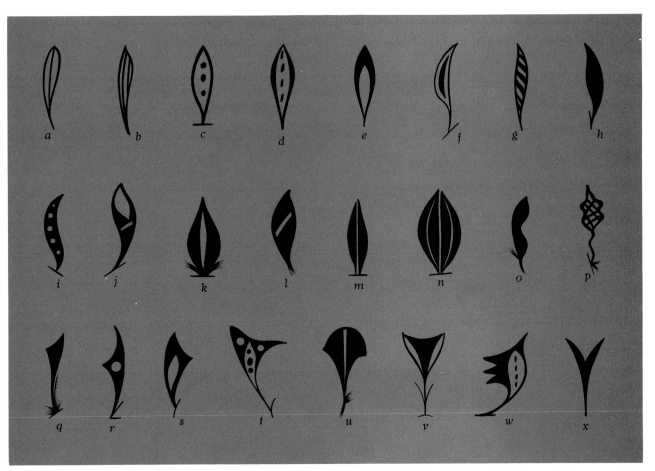

PLATE 81

PLATE 82

147

Plate 83. Floral and other motifs from Black-on-red ware. Only a few of the motifs in plate 83 are clearly recognizable as floral, such as *b, c,* and *e.* The others are more or less fanciful forms which, like the flowers, are placed at the end of stems.

Plate 84. Seedpods from Black-on-red ware. The seven motifs in plate 84 are identified as seedpods by form and by association with other related details. Thus the group *a, c,* and *e* have the outcurving tips usually associated with the device. In *b* and *f,* the multiple dots represent seeds; and in *d,* the lone dot has the same significance. The body of *g* with its cross bars of white is included because of its resemblance to forms in the contemporary Polychrome ware.

Plate 85. Feather motifs from Black-on-red ware. With possibly one exception, the thirteen motifs of plate 85 are identified as feathers by their rounded tips, even when disassociated from other details of birds. This applies in particular to the straight-sided group, but also to such forms as those in *a, b,* and *f-i.* The two unusual forms in *l* and *m* are not so readily interpreted by potters as either feather or leaf. In *k,* the three stubby upper motifs also cause some confusion among potters in identifying them as either short feathers or long clouds.

Plate 86. Lazy feather motifs from Black-on-red ware. The two motifs in *a* and *e* are most readily identified as turkey tail feathers, and even the fringed variation in *b* may be so termed. In *c* and *d,* however, opinion may vary among potters regarding their interpretation as feather or leaf.

Plate 87. Cloud motifs from Black-on-red ware. As compared with the cloud motifs of the preceding Black-on-cream ware, the group in plate 87 shows a more marked diversity of band arrangements beginning with the most commonly used type in *e* and continuing through the two outer rows to the most ornate form in *z.* In the group of cloud banks the two examples of inept drawing (*j* and *s*) contrast with the clever designing throughout most of the others. In *n,* the artist has produced an unusual combination of rain-far-off, within the clouds, and rain lines below. Whether or not with intent, the effect of a grinning face is produced in *p.*

Plate 88. Rain-far-off motifs from Black-on-red ware. The often used rain-far-off motifs of varying sizes, shown more or less formalized in plate 88, add but little to the variations of those in the Black-on-cream series, although the inclusion of a rain line in *j* is quite unusual.

Plate 89. Miscellaneous free motifs from Black-on-red ware. With only a few minor exceptions the nineteen free motifs of plate 89 are composed basically of vegetal details, or are at least embellished by them. The exceptions include the stars in *g* and *h,* the unidentified crooked motif in *k,* the rain-far-off and clouds in *m,* the clouds in *s,* and the aimless space fillers in *a* and *l.*

PLATE 83

PLATE 84

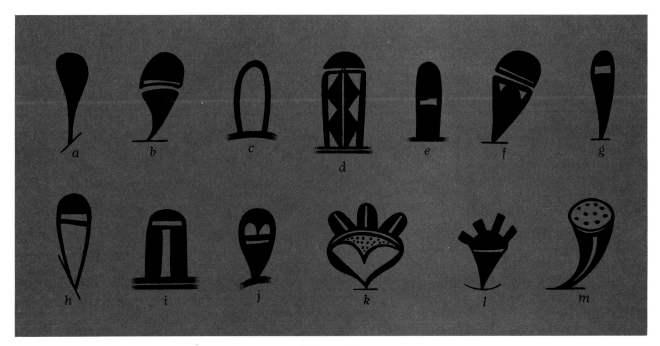

PLATE 85

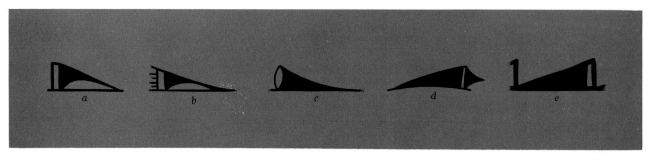

PLATE 86

PLATE 87

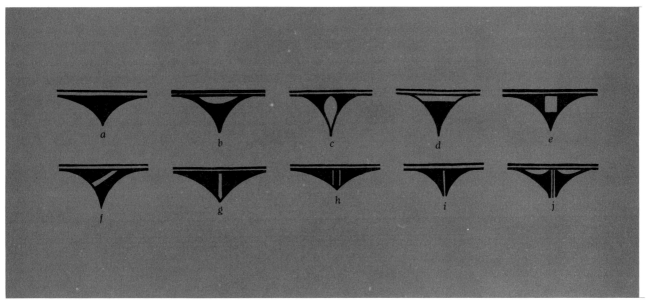

PLATE 88

PLATE 89

151

Plate 90. Minor stylized bird forms from Black-on-red ware. Since for several decades the production of Black-on-red ware was contemporaneous with that of the later stages of Black-on-cream ware, there is a noticeable similarity in the bird forms of the two. With the exception of two (*a* and *b*) all the minor bird forms of plate 90 are attached to banding lines or to details of major devices. Two stylized forms (*d* and *e*) are derived from pre-Spanish or early post-Spanish wares, in which the head survives as a mere crook. Legs are omitted in all the forms except *b*. An occasional absence of the eye dot in such minor figures might be considered an oversight, but its consistent omission in the lower four is quite unusual.

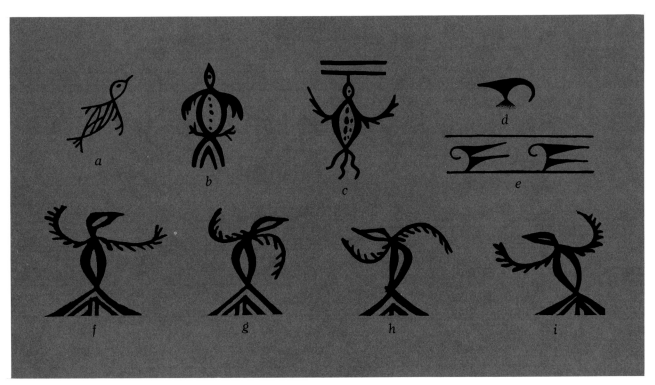

PLATE 90

153

POLYCHROME WARE

Plate 91. Transition. The group of design details in this plate represents what is believed to be the earliest experiments of the San Ildefonso potters with the use of red to enliven the monotonous effect in their black and cream ware. No effort was made to devise new motifs, for the available specimens show only the adornment of the details of the ordinary motifs within or attached to bands. Thus the early attempts were with the use of dots bordering, or within, black lines as in *b;* straight lines as in *c;* and wavy or scalloped as in *d-g* and *i*. After considerable experimenting with free motifs in red the potters progressed toward filling in outlined spaces of the black designs, some of them adjoining forms of solid black. But once they learned by experiment or hearsay or by observation of the more sophisticated use of red by the potters of the western pueblos, the potters of San Ildefonso made good progress in the use of paired black lines to separate masses of red and black.

Plate 92. Single, detached motifs from bowls and jars (comparatively rare). Conforming with the sequences adopted for the preceding plates, the Polychrome series begins with detached motifs, mostly within bands, used singly or alternating with other motifs attached or detached and usually of contrasting size.

Of the fifteen designs, eleven are basically static, although in *l* there is a minor dynamic detail in its central group of volutes. Three well-planned bilaterally symmetrical arrangements appear in *j, k,* and *m* in decided contrast with the crudities of *g* and *i*. The remaining four designs (*d, f, n,* and *o*) are dynamic, varying between the well-designed rotational symmetry of *f* and the more crude attempts in *n* and *o*.

Of the identifiable component details in the entire group of fifteen, there are eight examples of leaf, four of rain-far-off, four of volute, two of seedpods, and strangely only one of clouds (*c*). Among others there is also one each of terrace, lightning, and checker.

Plate 93. Repeated, bilaterally symmetrical, free motifs in bands. As in plate 92, the designs are shown without the enclosing lines of bands which in a few instances determine the relative levels of such upper details as those in *e, f,* and *m*. In eleven of the designs there is an intentional bilateral balance of form and use of color. In *c,* however, an unsymmetrical use of black and red is repeated in each triad. In *b,* the diagonal divisions between black and red give a dynamic quality to the otherwise static rectangles. Variety is produced in *g* by a regular alternation of the relative positions of black and red in each unit. Bilateral symmetry is well maintained in the complex design of *m,* from a large storage jar.

In the entire group there are seven various leaf forms (*d, f-h, j, l, m,* and possibly *k*); two of clouds (*f* and *m*); one each of rain-far-off (*i*), terrace (*m*), rain lines (*m*), star (*l*), and possibly seedpod (*g*). The meaning of the motifs in *a* and *c* is not clear.

PLATE 91

155

PLATE 92

156

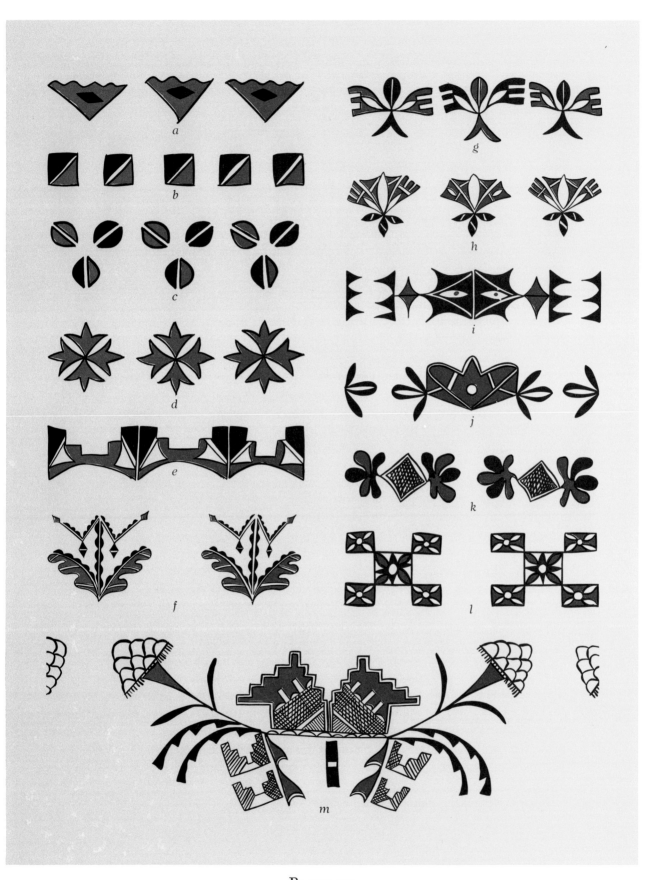

PLATE 93

157

Plate 94. Repeated dynamic free motifs in bands. The majority of the fifteen designs of plate 94 are from the neck or body bands of water jars. Only rarely have the border lines influenced the size or layout of the motifs themselves. Considerable variation is found in the relative spacing of the repeated motifs, the extreme width between the units of *f* contrasting markedly with that of *k* and particularly that of *l* in which the effect is of a continuous band.

The component elements consist of eight cloud forms, five leaf, three rain-far-off, three volute, and two checker.

Plate 95. Alternating free units within bands. Alternating static with static is shown in *a-d* and *j*; and alternating static with dynamic is shown in *e-i*. Of the five designs in the latter group, the alternating motifs in *e* are fairly equal; in *f-h*, the dynamic units are major; and in the crude drawing in *i*, the dynamic unit is minor.

Static units attached in chain. The entire group of five in *k-o* is structurally static. Of the three lanceolate chains, the simplest use of color is that in *k*. The easy progress from link to link is somewhat retarded in *l*, while in *m* the oblique division within each unit gives a decidedly dynamic quality to the chain. The simple alternation of color in the astroid units of *n* is much more effective than that within the diamonds of *o*.

Leaf forms predominate in the entire group, those in *d* and *h* being of major importance; next are the cloud banks in *i* and *j*.

Plate 96. Static and dynamic units in chain. Continued from plate 95 are six designs (*a-f*) more elaborate in structure and detail. Though crude in drawing, the obvious intent in *a* and *b* is for upright static units; and the placement of the black checker in *a* gives a dynamic twist to the diamonds. The use of the terrace and stripes within the diamonds of *g* adds confusion to the unbalanced diamonds. The more regular drawing (*h*) is also thrown out of balance by the upturned leaf forms.

In five designs (*i-m*), the dynamic layouts are well conceived and executed. In *n*, from a large storage jar, the basic diamond figures are static, but the placement of the enclosed terraces and black elements, combined with the volute-tipped appendages above and below, gives a sense of unbalance and movement to the band.

Plate 97. Alternation of unlike elements in chain. Static elements are used in *a-l*. The favorite arrangement of major alternating with minor appears in six (*a-d*, *g*, and *h*), while an approximate balance is found in *e*, *f*, and *i*. Following these are three with alternations of static and dynamic (*j*, *k*, and *m*). In *k*, the majors entwine about small disks; in *m*, they are separated by small and somewhat distorted astroids in black. Only one design (*l*) is dynamic throughout.

Plate 98. Repeated free motifs, both static and dynamic, closely bordered by banding lines. The designs are similar to those in plate 94 but are more closely bordered by the banding lines; and in a few instances (*f*, *g*, and *l-n*) are supplemented by border motifs. As a group the units are closely spaced, the greatest freedom appearing in *c*. Seven designs (*a-g*) are static, and nine (*h-p*) dynamic. In three instances (*l-n*), the designs are accompanied by static border bands.

As usual, leaf forms predominate, followed by cloud, terrace, and rain-far-off. The appearance of lightning in *j* is unusual. Several of the components have not been identified, including the black device in *m* and the plump, bipartite motifs in *n*.

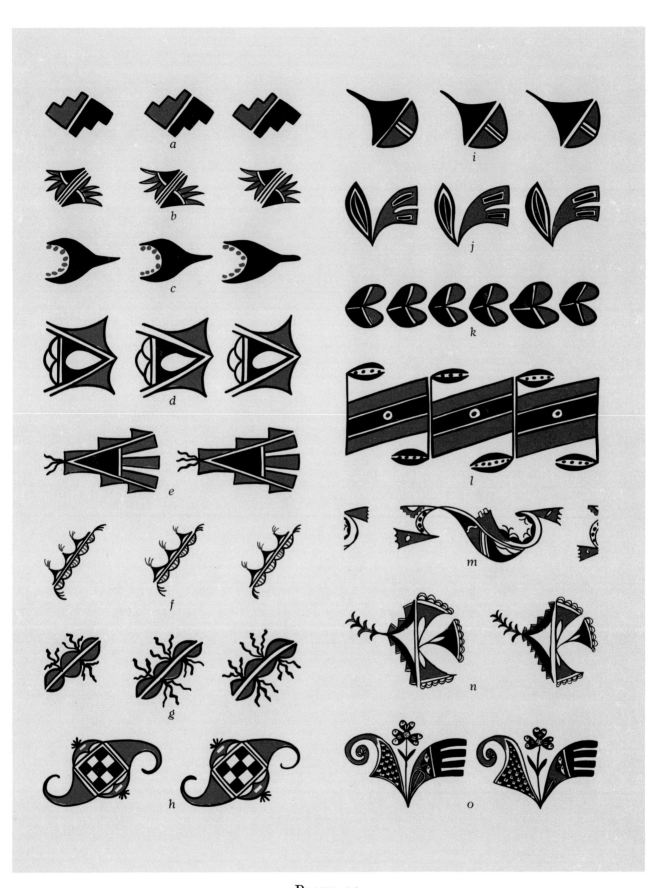

PLATE 94

159

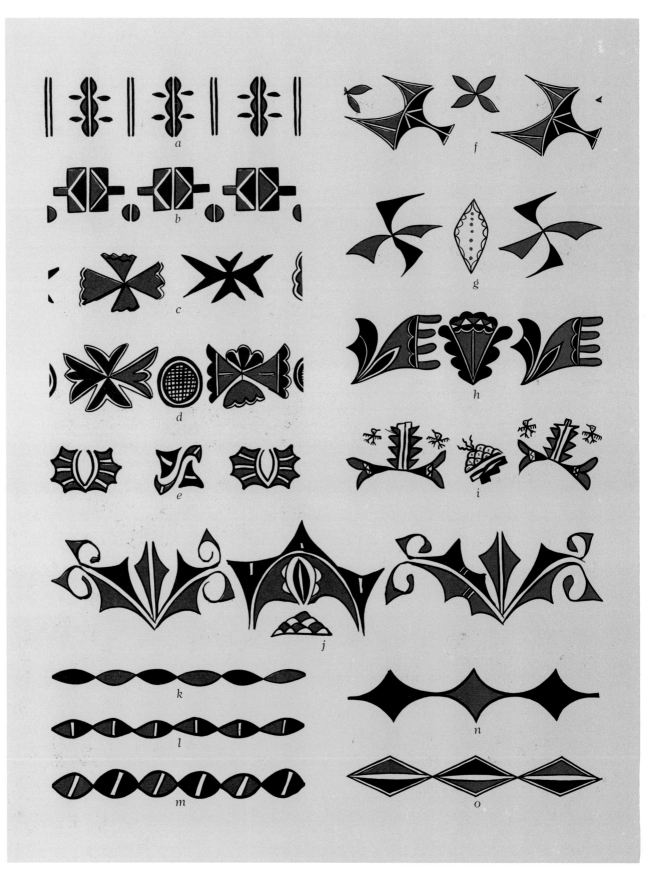

PLATE 95

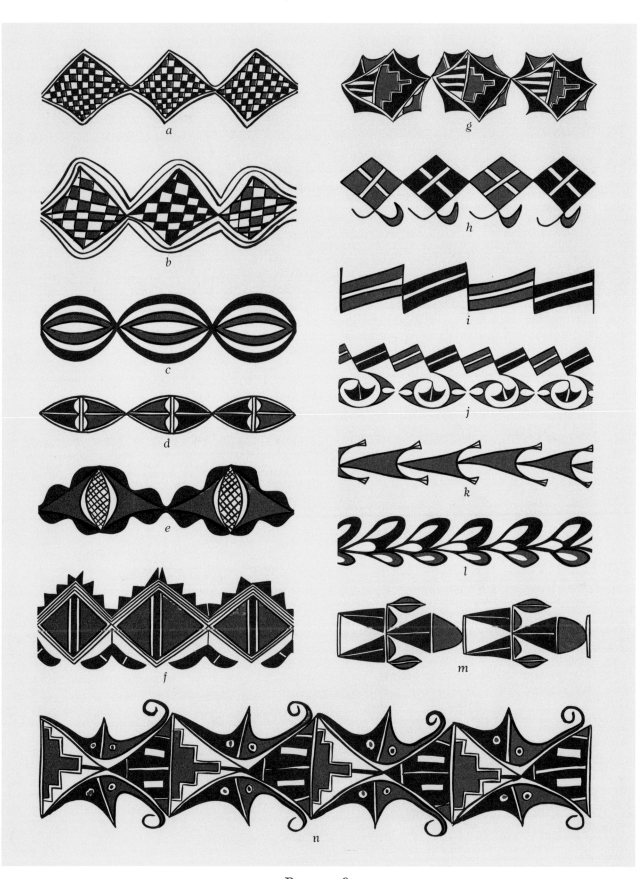

a

b

c

d

e

f

g

h

i

j

k

l

m

n

PLATE 96

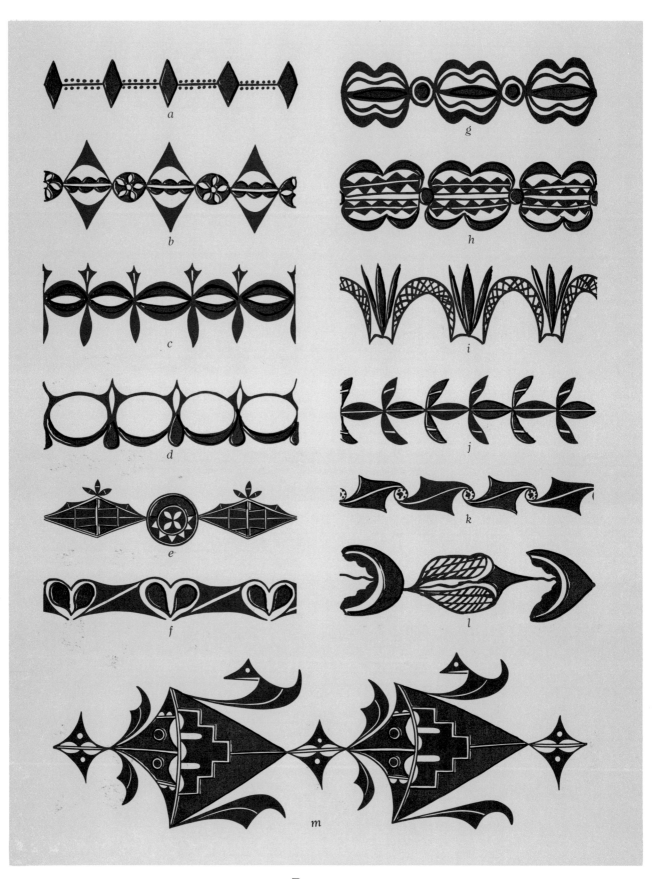

PLATE 97

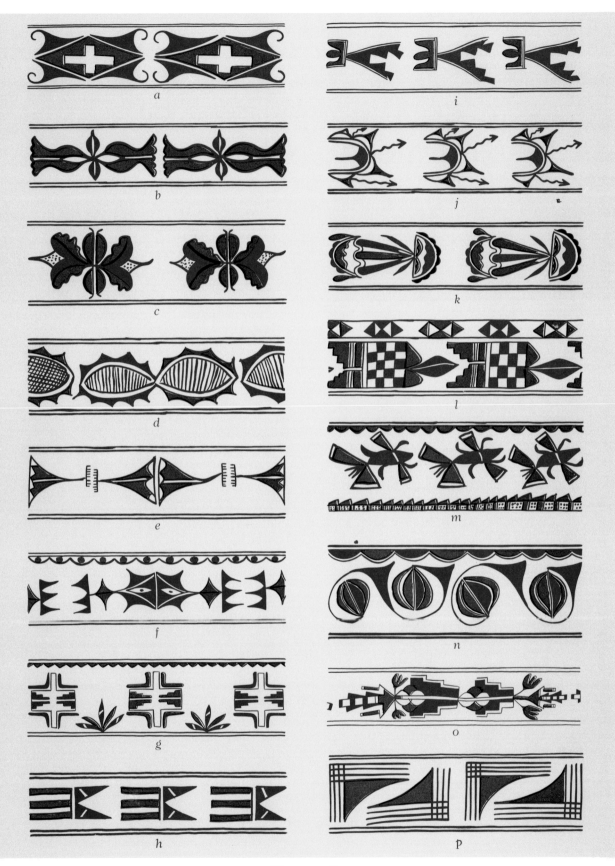

a

b

c

d

e

f

g

h

i

j

k

l

m

n

o

p

PLATE 98

163

Plate 99. Free static and dynamic units, in chain, closely bordered by banding lines. The three static designs (*b*, *e*, and *f*) resemble those in plate 96, where they are shown without banding lines. The diamonds in *e*, like those in plate 96, are given a dynamic twist by the use of the inner oblique bands.

Considerable variety is shown in the dynamic group, beginning with identical repeated motifs in *a-c*, and less orderly in *d*. Major and minor dynamic motifs alternate in *g*, while in *h* and *i* the minors are static. The precise layouts of *h* and *i* identify them as the product of the artist responsible for a similar design in plate 97*m*.

Of the component elements, the leaf motif predominates, followed in frequency by eye, terrace, and volute.

Plate 100. Free, continuous static motifs in bands. In each of the fifteen designs of plate 100, the basic arrangement is a continuous static band including only a few examples of unadorned zigzag, such as *d* and *e;* crenellated in *c*, and wavy in *g*. Otherwise the remaining nine consist of zigzags with accessory details which tend to obscure the basic arrangements. Thus in *a* the single-line zigzag is minimized by the horizontal line and resultant triangles, while in *h* it is even more subordinate to the figures built upon it.

Plate 101. Continuous motifs in bands. Three additional designs of the zigzag series are included in plate 101. The conventional right and left oblique lines are used in *a* and *b;* and in the more dynamic combination of vertical and right oblique in *c*, the crossing with black produces a simple but effective pattern. The static effect in *a* is lessened by the use of a bird, and in *b* by the dynamic attachments to the zigzag.

Following these are three developments on wavy lines in *d, l,* and *m; d* and *m* were obviously conceived by the same potter.

In the remaining eight figures (*e-k* and *n*), the basic motif is a band of attached scallops suggesting rainbows that curve upward in five and downward in three.

Several unusual details are used, such as the vortex of lines in *e* and the crossing of arcs in *l*. Of the familiar components, leaf appears in six, and rain-far-off in only one.

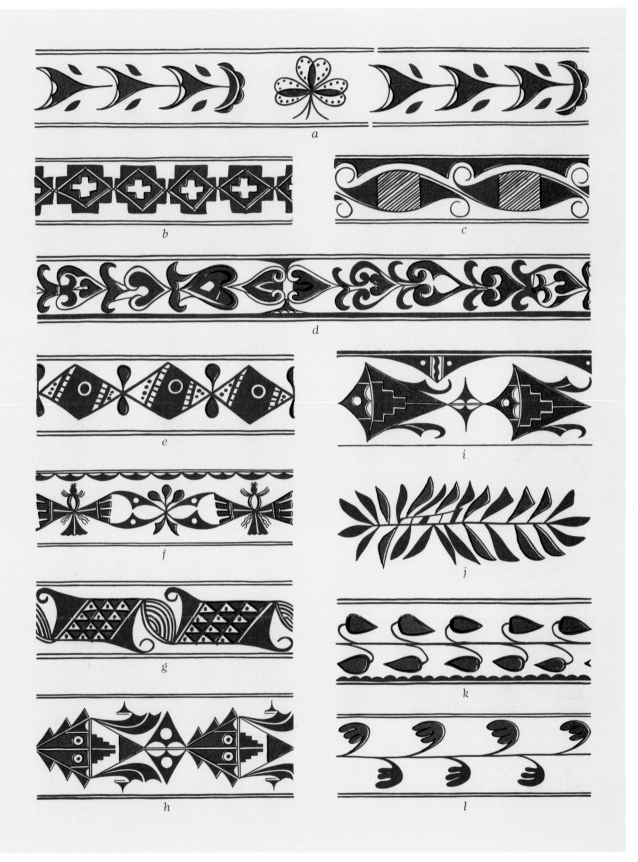

a

b

c

d

e

f

g

h

i

j

k

l

PLATE 100

PLATE 101

Plate 102. Free continuous bands. Four figures (*a* and *c-e*) are a continuation of the group in plate 101. They include but one basic wavy line (*d*), and two arching scallops (*a* and *b*), and two dipping (*e* and *f*). The static layout is maintained in *a* and *c*, but given a dynamic thrust by the appendages of *e* and *f*.

Among the accessories, rain-far-off, leaf, and open-space cloud are frequently used.

Repeated static motifs, pendant from upper banding lines. In the preceding plates there has been evidence of a desultory use of occasional motifs attached to upper banding lines. In plate 97, *f* marks the beginning of an extensive series of border arrangements, either pendant or upright, which in many instances provide the sole, or at least the major, decoration of the bands. The twelve static forms (*g-r*) include the use of pendant feathers in *g-i*; the terrace in *k-n* and *q*; triangles in *o* and *p*; and leaf forms in *r*. In only one (*m*) is there a departure from purely static design.

Plate 103. Static motifs pendant from upper banding lines. Continued from plate 102 are six pendant motifs (*a-f*). In three (*a, b* and *c*), the narrow interspacing gives, at first glance, the effect of continuous bands. Bilateral symmetry of the units is well maintained in the layouts of all except *e* and *f*. In *e*, there is a deliberate unbalance in each unit through use of the cloud bank at left and leaves at right, and also by the uniform direction of lazy leaf forms on both right and left volutes. However, as viewed on the ancient water jar itself, the effect as a whole is typically free and easy San Ildefonso at its best. In contrast, the off-balanced motif in *f* approaches the limit of crudity.

Upright static motifs placed on lower banding lines. As shown in the ten designs (*g-p*), the upright stance seems to favor the use of vegetal motifs, feather, and terrace. Bilateral symmetry is maintained in most of the designs. One exception, in *o*, needs explanation. The use of an odd number of repeats has made it necessary to break the rhythm by matching the black unit at the left or the red unit at the right or, in deference to both, to split the final unit at the middle. The potter chose the last alternative.

Plate 104. Dynamic motifs pendant from banding lines. Of the sixteen designs in plate 104, all but the final three (*n-p*) show a decided trend from upper left to lower right, due, according to some potters, to the comparative ease in laying in the major lines rightward rather than leftward as the vessel is held by the left hand either in the lap or on the table.

The only alternation in color of units is that in *a*. Otherwise there is a notable uniformity in the repeated units of each design, the most erratic being the variants in *e*. In this also, the adjoining of red and black is unusual.

The inverted figures in *j* are apparently intended as *avanyus,* in which case the dots would signify rain. The usual components, both major and minor, range from leaf, eight; rain-far-off, five; cloud and open-cloud space, four each; feather, three; eye, two; and seedpod, one.

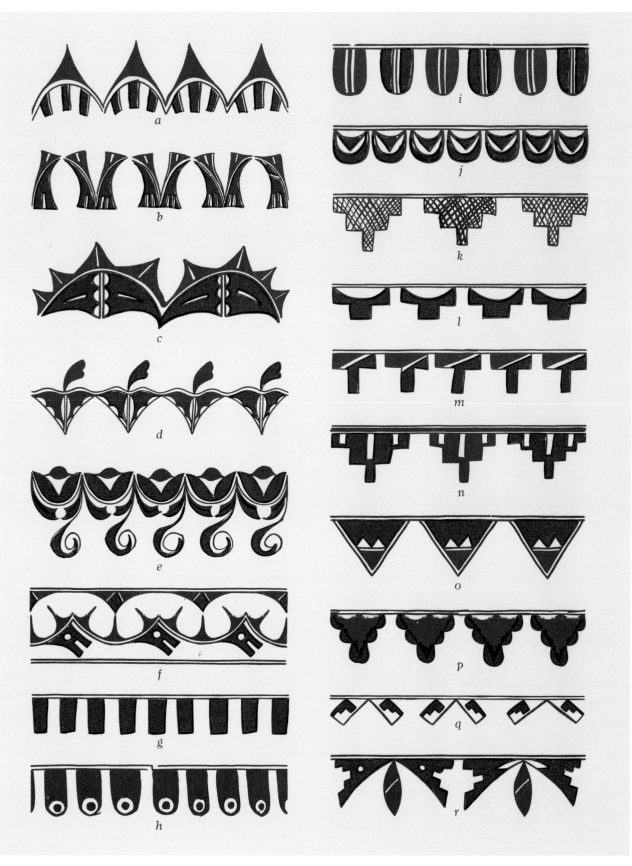

PLATE 102

PLATE 103

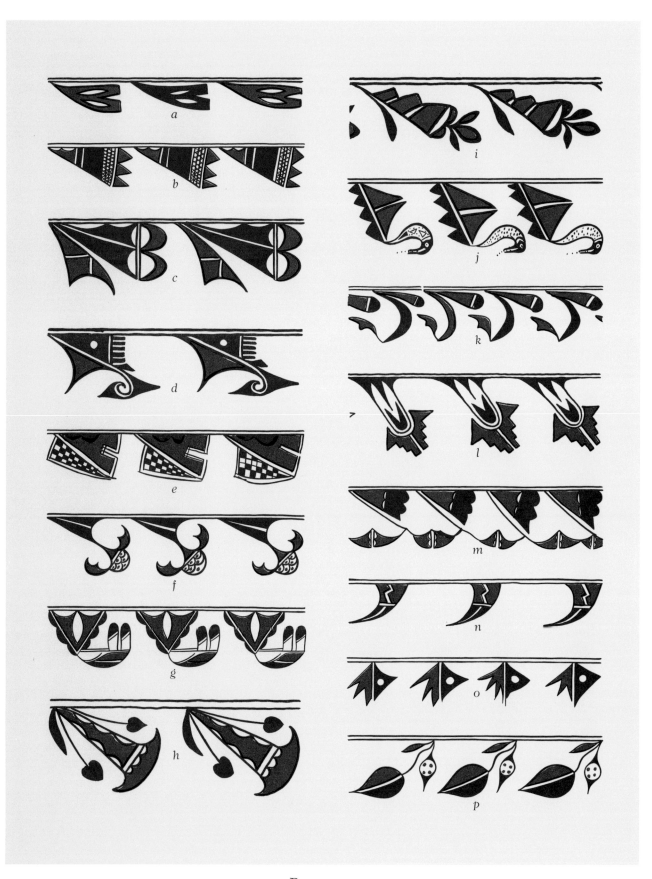

PLATE 104

171

Plate 105. Dynamic motifs pendant from upper banding lines. A continuation of the series of pendant designs in plate 104 is shown in plate 105*a-l*. With the exception of *a* and *g*, in which the primary structural lines are vertical, there is a leftward down-thrust in most of the others, particularly noticeable in the simple arrangements of *b*, *h*, and *i*. The arrangements become more complex in *h-j* with the inclusion of minor static elements and with the use of major free motifs in *k* and *l*.

Dynamic motifs extending upward from lower banding lines. The five simple motifs in *m-q*, slanting upward to the right, are all vegetal in concept.

Plate 106. Repeated dynamic motifs extending upward from lower banding lines. Of the eighteen designs of plate 106, all show a major direction of units to the upper right. Four (*a*, *d*, *e*, and *k*) show use of alternations in color of repeated units, but with these few exceptions there is a constant preference for use of identical form and color in the units of each design. As in plate 105 the prevailing basic motif is the leaf, the only possible exceptions being the paired units and the black motifs of *h* which might qualify as either leaf or feather. In most of the arrangements, the leaf spreads well above the bounding line; the nearest approach to the lazy position is that in *d* and *o*.

With so few accessories in use, the range of identifiable details is limited to rain-far-off, three; eye and dots, two each; and cloud bank, rain lines, checker, feather cluster, and possibly seedpod (*n*), one each.

Plate 107. Repeated dynamic motifs extending upward from lower banding lines. The entire group of nineteen designs provides a continuation of the dominant direction, to the upper right, as shown in the two preceding plates, but with greater variation in their use. Variants of leaf forms from realistic to abstract are used in all but two of the designs. The group is notable for the unvarying treatment of the repeated units in each design. Unlike the simple forms in plate 105, the left motifs in *a-d* are joined to the banding lines by pairs of curving lines. In *e* and *f*, the tips of the leaves touch the line, thus placing them in the more obviously lazy leaf group (*g-s*), except possibly three (*j*, *k*, and *q*), which are identified as lazy feather.

Plate 108. Dynamic motifs attached to lower banding lines. One additional lazy leaf arrangement appears in *a*. In addition, three more lively leaf motifs appear in *i-k*. The triangular forms of leaf also appear in *b* and *c*, but they are so bounded by accessories that they lose their significance. Otherwise the leaf is outnumbered by several devices attached to the banding lines lightly as in *l* and *n* or solidly as in *f*, *g*, and others. With the exception of such upright stances as those in *f*, *g*, and *m*, the prevailing direction (as in previous plates) is upward to the right. Not one example of color alternation in repeated units appears in the entire group. In *k*, the barbed black stems seem to span the band, but in most of the repeats they do not actually join the upper bands.

Plate 109. Dynamic motifs attached to lower banding lines. Continued from plate 108 are four additional variants of dynamic motifs, in three of which (*a*, *k*, and *l*) the dominant direction is upward to the right. In *b*, the similar layout is balanced by the group of feathers pointing

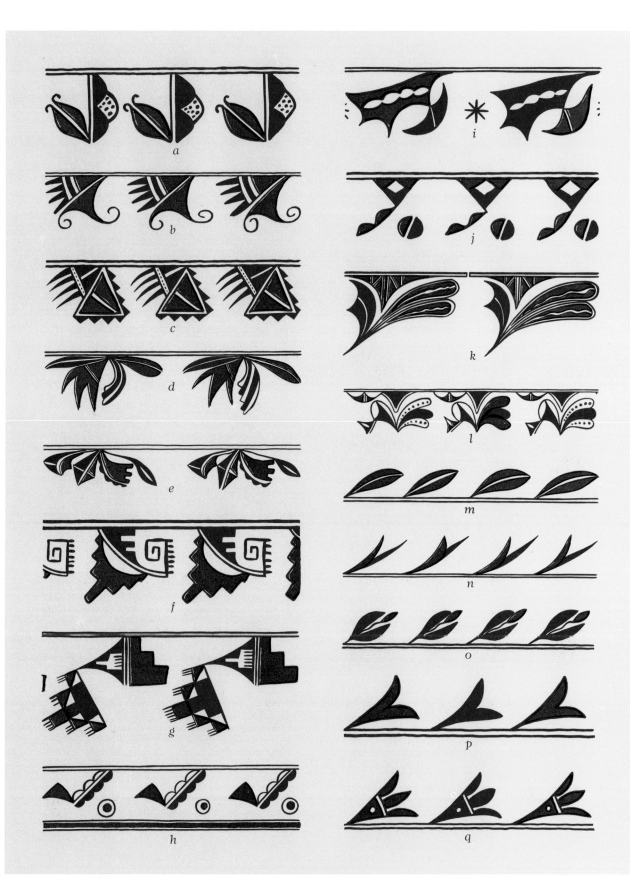

PLATE 105

173

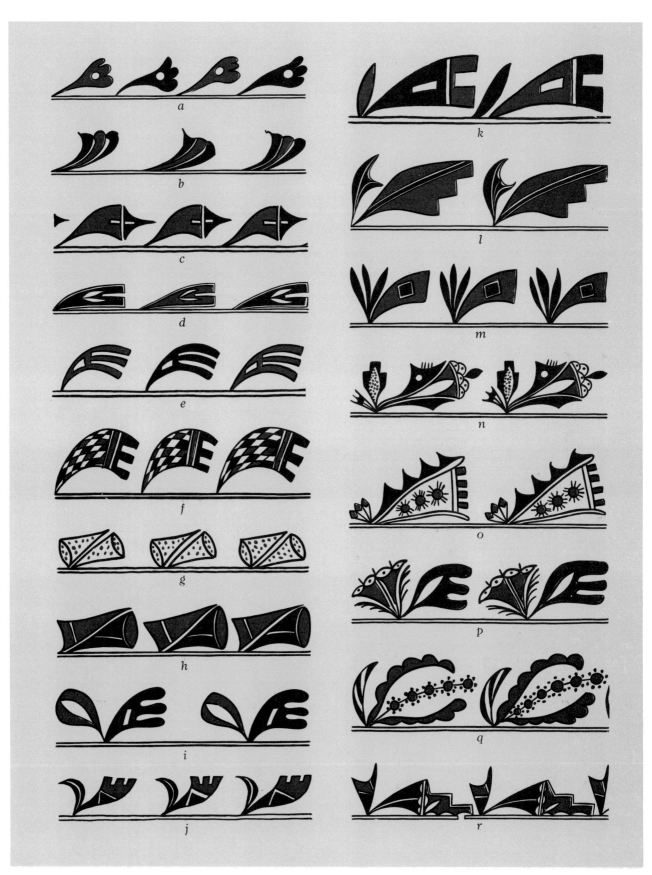

PLATE 106

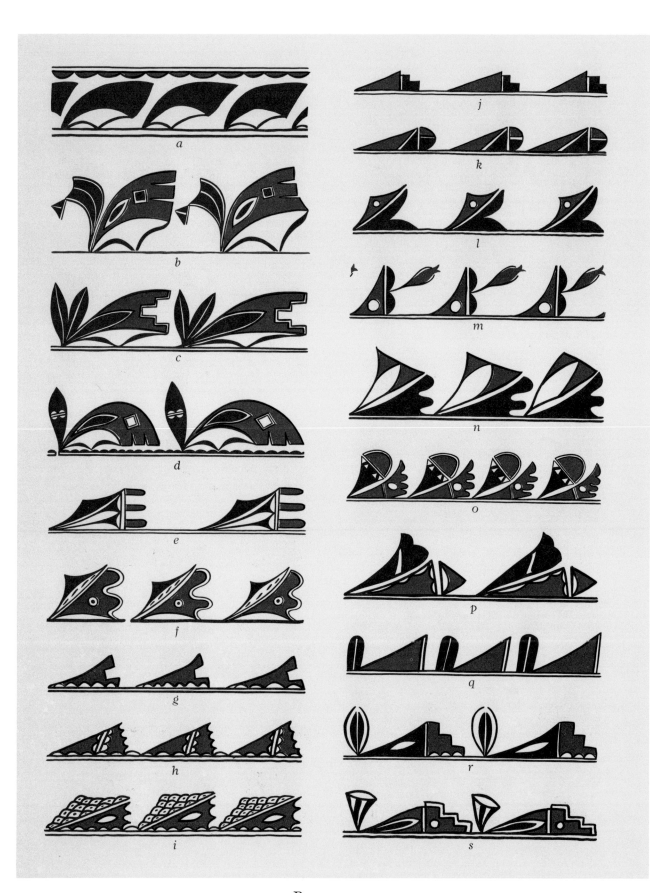

a

b

c

d

e

f

g

h

i

j

k

l

m

n

o

p

q

r

s

PLATE 107

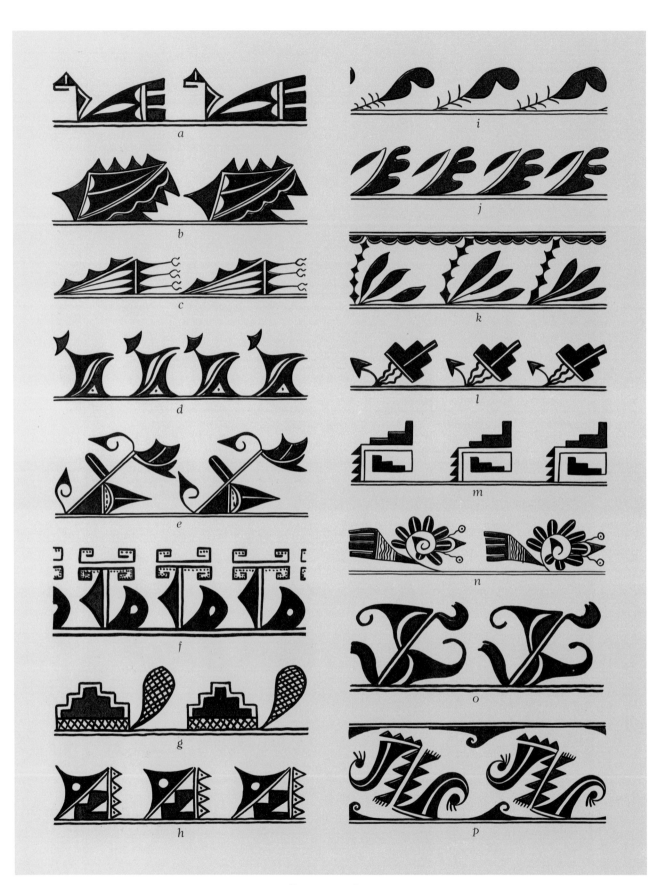

PLATE 108

176

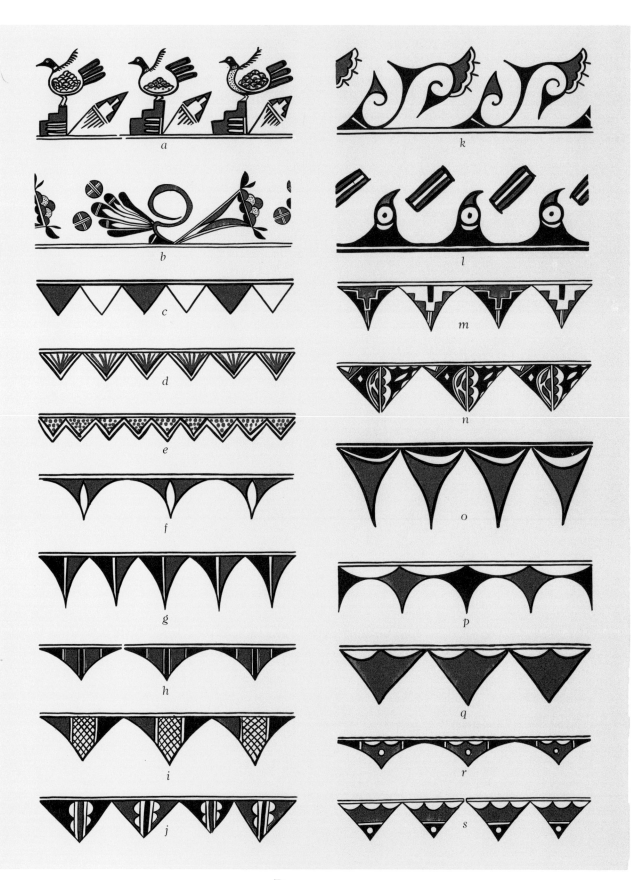

PLATE 109

leftward. Five accessory devices appear in *a* — bird, cloud bank, terrace, dots, and rain lines. And in *b*, there is an unusual grouping of feathers and disks. The double volutes in *k* and the birdlike beak in *l* are unusual.

Adjoined static motifs pendant from banding lines. The fifteen adjoined static motifs (*c-j* and *m-s*) are part of a series including seventeen in plates 110 and 111. The group includes nearly an even number of rectilinear and curvilinear forms. Interpretations of the rectilinear forms differ between cloud and rain-far-off. In either case, however, the rain lines in *d*, the rain drops in *e*, the cloud spaces in *j* and *s*, and the red clouds in *n* leave no doubt as to the constant concern shown for rainfall. In constrast, the curvilinear forms from the simplest in *f*, *g*, and *o* to the more complex in *i*, *m*, and *r* are more definitely known as rain-far-off.

Plate 110. Adjoined static motifs pendant from banding lines. Continued from plate 109, the triangle and rain-far-off appear as basic motifs in nine of the sixteen designs, together with three of cloud (*a*, *b*, and *m*), two of crisscross (*h* and *i*), and one each of terrace (*c*) and zigzag (*l*). In *l*, the basic terrace alternates with seedpod; and in *n*, the terrace within rain-far-off with bird in cloud bank. Of the minor details, there are four examples of leaf, three of crisscross rain lines, two of clouds, and one each of numerous others.

Plate 111. Adjoined static motifs pendant from banding lines. Supplementing the static series in plate 110, one additional design is shown in *a*. In addition are five figures, basically static but with dynamic appendages that more or less dominate the static combinations. The basic rain-far-off motif appears in *c* and *d*, and the triangle in *f*.

Adjoined static motifs placed above banding lines. The small group (*g-n*) includes five arrangements varying from the simple motifs of *g* and *h* to more complex arrangements in *i* and *k*; in all of them bilateral symmetry of units is maintained. In the three following (*l-n*), use is made of supplementary dynamic devices including the birds in *m*. In the entire group, the basic motifs are triangles, rain-far-off, the cloud in *m*, and the apparent rainbow in *n*.

Adjoining dynamic motifs pendant from banding lines. The last three designs (*o-q*) are of simple dynamic pendant motifs with a major trend to the right. These mark the beginning of a larger group in plate 112. The meaning of the triangular units in *o* is not clear, but in *p* and *q* the use of the lazy feather is quite evident.

Plate 112. Adjoining dynamic motifs pendant from banding lines. Following the three designs in plate 111 (*o-q*), the fourteen designs in plate 112 (*a-n*) comprise a group in which the major trend is toward the lower right and which vary in the use of simple units, as in *a-i*, to more complex arrangements. In only two designs (*e* and *j*) is there a use of appendages with a leftward trend. Beginning with *o*, the major direction changes to leftward in the group of six; a system that is followed throughout the seventeen designs in plate 113.

Among accessory motifs are eight examples of leaf, three of cloud, and two of terrace.

PLATE 110

179

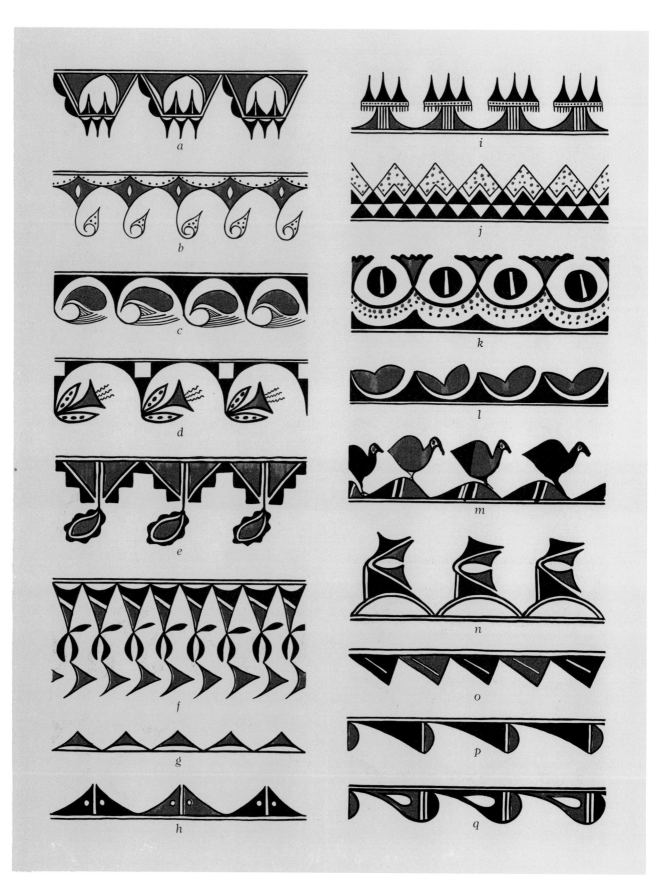

PLATE 111

180

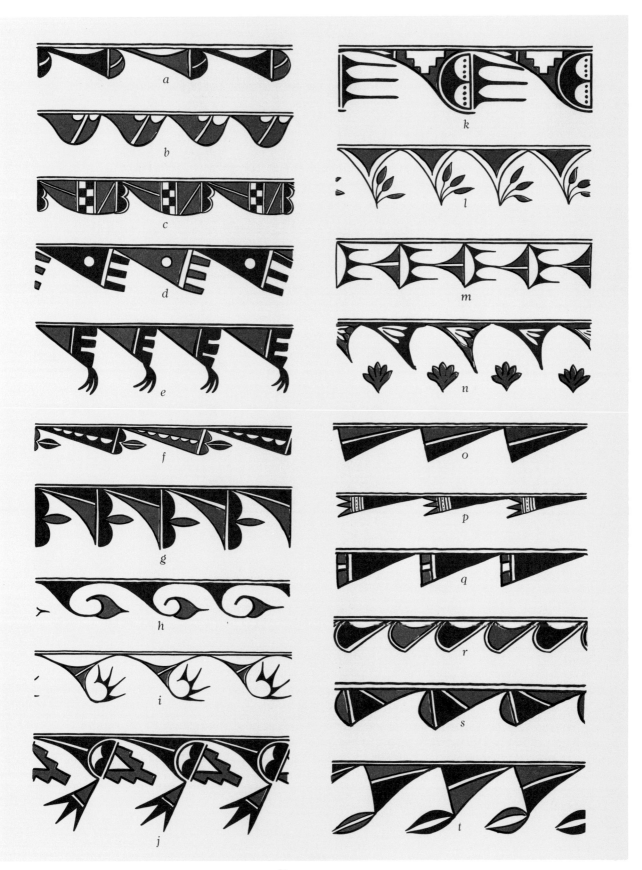

a

b

c

d

e

f

g

h

i

j

k

l

m

n

o

p

q

r

s

t

PLATE 112

Plate 113. Adjoining dynamic motifs pendant from upper banding lines. The leftward trend of the six designs in plate 112 is maintained throughout the seventeen designs in plate 113, with the possible exception of *o* in which, though the long straight structured lines conform, the resulting leaf motifs themselves appear to be facing right.

Of the identifiable minor devices, there are four each of leaf, volute, and open-cloud space; three each of eye and rain-far-off; and two each of cloud and rain lines.

Plate 114. Adjoining dynamic motifs based upon lower banding lines. In the entire group of twenty designs, the major movement is upward to the right. Alternation of red and black appears in only five (*a, f, g, p,* and *t*). The major motifs are lazy forms of leaf and feather with a few such as *d, j, l,* and *m* that might serve for either. The use of minor accessories seems only to confuse the basic structure of *m-o*. Although the group (*q-t*) is equally complex, the use of solid blacks gives them greater distinction.

Among the few unusual minor motifs used, the free cloud banks in *q,* the combinations of leaf and rain-far-off in *r,* and the tripartite leaves of *t* are outstanding.

Plate 115. Adjoining dynamic motifs based upon lower banding lines. Additional designs with upward movement to the right, as shown in plate 114, are included in *a-c* of plate 115. Following these is a group of ten (*d-m*) in which the major direction is leftward. These, beginning with simple forms, lead to more complex arrangements in which, with one exception (*l*), a fair degree of regular repetition is maintained. Alternation of red and black is used in only one (*d*).

Alternating static motifs developed on lower banding lines. Beginning with *n* is a group of five designs in which various means are used in the alternation of unlike units, the series extending through plate 116. Additional alternation of red and black appears in *n* and within the leaflike units of *p*.

Plate 116. Alternating static motifs developed on either upper or lower banding lines. Two of the designs in plate 116 (*a* and *l*) are pendant from upper banding lines, that in *a* consisting of plant forms alternating with crude representations of the American flag, a rare example of digression from purely Pueblo design. In *l,* the alternation is between free units, with those attached above. The drawing also includes a complex variant of the rarely used line-break. The remaining ten designs are based upon the lower banding lines, and in most instances show the alternation of fairly even-sized motifs, the greatest inequality being that in *j* where there is also an unbalance in the three major figures. The only example of alternation of red and black is that in the terraces of *d*.

Plate 117. Mixed group of designs attached to upper or lower banding lines. In the mixed group of plate 117, five designs (*a-d* and *h*) are pendant, and three (*e-g*) are attached below. Repeated, identical, major units occur in two pendant arrangements: static in *b* and dynamic in *d* and *e*. Alternation prevails in the dynamic arrangement of *c,* static in *g,* and mixed in *f* and *h*.

Several unusual minor features occur, such as the profusion of minute rain-far-off motifs in *a,* the large volutes in *d,* the disks and peacock feathers in *f*. (The bird is known because of its presence at a nearby mission.)

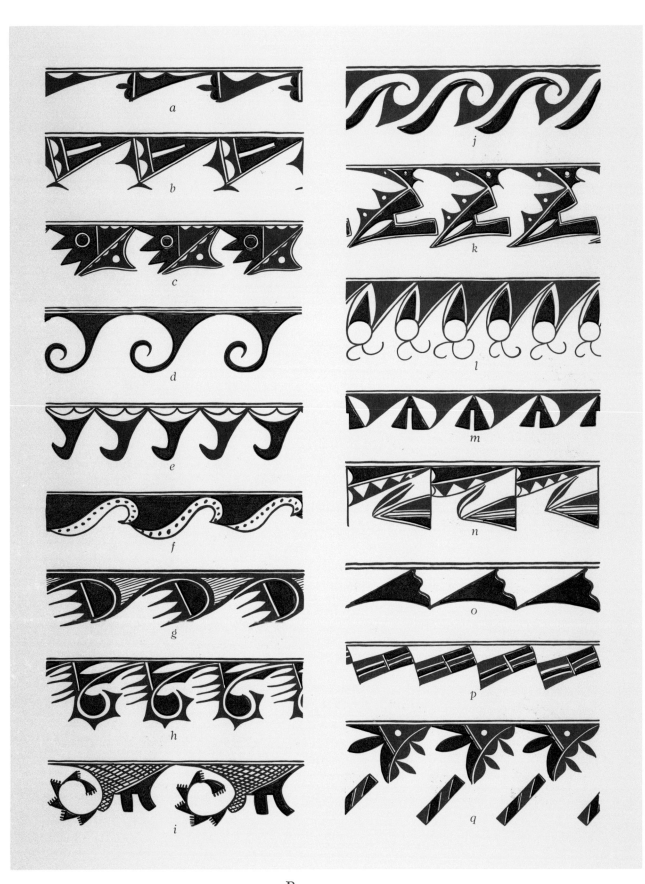

PLATE 113

183

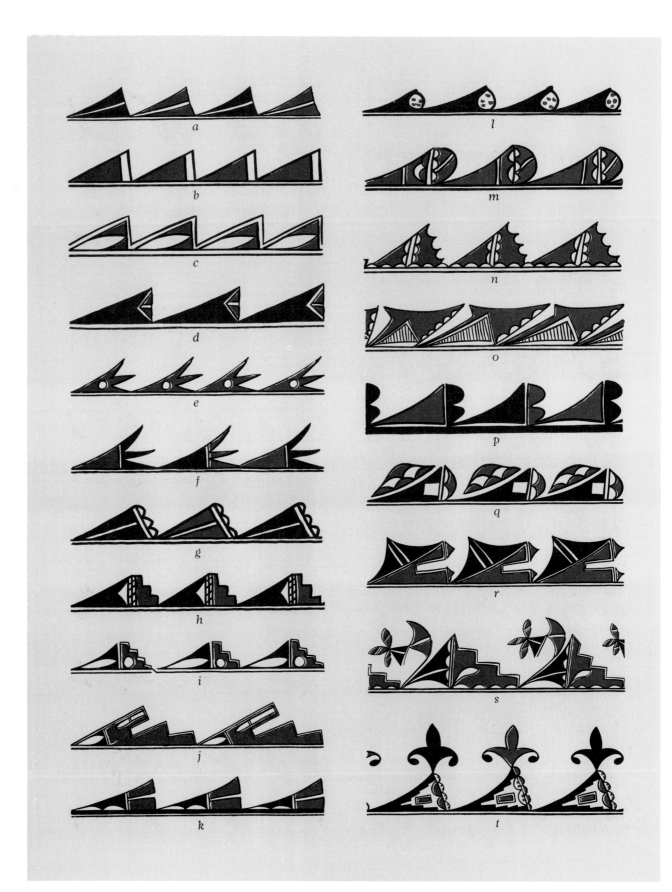

PLATE 114

184

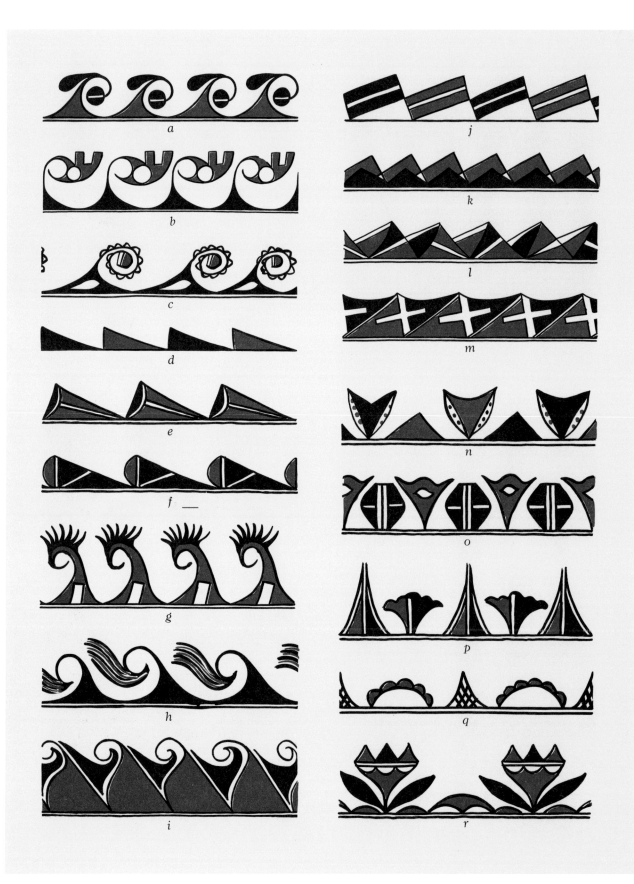

PLATE 115

185

PLATE 116

PLATE 117

Plate 118. Mixed group of designs attached to upper or lower banding lines. In *a*, the major, pendant static motif alternates with minor dynamic details. In *b*, the major motifs are dynamic, attached lightly to the lower banding line, and alternating with minor dynamic units. Volutes and rain-far-off provide the principal adornments of the two.

Alternation of unlike static motifs in continuous, pendant bands. Bilateral symmetry is preserved in the fourteen designs (*c-p*). In some, such as *e* and *f*, the major accent is in the pendant leaves; in others (*d, h,* and *m*) there is a more even balance of interest. In only one (*l*) is there a color alternation in the major motifs. Leaf and cloud motifs prevail throughout the group, followed by rain-far-off and terrace.

Plate 119. Alternation of adjoined motifs, mostly static, and a pendant form in upper banding line. Of the group of static motifs (*a-j*), exact repetition of details is used in *c, d,* and *f-i*. In *a*, there is an alternation of color and minor details of the three triangular units. The pendant forms in *e* may not have been intended as dynamic, but in *h* there is a deliberate use of paired oblique lines in the three triangles. The exceedingly complex arrangement in *j* is well handled; bilateral symmetry is maintained, even to the reversal of color in the minor terraces, to contrast with the red of the middle and the black of the two outer ovals. The design is further distinguished by the rare use of a line-break in the middle of the upper band. In the four remaining designs (*k-n*), the continuous pendant borders are static but alternating with dynamic units placed between cloud or terrace, or, as in *n*, attached to the static units of rain-far-off. The minor stepped units also add to the dynamic effect.

Plate 120. (The text explaining the details of plate 120 was not available. Since Dr. Chapman knew exactly what he wanted to say in presenting these designs, an explanation by another would be presumptive.)

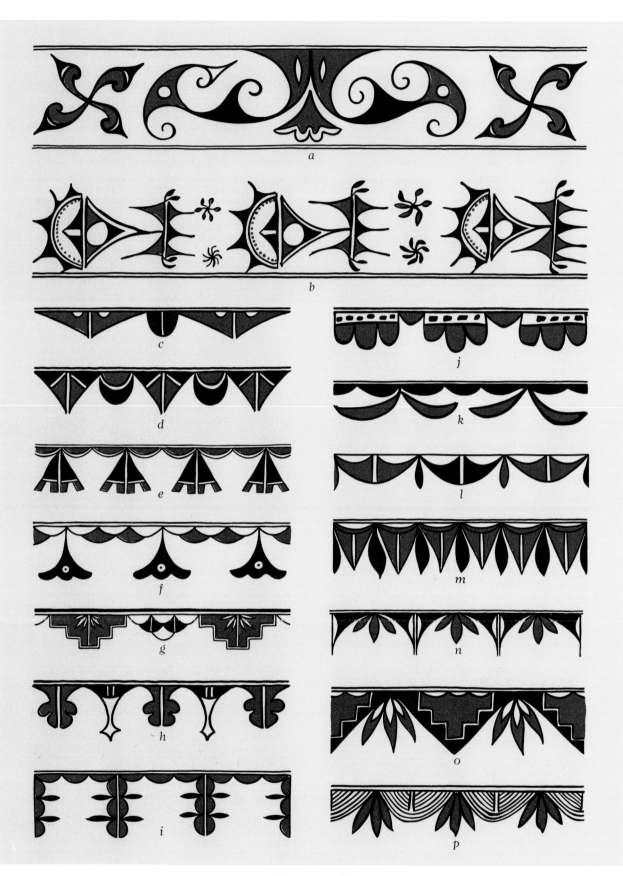

PLATE 118

PLATE 119

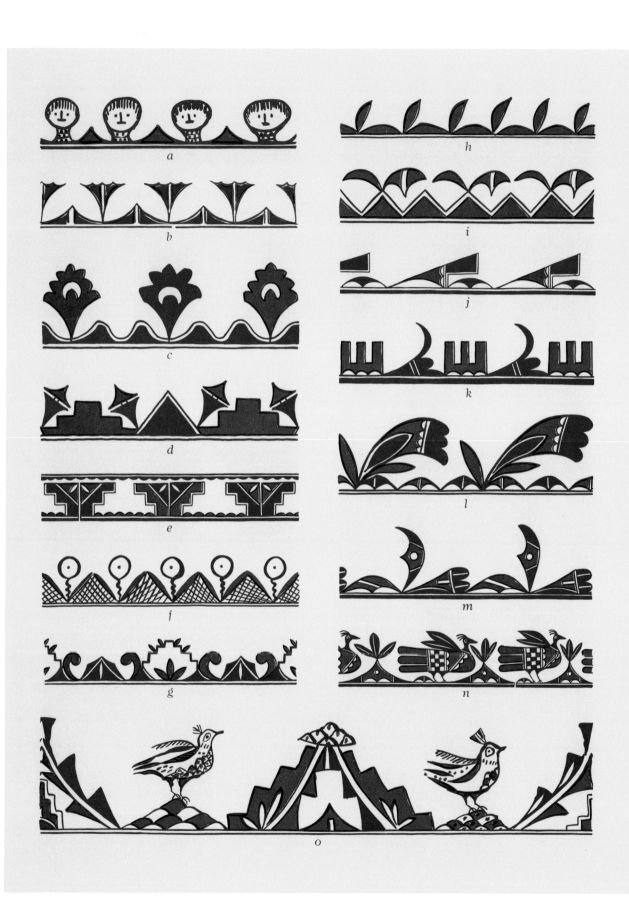

PLATE 120

191

Plate 121. Alternation of adjoining dynamic motifs pendant from upper banding lines. Of the thirteen designs in this group all but two (*l* and *m*) have a uniform trend downward to the right, with the possible exception also of the complex arrangement in *j*, which has no major direction. In most of the designs there is a decided contrast in size of major and minor motifs. No notes accompany the sketch from which *i* was drawn. Very likely the middle motif was the last to be drawn and, with insufficient space, the serrate detail was used in place of the triangles. If so, a view of the opposite side of the vessel would show a repetition of the two end motifs.

Alternation of adjoining dynamic motifs based upon lower banding lines. Appended to the above group are four upright dynamic motifs (*n-q*) with the major trend to the right.

Among minor motifs used throughout the above two groups, the leaf, appearing in fourteen of the seventeen designs, is followed by two each of terrace, volute, and eye; and only one each of cloud, feather, seedpod, rain-far-off, checker, and disk.

Plate 122. Repetition of static motifs pendant from upper banding lines and closely bordered or adjoined by a secondary row. In the group of nine designs (*a-i*), the secondary motifs of *c-f* do not touch the upper band. In *e*, however, the composite lower band outweighs the cloud border above, and in *f* the cloud border is even more subordinate to the ornate band below. The dynamic layout in *o* is far more complex than that of *h*, for though it is lightly pendant from the upper banding line, the major interest is in the succession of upper and lower volutes which unite to form the sigmoids tipped with heavy black; the joining of the sigmoids with red also gives substance to the continuous band. The crude design in *g* and the more finished one in *h* are rare instances of the omission of paired lines separating black and red. In *g* and *h*, the dynamic volutes conflict with the basic static motifs above them, and in *i* they serve to border the continuous expanse of red between the upper and lower motifs.

Plate 123. Single units of repeated complex static arrangements attached above or below. For variety the ten designs of plate 123 are of single units only, thus reproducing in greater size the details of several more complex arrangements, such as those in *d, e, i,* and *j*. Six of the designs are upright, and four pendant from the upper banding lines. Bilateral symmetry is preserved in the major layouts but is confused by dynamic details in *e, i,* and *j*.

Familiar details are used in every figure, their relative frequency varying from six of leaf, to fewer of cloud, rain-far-off, feather, and eye, with only one each of eye and *avanyu*. The latter attached to the cloud bank in *d* may also have the significance of lightning.

Plate 124. Like motifs attached above and below to banding lines. (The text explaining the details of plate 124 was not available. Since Dr. Chapman knew exactly what he wanted to say in presenting these designs, an explanation by another would only be presumptive.)

Plate 125. Continuation of like motifs above and below in a and b.

Alternation of repeated motifs, unlike above and below. Static in *c-e*; dynamic in *l*; and both static and dynamic in *f-k*.

Alternation of adjoined motifs above and below. Static in *m* and *n*.

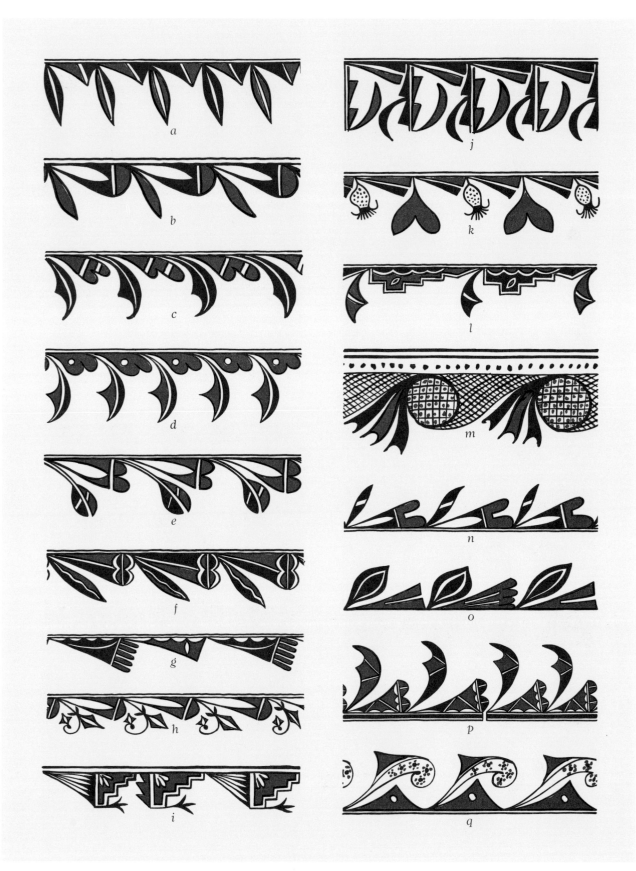

PLATE 121

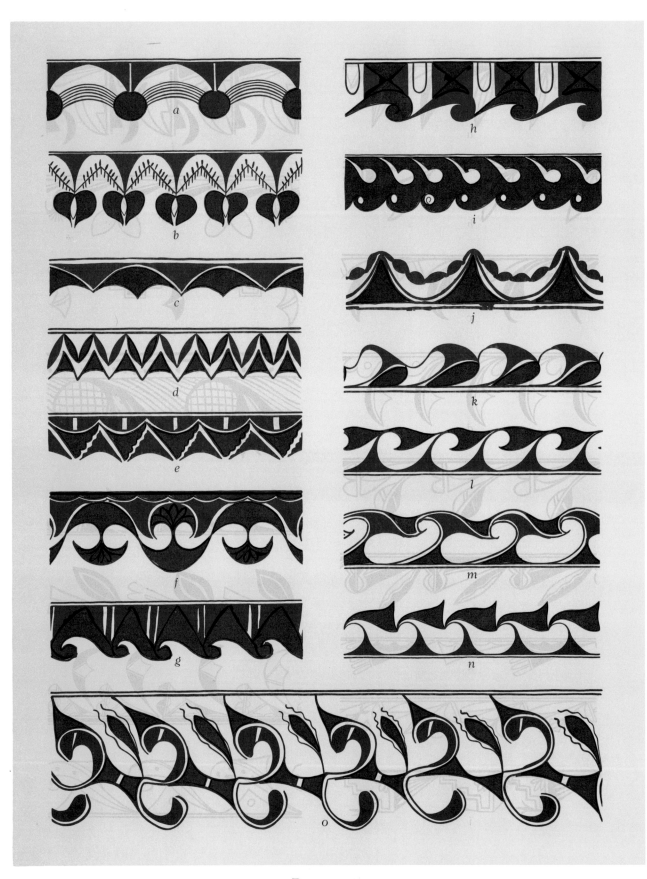

PLATE 122

PLATE 123

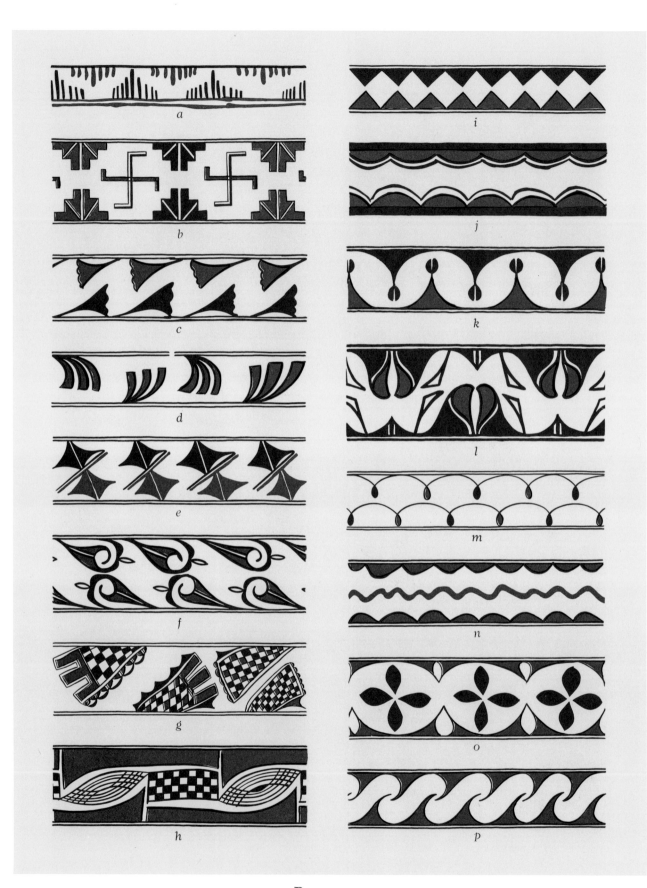

PLATE 124

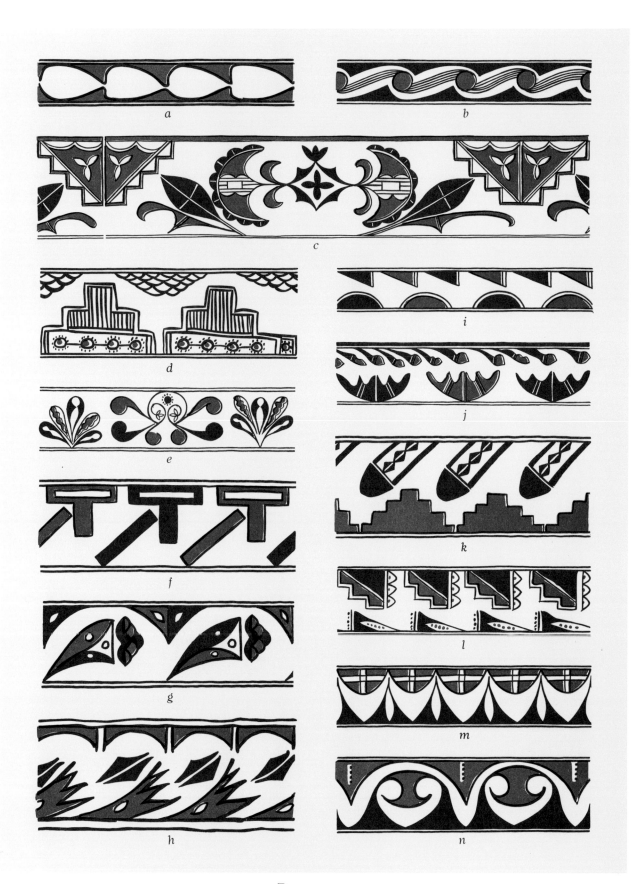

a

b

c

d

e

f

g

h

i

j

k

l

m

n

PLATE 125

Plate 126. Combination of adjoined motifs above and spaced motifs below. Static in *a, g, h,* and *k;* dynamic in *b* and *c;* and both static and dynamic in *e, f, m,* and *n.*

Plate 127. Continuation of adjoined pendant motifs above, with spaced motifs below. Five additional examples of the group in plate 126 with adjoined motifs above and spaced motifs below appear in plate 127, including one static and dynamic in *a* and four static in *b-e.*

Spaced or adjoined pendant motifs above, meeting with others below — placed upright and spanning the intervening space. In four (*f-i*) both pendant and upright motifs are spaced; in five (*j-n*) they are adjoined. Beginning with simple leaf motifs in *f,* the series includes other static layouts in *g* and *h,* three combinations of static and dynamic in *i-k,* as well as three with dynamic units both above and below.

Plate 128. Upper and lower motifs united by other intervening motifs. Various means are used to unite the pendant and upright motifs. In *a,* the medium is an open-space zigzag; in *c,* the medium consists of the small triangular motifs between cloud band and large leaves. In the group of six designs (*d-i*), the intervening motifs are formed largely by the volutes of the upper and lower motifs. In *k,* the intervening rectangular motif adjoins, laterally, the upper and lower zigzags. In *m,* obviously the paired spanning lines were first drawn; and then, at left, the upper, lower, and intervening motifs were added. At right, however, the unit is clearly one of spanning. Its complex details, and the leaves at left and right, add a dynamic touch to the entire layout.

Plate 129. Repeated, spaced motifs spanning band. Static in *a, b, e,* and *g;* dynamic in *h-m, p,* and *q.*

Spanning static motifs alternating with unlike motifs. Static in *c, d,* and *f;* alternating in *n* and *o.*

Plate 130. Repeated, spaced motifs spanning band. Dynamic without minors in intervening spaces in *a-c* and *g,* with minors in *d-f.* Adjoined repeats of like motif spanning band: static in *h-k,* dynamic in *l-p.*

Plate 131. Adjoined repeats of like motif spanning band. The series in plate 130 is continued through *a-c* of plate 131.

Adjoined units based upon zigzag spanning bands. In ten designs the simple zigzag or wavy arrangements produce a bilateral symmetry (*d-j, n, o,* and *q*). In four others (*k-m* and *p*), added details give a decided dynamic effect.

Plate 132. The zigzag arrangements in plate 131 are continued in four designs (*a-d*) of plate 132. Bilateral symmetry has been maintained in *d* but is lost in *a-c* by use of dynamic details.

The static group includes one stepped device in *e,* and five crisscross devices in *n-r.* The alternation of colors in *n* and *p* does not lessen their static effect; but in *r,* where it occurs within the diamonds, there is a decided unbalance.

In the dynamic group (*f-m*) are variations, from the simple serrate arrangements of *e* and *f* to the more complex group in *h-m.*

In such groups, based mostly upon abstract geometric layouts, very few named motifs are used. There are four of feather, three of leaf, and two each of cloud and terrace.

PLATE 126

199

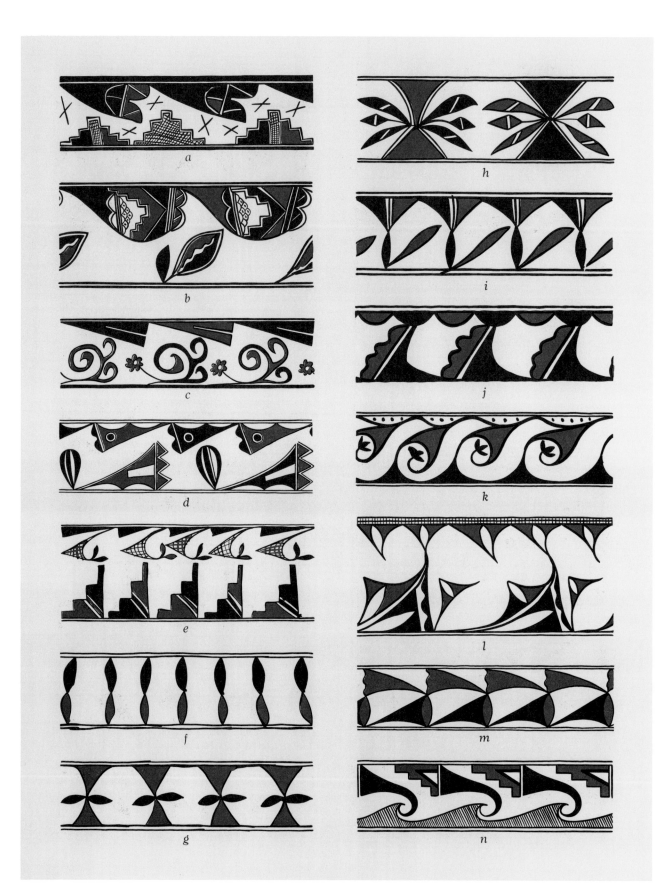

PLATE 127

PLATE 128

201

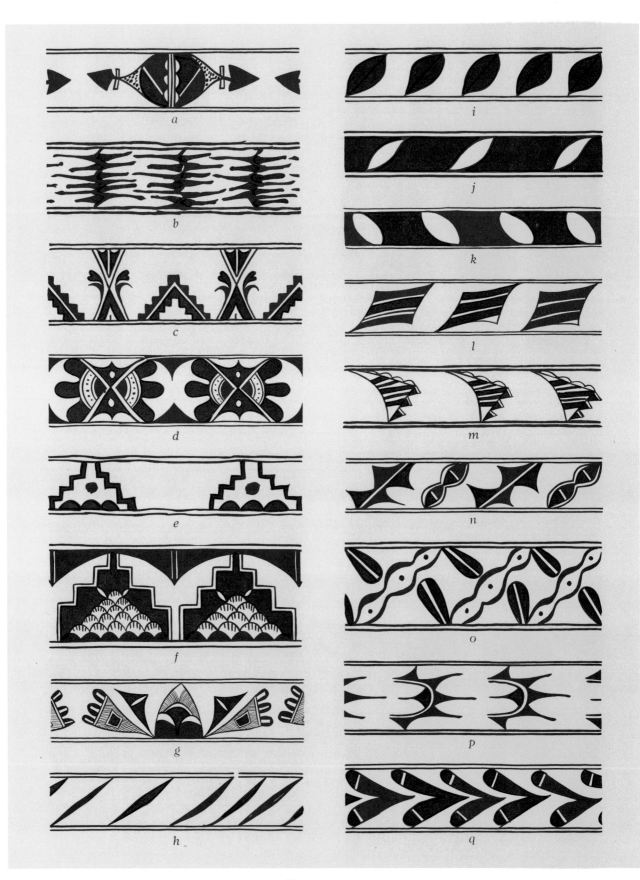

PLATE 129

a

b

c

d

e

f

g

h

i

j

k

l

m

n

o

p

PLATE 130

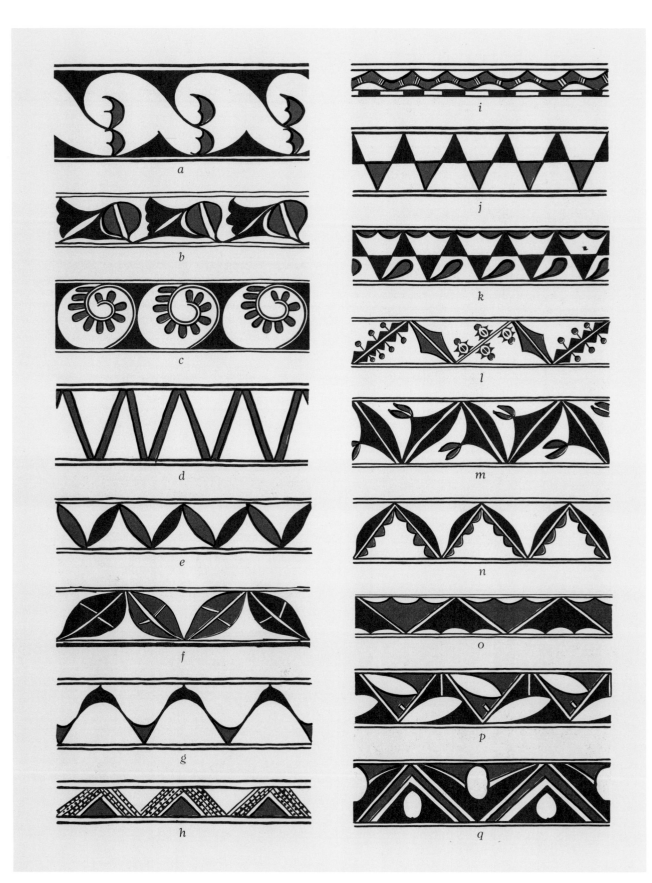

a

b

c

d

e

f

g

h

i

j

k

l

m

n

o

p

q

PLATE 131

a

b

c

d

e

f

g

h

i

j

k

l

m

n

o

p

q

r

PLATE 132

205

Plate 133. The series of adjoined, static, crisscross arrangements shown in plate 132 is continued in six designs (*a-f*) of plate 133. Of these, the crisscross dominates in *a*, but the remaining designs show by stages a tendency toward centering the interest on the diamond spaces. A minor eccentric detail in *f* disturbs the otherwise bilateral symmetry.

Miscellaneous group of abstract geometric spanning units in continuous bands. The group of five (*g* and *i-l*) includes various continuous bands with use of triangles, crisscross, and rhomboid in dynamic layouts. These are followed in *m-q* by a group of simple static arrangements, including rectangles in *m-o*; and two (*p* and *q*) which are based upon the crisscross, developed in paneled spaces produced by single vertical lines.

A minimum of named details is used in the whole geometric group; the only recognizable details are the clouds in *i* and *k* and rain-far-off in *h*.

Plate 134. Two static motifs of the series in plate 133 appear in *a* and *b* of plate 134.

Dynamic motifs spanning bands. The group of six dynamic figures (*c-h*) includes five using repeated units, and one with them adjoined. The simple effective layout in *h* is the only one of its kind.

Motifs developed on paired lines dividing the band into panels. Although the paired lines in eight motifs (*i-p*) serve as panel dividers, the bilaterally symmetrical designs produced on them minimize the effect of paneling.

Plate 135. Static motifs developed on paired or multiple lines dividing bands into panels. Of the twelve designs in plate 135, bilateral symmetry is used in the panels of *a, b,* and *d-h*. Two entire panels appear in the full-width design of *a*, while one whole panel and two half-panels are shown in *h*. A middle panel and two half-panels appear also in *e*. In *i-k*, an alternation of the unlike spanning motifs produces an asymmetrical arrangement in each panel. However, the bilaterally symmetrical motifs themselves are the dominant features, and the multiple-line paneling arrangement is decidedly secondary. A minor defect in the full panel of *i* and the rotating effect of the black leaves in *j* give a slight unbalance to their otherwise bilaterally symmetrical panels.

Among the accessory details are seven uses of cloud, five of leaf, four of feather, with fewer of rain-far-off and seedpod.

PLATE 133

207

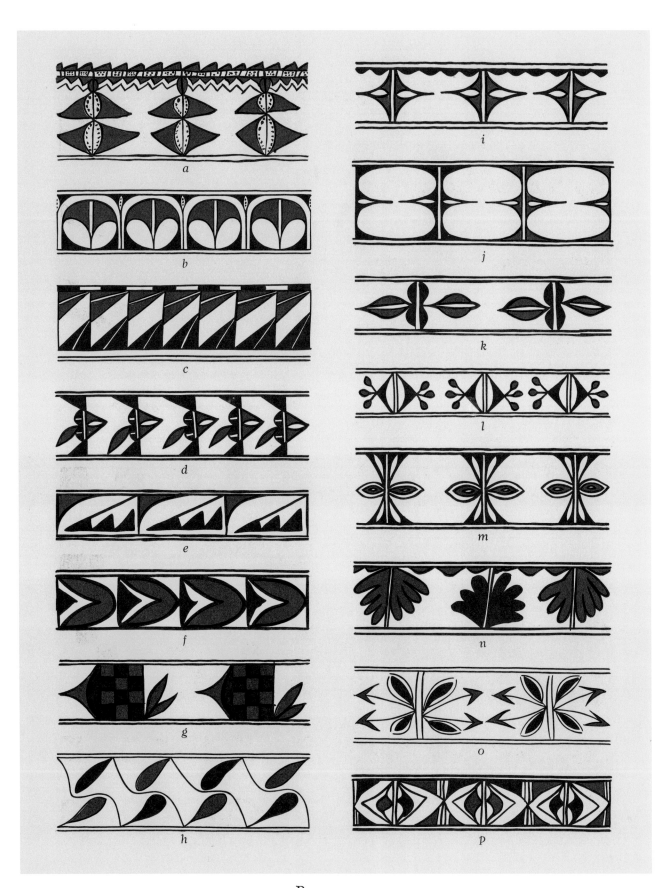

a

b

c

d

e

f

g

h

i

j

k

l

m

n

o

p

PLATE 134

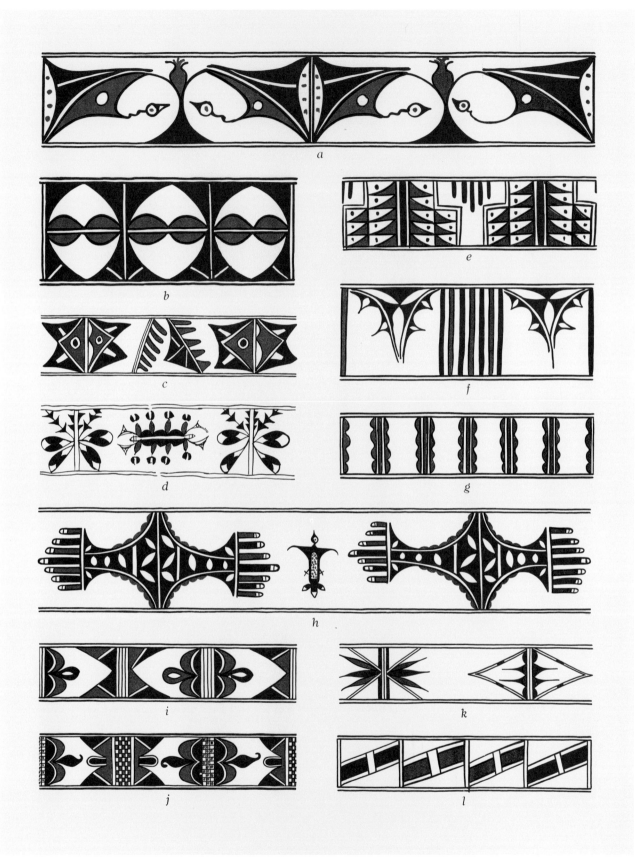

a

b

c

d

e

f

g

h

i

k

j

l

PLATE 135

Plate 136. Static and dynamic motifs in panels. Paneling is used throughout the series of thirteen designs in plate 136. Paired lines are used as panel dividers in most of the designs, the only exceptions being in the use of triple lines in *j* and *k* and quadruple lines in *i*. If only the paired lines are considered in the paneling of *l*, then the intervening checkered spaces might be considered as filling narrow, upright panels. However, in effect, they appear as parts of the extended bilaterally symmetrical motif at the middle. Combined static and dynamic motifs are repeated in the panels of *a*, and dynamic only in *b-f* and *i-k*. In four others (*g, h, l,* and *m*), static panels alternate with dynamic. In the first three, the static panel is shown between two dynamic panels; in *m*, the order has been reversed for comparison. A partial line-break appears at the left in *l*.

Plate 137. Static and dynamic motifs in panels. The use of multiple-vertical paneling lines noted in plate 136 appears in *a-e* and *l*, including three added examples of the checker in *c, d,* and *l*. In contrast with the extreme width of the checker in *d*, the narrow form in *l* can hardly be called a panel.

Five additional arrangements of alternating static and dynamic motifs appear in *a-e*. A crude effect of bilateral symmetry appears in the two panels of *a* in contrast with the leaping does. Two whole panels are also shown in *c*, but in *d* only a portion of the panels is shown at left and right of the middle device.

The upright paneling lines of several of the designs (*e-h* and *l*) show some varying degree of inclination, caused either by inept drawing or, as in *g* and *h*, possibly by intent. In contrast, the paneling lines in *i-k* are clearly slanted with the purpose of creating rhomboid panel spaces.

Minor motifs consist mainly of leaf, six; cloud, five; checker, three; and terrace, two.

Plate 138. Dynamic motifs in rhomboid panels. The well-designed figures in plate 138 are all based upon the use of paired, oblique paneling lines producing rhomboid interspaces. The preference for the direction from upper right to lower left is apparent; only one example, *m*, shows the opposite slant. Various degrees of inclination are used: the minimum in *h* and *m*, and the maximum in *f*. In the entire series, the motifs are placed on the paired lines.

Identical motifs produce rotational symmetry in nine designs (*a-d* and *g-k*). The use of the red motif in *f* and of unlike details in combination in those of *l-n* gives an added dynamic quality to the layout. In only one design (*n*) is there an alternation of dynamic and static units.

PLATE 136

211

a

b

g

c

h

d

i

j

e

k

f

l

PLATE 137

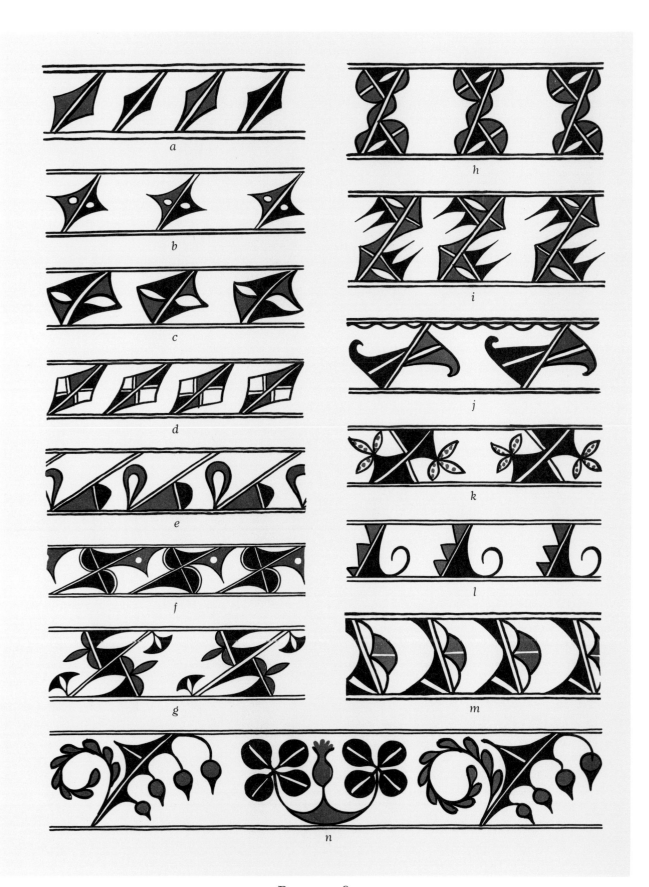

a

b

c

d

e

f

g

h

i

j

k

l

m

n

PLATE 138

Plate 139. Dynamic and static motifs within panels. Oblique paneling is continued in eight designs (*a-h*). In four of these, static motifs are used within the panels: free in *b* and *h,* and spanning in *a* and *f.* Paired, black lines are used in only four; the others (*d-g*) show varied use of multiple-line paneling. Following this group are two in which curved lines replace the usual rectilinear pairs; and one (*k*) in which an angular rectilinear variant is used.

Adjoined static motifs used above and below on paired median lines within bands. The only elaboration of the median band is that in *p.* Structurally identical motifs are used above and below in four designs (*l* and *o-q*) and unlike motifs in *m, n,* and *r.* In the latter, however, the terraces do not adjoin.

Plate 140. Static motifs used above and below on paired median lines in bands. The series in plate 139 is concluded in the first four designs of plate 140 (*a-d*). In *a* and *b,* as in plate 139, the motifs are free from the banding lines. But in *c* the upper motifs span the space between banding and median lines, while in *d* a more complex arrangement produces a series of four distinct motifs within three zones, the lower not attached below. An unusually consistent coordination is used in placement of units in adjoining bands, only a slight off-center variation appearing in *a* and *d.*

Combination of static and dynamic motifs above and below on paired median lines. In *e,* the simple arrangement might be considered in the static group of plate 139, but that the upper motifs appear to have an intentional twist to the left. The layout of *f* resembles that of *c* except that it is dynamic above and static below the median band. The combination is reversed in *g.* In the following five designs (*h-l*), both upper and lower motifs are dynamic. Spanning is used in the upper motifs of *h* and in the adjoined lower motifs of *k.*

Plate 141. Complex designs from water and storage jars. The complex bands from storage jars in *a-c* and *f* show the disinclination of the potters to use enlarged motifs to compensate for the much greater space available in decorating large vessels. This results in considerable irregularity in the repetition or alternation of overornate units, so closely spaced that they lose distinction when viewed on the jars themselves and can be followed only with difficulty even in the extended drawings. A certain degree of confusion also appears in the three bands from water jars in *d, e,* and *g,* particularly noticeable in *d* and *g.* The latter contains two loops, filled with red, a device that is all but nonexistent in San Ildefonso design.

Otherwise the familiar units of volute and leaf, both realistic and stylized, outnumber the other commonly used minor motifs.

PLATE 139

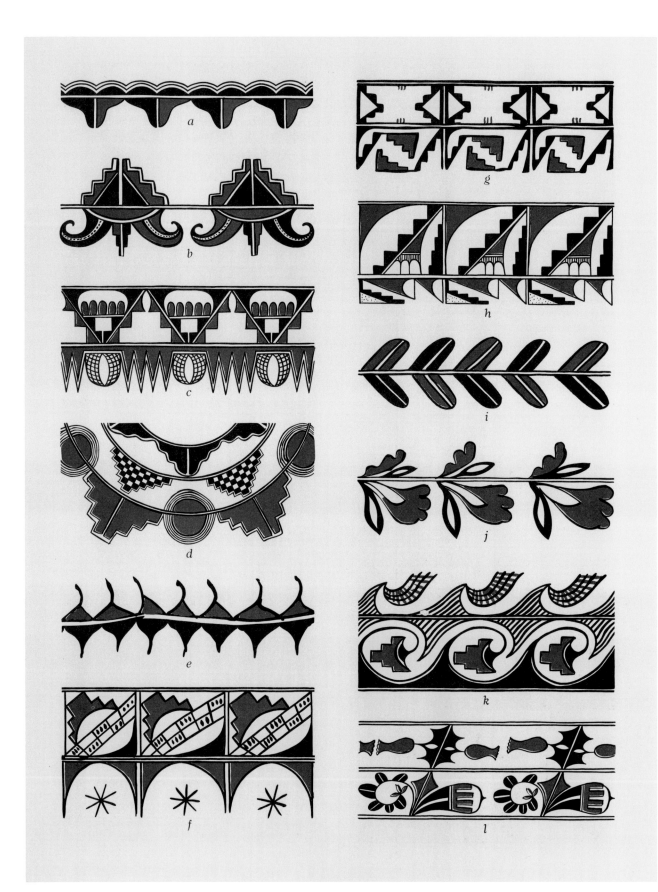

PLATE 140

a

b

c

d *e*

f

g

PLATE 141

217

Plate 142. Cloud bands, pendant and upright. From the beginning of this study cloud bands have commanded attention because of their great variation in form, color, and arrangement of details. As work has progressed it has seemed advisable to add to the collection (plates 142-144), even though in a few instances certain designs may appear out of sequence. No account has been kept of the scores of examples of the simple black form in *c*, as compared with more complex forms in *r* and *s*. The group in plate 142 includes, with only a few exceptions, the forms in which the cloud units appear as solid entities, against the banding lines, without intervening scallops (here termed cloud spaces) such as appear in *l-p* and *x*. Other devices such as those in *q-s* and *w* also detract from the simplicity of the units. Beginning with *y* each band is bordered by a scalloped line conforming with the cloud units. Static arrangements are used throughout with only two exceptions. In *t*, each unit is unbalanced by use of black and red. This is called "black clouds with red of sunlight on one side." In the other, the paired oblique lines give motion to the units.

Plate 143. Cloud bands, pendant and upright. The series of designs in plate 142 showing use of a scalloped border of clouds is continued through five designs in plate 143. Beginning with *h* is a group of ten bands showing the use of secondary clouds, pendant below the basic band. In three (*h-j*), the secondary clouds are limited to the alternate spaces between the basic units; in *k-q*, each interspace is used. The secondary row is given major importance in *l-q* by leaving the upper units as open-space clouds. Following are five designs (*r-v*), in which each extended, secondary cloud space is pendant from a pair of primary open-space clouds. The spanning is increased in *w* and *x*, so that the relative size of the open-space units is decreased. Two unusual arrangements appear in *y* and *z*: one complete, and two halves of open-space units. In *z*, each pair of upright open-space units is spanned by a complete cloud motif; and it, in turn, by a bordering pair of black clouds. In the entire series, five designs (*b*, *j*, *p*, *w*, and *y*) contain dynamic details that remove them from the static class.

Plate 144. Cloud bands, pendant and upright. The twenty-one designs in plate 144 include a greater variety in combinations including those of the cloud motif itself and those with the addition of related and unrelated motifs. Bilateral symmetry is maintained in most of the layouts; the minor use of oblique lines appears only in *a*, *i*, and *s*. Added complexity appears in the emphasis on the scallops in *a* and *f*; the clustering of the cloud forms in *b-d*; and the triple rows in *e*. The use of the meaningful rain lines in *g*, and perhaps in *i* and *j*, as well as vegetal motifs in many others is considered most appropriate by the artists. Less self-explanatory are the unusual details in *h*, *n*, *o*, and *u*.

Plate 145. Detached cloud clusters used singly in static and dynamic arrangements. The use of detached cloud clusters is comparatively rare in Polychrome design. Most such devices are upright and static; the actual layouts of *i*, *m*, and *n* and the cloud clusters themselves in *p* are essentially bilaterally symmetrical, though placed obliquely. One exception, however, is in the leaning clusters of red rain lines at the left in *m*.

In relative frequency of use, rain dots appear in eight designs, rain-far-off in seven, leaf in five, rain lines in four, lightning, followed by terrace, and feather.

Plate 146. Interior designs from bowls. The exterior designs from bowls, being essentially confined to bands, have been commingled with those from water and storage jars in the preceding plates. Unlike the bowl designs from other pueblos such as Zia and Zuñi, there is no appreciable distinction made by the San Ildefonso potters in the choice of motifs and arrangements for each

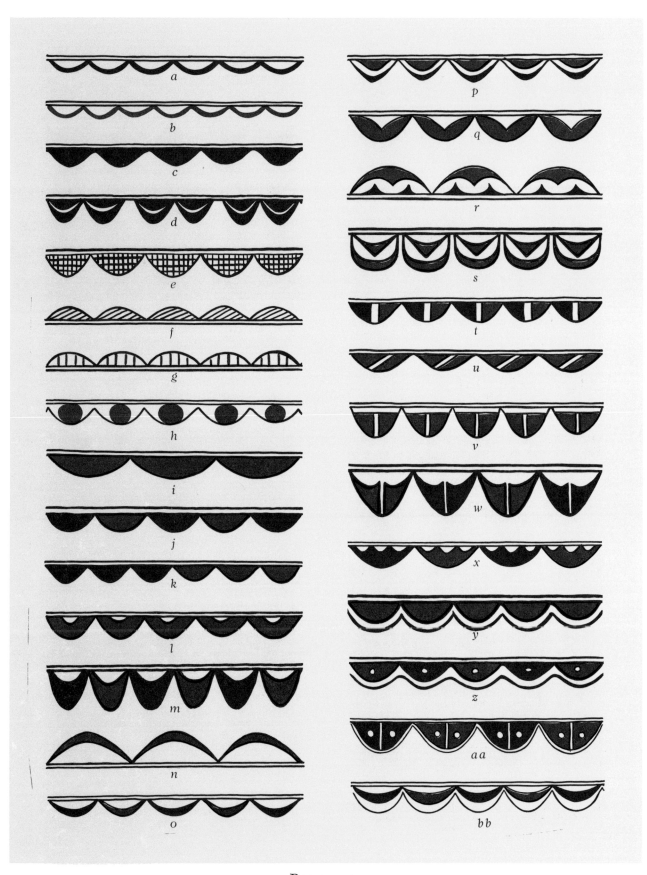

PLATE 142

219

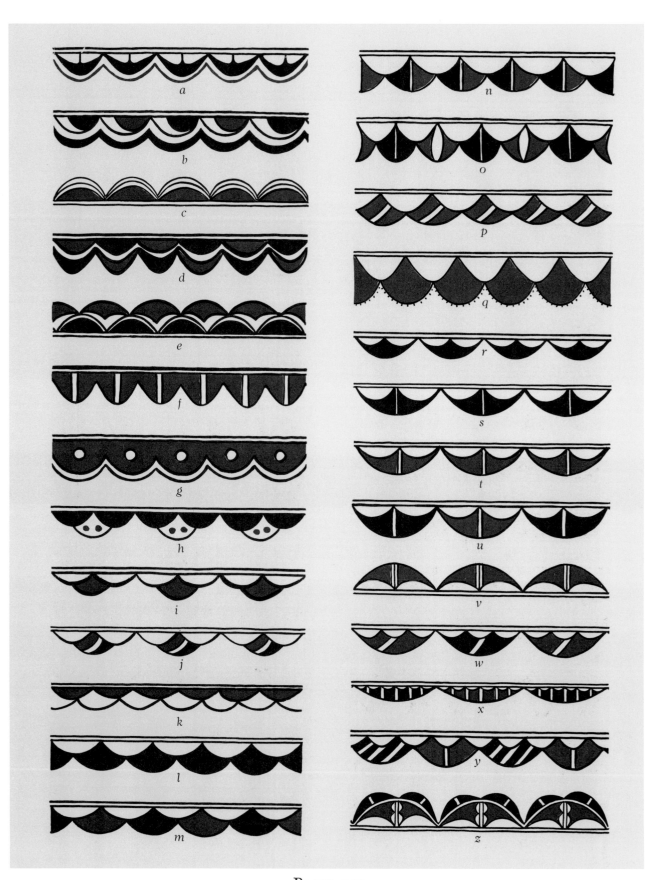

PLATE 143

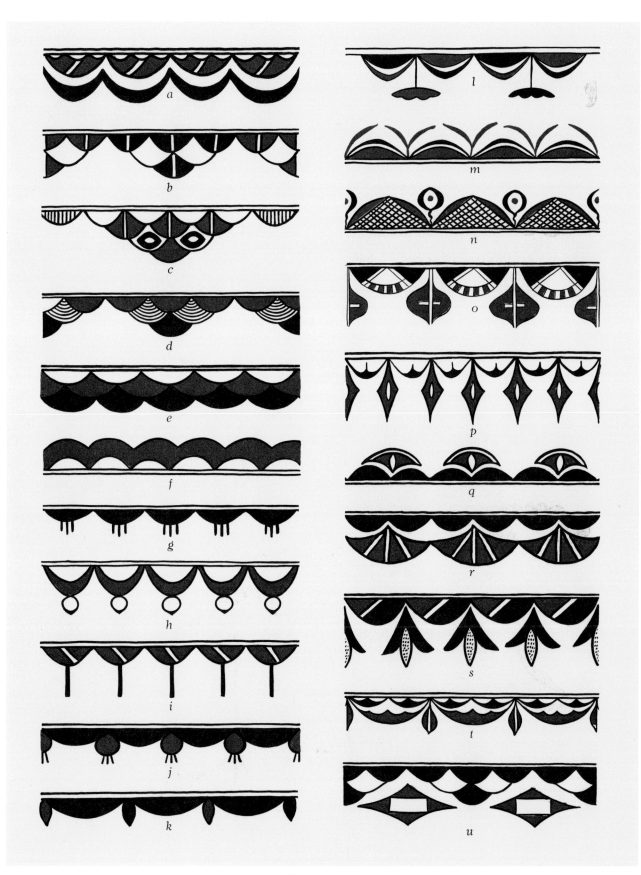

PLATE 144

221

PLATE 145

222

PLATE 146

223

of the three forms of vessels. But for the interior decoration of bowls, problems present themselves in adapting the familiar San Ildefonso motifs and arrangements for use within circles. The nine designs in plate 146 show various means of using static arrangements for this purpose. The simplest are those in *e, f,* and *i,* in which detached motifs are centered at some distance from the banding lines. In *g,* they are placed bordering a central disk. Repeated separate motifs also spring from the banding line in *c,* but they are so carelessly spaced that two minor units are needed to give continuity. Adjoined, repeated motifs are commonly used to border the rim, as in *a, b, d,* and *h.* Within such borders appear the detached central layout in *h;* the attached arrangement in *d;* and the four arms in *b,* spanning the space between rim and central disk.

No new motifs appear in the group. The two most frequently used are six of cloud and four of leaf.

Plate 147. Interior designs from bowls. The group of eight designs in plate 147 includes five dynamic units (*a* and *c-f*) and three of the combined static and dynamic units (*b, g,* and *h*). Three of the dynamic group (in particular *c-e*) show to great advantage the very lively effect produced by dynamic units within circles rather than in the extended horizontal bands of jars as shown in preceding plates. In contrast the three widely spaced free motifs of *a* lack the concerted motion of those in the well-designed layout of *c.* In *e,* though the cloud motifs are structurally static, they are given the effect of motion by their oblique open spaces. In the mixed group, the static cloud band in *b* is subordinate to the four free designs; in *g,* the major portion is static, with dynamic motifs confined to the central disk. A more even balance between the two modes is used in *h.*

Plate 148. Interior designs from bowls. Bilateral symmetry is used in the well-planned, static designs of *e, g,* and *h,* though the execution in *e* and *g* is decidedly carefree. Of the two dynamic designs (*a* and *f*), that in *a* with its rotational symmetry contrasts with the crudely designed and finished motifs in *f.* Minor dynamic details in the otherwise static layouts of *b* and *c* produce a slight unbalance, as compared with that in the most erratic combination of *d,* in which the major layout is partly attached and partly free. The use of ornamental details within the central disks of *d, e,* and *h,* like that of *g* and *h* in plate 147, is apparently a special attribute of designs in which static and dynamic motifs are combined.

The use of the familiar motifs is more evenly distributed than in most of the preceding plates; their presence, in numerical order, is leaf, feather, cloud, volute, terrace, and lazy feather.

Plate 149. Interior designs from bowls. The only static figure in the group of five is that of the bird, in *e,* which happens also to be one of the very few designs known to have been copied from the art of another pueblo (Hopi). The one dynamic arrangement, in *a,* developed with rotational symmetry similar to that of *a* in plate 148, is undoubtedly by the same artist. The remaining three figures (*b-d*) are developed by the use of both static and dynamic details. A very satisfactory combination of the two appears in *b,* even though the four whirling "bird's heads" are opposed by six black terraces at the rim. Although the arc in *d* is bilaterally symmetrical and is opposed by the black fringe at the left, the intervening ornate bird adds unbalance to the layout.

The most remarkable design in the group is that of the four birds in figure *c;* an excellent example of the freedom used by many of the artists of a half-century ago. Considerable variance appears also in the angular border units, where the black figures appear in three groups of six, seven, and nine. However, perhaps by chance, the cloud units appear in an even number of repeats, so that there is an unbroken alternation of red and black.

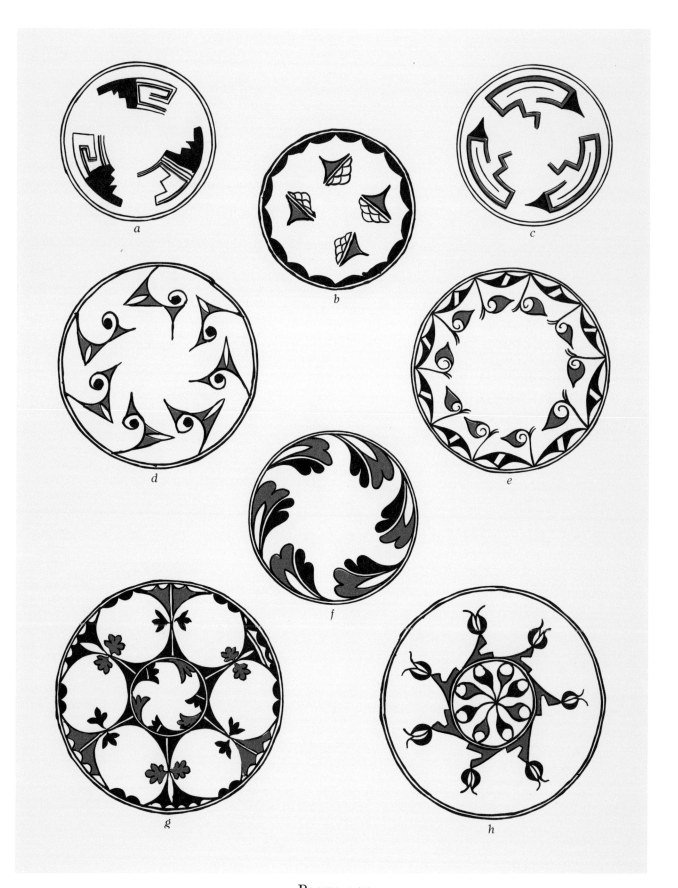

a

b

c

d

e

f

g

h

PLATE 147

a

b

c

d

e

f

g

h

PLATE 148

PLATE 149

Plate 150. Exterior designs from Ceremonial bowls. Comparison of designs from Polychrome Ceremonial bowls with those of the preceding Black-on-cream and Black-on-red wares shows a very consistent adherence to the old symbolism, expressed in the new combinations of black and red. The major exterior decoration is applied with reasonable deference to bilateral symmetry, influenced largely by the terraced rims of oval Kiva bowls. In contrast, the dynamic arrangement in *b,* from one side of a rectangular Ceremonial bowl, shows an unusual use of rotational symmetry.

As in the previous wares, several of the designs may be the work of aged and unskilled artists who were more learned in the performance of rituals than in painting the symbols associated with them. The importance of the *avanyu,* both curvilinear and rectilinear, is evident by its appearance in pairs in each of the seven figures. Other motifs such as cloud, lightning, star, terrace, and rain lines follow in importance.

The coniferous tree in *a* and the birds in *d* and *e* are rarely used in such Ceremonial compositions. Red leaves in *a* and the sprays between black clouds in *f* are apparently the only minor vegetal motifs.

Plate 151. Exterior and interior designs from Ceremonial bowls. Seven additional designs from the exteriors of Ceremonial bowls are included in *a-g.* In these the usual pairs of *avanyus* appear in four designs (*a-c* and *e*) and an unusual lone figure in *d.* The bears in *e* and *f* and the realistic corn plant in *b* are also of rare occurrence. The three designs in *h-j* are from the interiors of bowls. A formal representation of corn also appears in *h* and is quite unlike the realistic plants in *i.* In addition to the rain lines in *a, d,* and *f,* moisture is also represented by the tiny dewdrops in *b.*

Among the other familiar minor motifs, cloud and terrace take precedence over feather, star, and rain-far-off.

Plate 152. Exterior designs from Ceremonial bowls. The six designs in plate 152 are all from the exteriors of Ceremonial bowls. Bilateral symmetry is used in the layouts of the portions placed below the single terrace in each of *d, e,* and *f.* In *a,* however, though the symmetry is preserved below both the triple terraces and the pendant cloud clusters of the intervening spaces, the layout as a whole is made more informal by the use of hummingbirds at the left of the corn plants. In *b,* the slight degree of balance in the corn plants is almost lost in the antics of the groups of Koshare, who participate in ceremonies relating to the corn dance. The arrangement is reversed in *c* where the symmetry of the formal arrangements of familiar rain symbols clashes with the informal use of the deer within a scalloped border. There is also an unbalanced use of black and red in the terraces. The Koshare appear also in *d;* but in *c* and *f,* the figures represent the Chifoneti who substitute occasionally in the ceremonies at San Ildefonso, their distinguishing feature being the bifurcated cap.

a

b

c

d

e

f

g

PLATE 150

a

b

c

d

e

f

g

h

i

j

PLATE 151

a

b

c

d

e

f

PLATE 152

231

Plate 153. Leaf forms from all types of bowls and jars. At the beginning of this study it became evident that leaf forms used in San Ildefonso Polychrome ware exceed in number and variety those of any other motif of importance in Pueblo design. And if we consider the countless repetitions of the most simple forms, a complete census might show that the leaf actually outnumbers the total of all other motifs used. In this they exceed by far the leaf variants recorded for any of the other pottery-making pueblos.

To record fully the many variations in form, color, and minor decorative details of each of the basic leaf forms would serve only to repeat what has been disclosed of their use in the preceding plates. Therefore, to conserve space, a selection is shown enlarged in plate 153 and is sufficient to indicate only major basic variations in form, beginning with the simplest and most realistic and ending with one variation, equally realistic but more complex.

Not included are the simple black forms derived from Black-on-cream and Black-on-red wares, which though not Polychrome in themselves yet are used effectively in association with motifs in which red predominates. For comparison, most of the forms are shown upright, though the group of six (*s-x*) is often shown in the lazy position.

Plate 154. Additional leaf forms. A selection of twenty-four well-designed, fanciful forms of leaves is shown in larger scale than those appearing in the many preceding plates. They are arranged in three groups: pendant (*a-h*); lazy (*i-l* and *o*); and in a miscellaneous assortment (*p-x*). Of the total, good bilateral symmetry is used only in *p* and *x*, though it is approached somewhat in several of the miscellaneous group. Considerable variation appears in the dynamic group, including the use of sigmoid curves in *s* and the in the two outer leaves of *w*.

Plate 155. Miscellaneous vegetal forms. The group of twenty-four designs includes five horizontally extended motifs; nine free, including formal and informal; and ten attached to banding lines. In the extended class (*a-c, e,* and *f*), the extreme of realism in *c* seems out of place with the extreme of fanciful details predominating in *e* and noticeable in *a*. Even in *b* the well-designed layout includes unrealistic forms of doubtful meaning. The free group includes only a few fairly informal arrangements, as in *g* and *i*. The others show a predominance of formal arrangements in bilateral symmetry, as in *p, r,* and *s,* and quadrilateral, as in *d, h,* and *m*. Bilateral symmetry is maintained in most of the attached groups, the two marked deviations being those in *o* and *n*. The two most complex of the group, *t* and *w*, are outstanding examples of the assemblage of numerous details, vegetal and otherwise, into arrangements that because of their bilateral symmetry bear fancied resemblance to such life-forms as butterflies and which in early Polychrome times were so known.

Otherwise the symmetrical arrangements, both free and attached, are generally conceded to be mainly vegetal in concept. Variants of the seedpod appear in *n, p, r-u,* and *w*. Other details, not essentially vegetal, such as the volutes in *a, o,* and *t* and the black clouds in *l, t,* and *x* give variety to the composite forms.

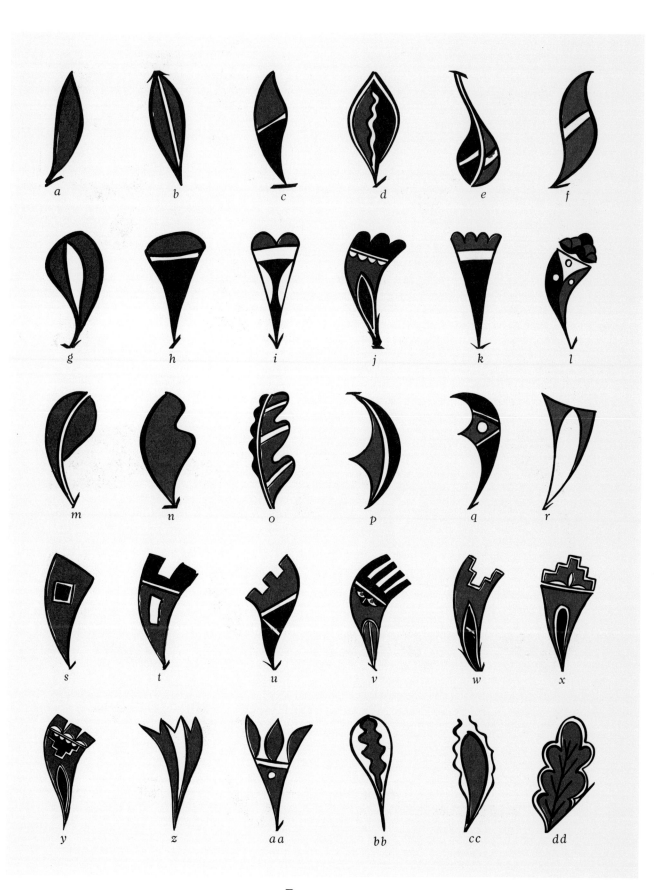

PLATE 153

233

PLATE 154

234

PLATE 155

Plates 156 through 162. Birds. The frequent use of birds in association with other motifs in many of the preceding plates bears evidence of at least a token recognition of their symbolic importance, as well as an appreciation of their enlivening effect because they afford the potter great freedom in composing the details of body and appendages. Of the eighty-four designs in plates 156 through 162, no two are identical and seldom is one made to represent any particular species. Instead they are fanciful creatures designed to take their place with other stylized motifs, most of which denote an underlying concern for the welfare of the Pueblo. Though the bird is used most frequently in water jars and food bowls, it is found also on numerous larger vessels where greater space permits relatively large figures. As a group they show considerable variance. They begin with primitive forms derived from earlier wares, include fairly realistic and stylized forms developed within the Polychrome period, and close with a few later styles influenced apparently by techniques originating outside the Pueblo. Of the seventy-nine birds shown in lateral view, more than seventy percent face the right, a predominance that appears in most Pueblo ceramics and reaches a maximum of over ninety percent in the pottery of Santo Domingo.

Throughout the series the great majority of the birds are drawn with fairly realistic forms of body, head, beak, and eye, the latter shown usually by a dot within a circle. Only rarely do two eyes appear in a lateral view, as in plates 156*d* and 159*g*, the latter a sophisticated adaptation of an ancient trait.

In more than half the figures the head is adorned by some form of crest, varying from mere lines indicating plumes to more formal upright devices. Wings afford opportunity for more fanciful devices, represented singly or in pairs. Tails appear in even greater variety. Legs are represented throughout with greater realism. In several instances the feet are omitted. In most of the designs, the feet are drawn with three toes; in a few instances, four or even five may appear.

Plate 156. Birds. Beginning with plate 156, the birds in six designs (*a-c* and *g-i*) show a derivation from earlier San Ildefonso forms, in black only, including those in flight and two dancing on the banding lines. The latter (*a* and *c*) and also *g* are shown considerably enlarged. Aside from the foregoing group, the body forms of the thirteen designs (*d-g* and *j-r*) represented in the lateral view are fairly realistic, a trait that appears also in plates 157 and 158.

Plate 157. Birds. The sixteen birds in plate 157, all in the lateral view, show preference for a reasonable degree of realism in body form. Of the appendages, the wings are omitted in *i*, *n*, and *o*; shown singly in *j-m*; by pairs in eight; and replaced in *g* by a bifurcated appendage. In most instances the paired wings are identical in structure, but considerable variance is apparent in the use of color of several and of both form and color in *c*. Between the most realistic use of tail feathers in *g* and the equally fantastic creations in *f* and *j* are several designs showing other variations in form and color. The most unusual in overall concept is the highly stylized form of *l*. A wide range of variation in the details of a procession of birds, from a single water jar, is apparent in four designs (*a*, *c*, *d*, and *f*), and also another example is that in the pair (*g* and *i*).

Among added decorative details, the cloud is most frequently used: in the bodies of seven and as a support in three.

Plate 158. Birds. The more or less natural body forms noted in plate 157 are continued throughout the group of sixteen designs in plate 158. The greatest deviation appears in the short-

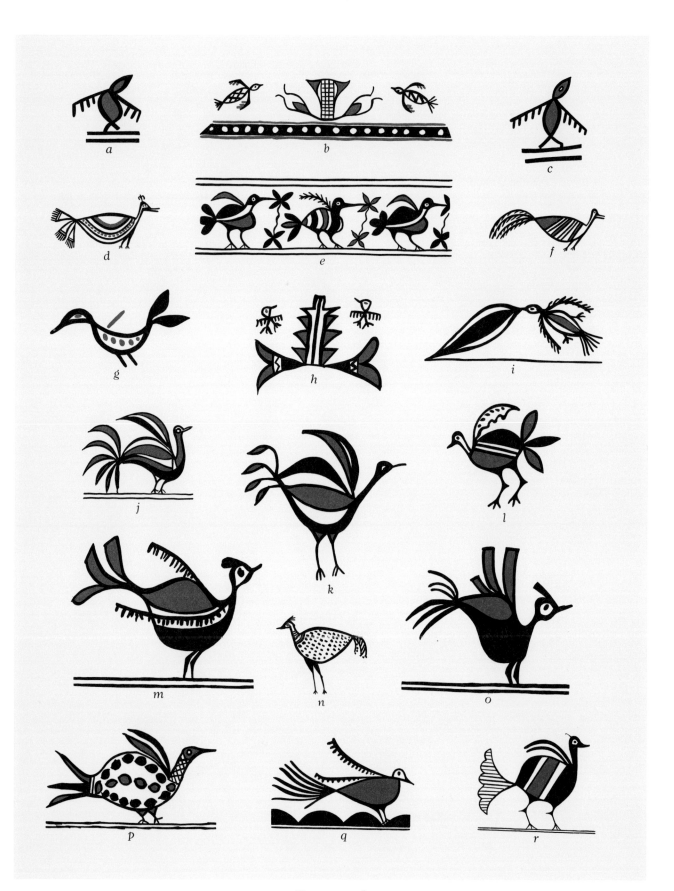

PLATE 156

PLATE 157

PLATE 158

239

ened bodies of *n* and *o*. Another example of variation in two designs from the same vessel is that in *a* and *c*. No wings are used in four of the figures. A single wing appears in seven, and pairs in three. An unidentified device serves in place of a wing in *o*. The unnatural position of wing attached to neck, as used in *l, n,* and *p,* is a possible derivation from the decorative art of the Keres pueblos. In *m,* a cloud bank is attached in the usual wing position. But if the device within the body is meant to serve as a wing, then the cloud bank might be regarded as a mere indication of the relation of all birds to the sky powers.

As in the preceding plates, the use of clouds in eight exceeds that of rain drops in seven.

Plate 159. Birds. The more or less rotund body forms of birds, noted in plates 156 through 158, are evident in *a* and *b* and, to a lesser degree, in *d* and *h*. In the remaining seven designs, the tendency is toward an extension of the upper and lower lines to confine both body and tail feathers. This radical change in form is due apparently to an influence from the pottery decoration of the western pueblos.

Plate 160. Birds. Five of the designs (*b, d-f,* and *h*) give added evidence of the variation in repeats of birds on one vessel. Still another instance appears in *i* and *l,* both from the same water jar. The crest and double device in the body of *j,* and also the feet on the stem, identify the figure as a crude imitation of a typical bird from Acoma pottery. Other unusual forms appear in *g, k, m,* and *n.*

Plate 161. Birds. Considerable variation in form and action appears in the twelve designs of plate 161. The two birds in flight are from one water jar. An unusual feature in the spread eagle of *g* is the heart, pendant from the neck, a device more commonly used in Hopi pottery decoration than in San Ildefonso. The sitting bird in *f* is a good example of consistent, fluent handling of a wide brush. The finer line work in *i, k,* and *l,* however, suggests the influence of Spencerian penmanship of the late 1800s. Three additional examples of the style appear in plate 162. The broad bill and web feet of *j* suggest a duck. In *h* is the only example encountered of the overpainting of a black line with red, as shown by the dotted band between tail and rear leg.

PLATE 159

a

b

c

d

e

f

g

h

i

j

k

l

m

n

PLATE 160

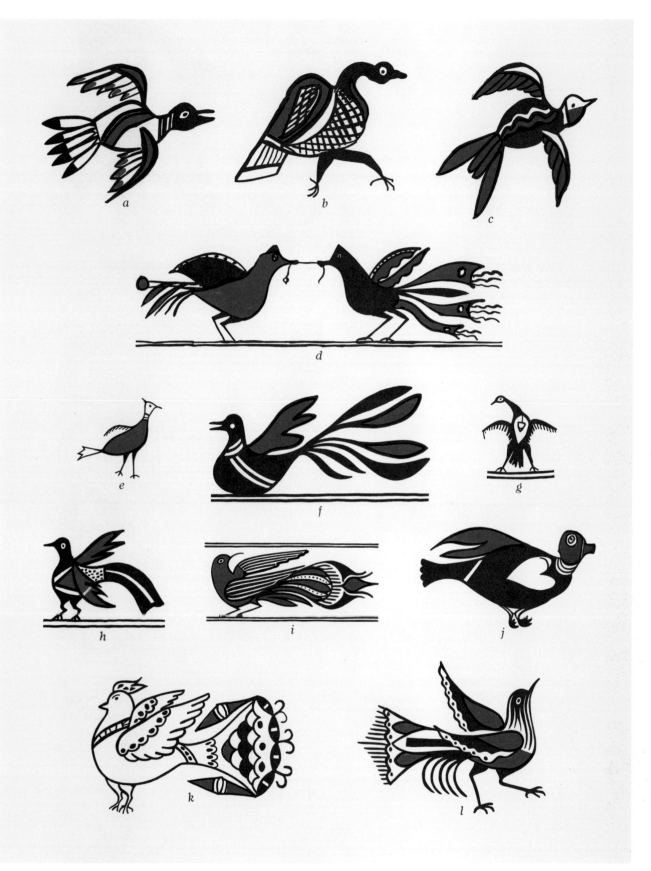

PLATE 161

243

Plate 162. Birds. A continuation of the apparent Spencerian penmanship style appears in *a*, *b*, and *d*. The ventral view in *c* is suggestive of the earlier Black-on-cream period. In *e*, the combination of realistic bird and abstract motif is most unusual.

Mammals. The use of mammals in San Ildefonso Polychrome decoration is exceedingly rare, as is evident in the small group (*f-j*) in which deer is the prime motif. The combination of fore-parts of deer with the intervening cloud bank is unique in Pueblo art. More common is the primitive representation of horns in the front view and on the side view of the head. The appearance of the heart line in *i* and *j* is rare in the Rio Grande pueblos, though it is a standard adjunct in Zuñi ceramics. The design in *i* is evidently a copy of the Zuñi type which, however, is never shown by them in red. An additional figure of a deer appears in plate 163*a*. The bear appears rarely in Polychrome decoration and almost exclusively on Ceremonial pottery. The example in *h*, however, is from a water jar for domestic use.

Plate 163. Miscellaneous life-forms. As a supplement to the group of deer in plate 162, the deer in plate 163*a* requires some explanation. It appears on a well-designed, small storage jar, with a typical arrangement of Polychrome motifs by one of the best artists. Because any definite information is lacking, it is impossible to determine whether this crude and primitive hunting scene was the volunteer work of an amateur, or a tongue-in-cheek bit of byplay by the artist himself.

The fish in figures *b* and *c* are realistic in form though given the prevalent fanciful adornment. The identity of the creatures in *d* and *e* is doubtful, as is that of the winged creatures of *f-j*.

Plates 164 through 170. (The text explaining the details of plates 164 through 170 was not available. Since Dr. Chapman knew exactly what he wanted to say in presenting these designs, an explanation by another would be presumptive. However, it is the feeling of those who have assembled the plates in the order indicated by Dr. Chapman that plates 164 through 170 were not intended to explain in detail any sequence of design features but rather to present additional designs found on San Ildefonso pottery.)

PLATE 162

245

PLATE 163

PLATE 164

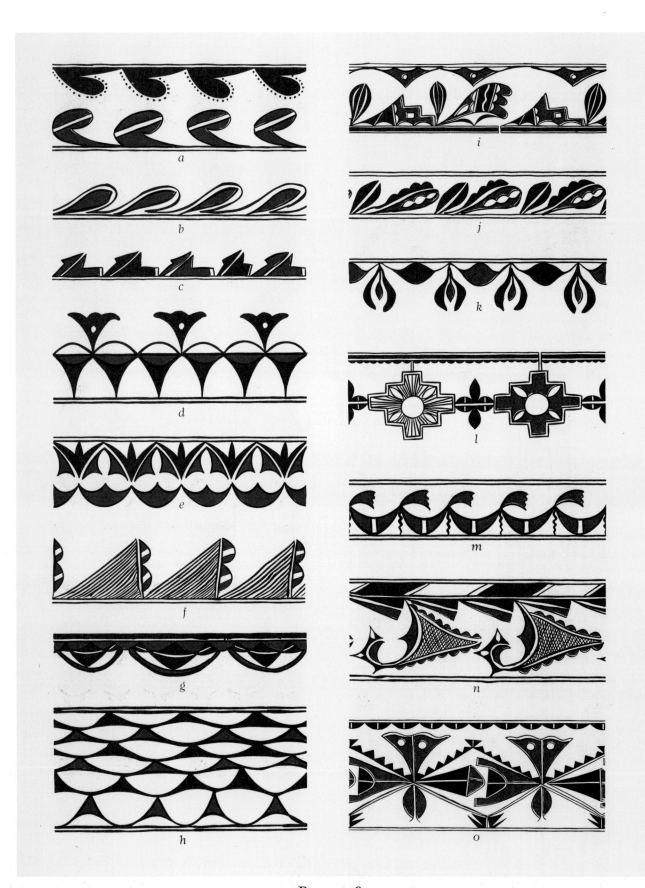

PLATE 165

248

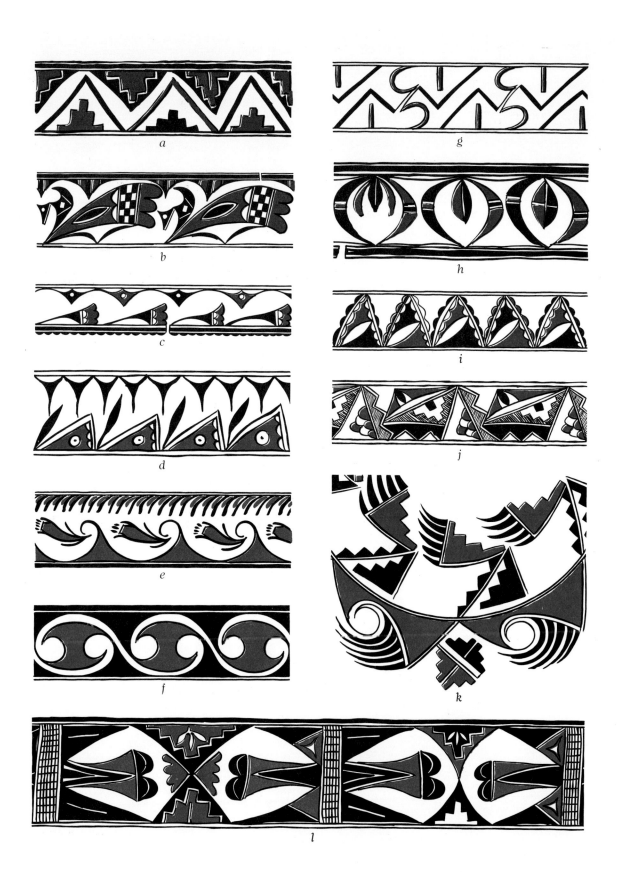

a

b

c

d

e

f

g

h

i

j

k

l

PLATE 166

PLATE 167

a

b

c

d

PLATE 168

a

b

c

d

e

f

PLATE 169

a

b c d

e f

g h

i j k

PLATE 170

MATTE-ON-POLISHED-BLACK WARE

Plate 171. Some of Julian Martinez' early experiments with use of matte motifs are grouped in plate 171*a-d.* These vary from mere lines in *c;* combinations of lines, dots, and clouds in *a* and *d;* and terrace with crosshatch in *b.*

In his original version of the *avanyu,* Julian used the simple, single "horn," as in *f* and *i.* But not until he confined the polished *avanyu* within a band, did he add the triple-pointed appendage to the horn (*g, h,* and *j*). At the same time he also devised both the triple-cloud cluster for the spaces above the *avanyu,* and the "fins" on the lower part of the body of the *avanyu,* as shown in *k.* An unusual use of the motif within a bowl is shown in *l,* which was designed by Santana.

In Julian's adaptation of a feather motif from an ancient Mimbres bowl (*m*), he made a wise choice in reversing the combination of Black-on-white by leaving the feathers in polished black and thus reducing the areas of matte to minor use as background.

Plate 172. Designs painted in matte, within bands. Use of motifs in matte is shown in the entire group of fifteen bands in plate 172. The motifs in twelve of the designs are easily recognized as literal adaptations from the design systems of the three preceding San Ildefonso wares. Included are cloud, terrace, leaf, rain-far-off, checker, and bird. In four others, Julian and other artists have used abstract geometric motifs from the Black-on-white wares of the early prehistoric period.

Plate 173. Of the fourteen designs in plate 173, eight are rendered as lunettes, thus giving a better idea of the relative proportions of the design elements at the upper and lower borders than is possible by use of straight bands. Throughout the group the motifs chosen by Julian and others are mostly devised through Julian's early study of the design systems of ancient Black-on-white wares. Two other motifs, of later origin, are the large feathers adapted by Julian from Zuñi pottery, one appearing in *g* and two in *n.* The only recognizable motifs from preceding San Ildefonso wares are rain-far-off in *b* and *h,* done in matte, and the leaf spaces in polished black (*c*). In all the designs, the motifs rendered in matte are mostly so proportioned and arranged with reference to the intervening spaces in polished black that the eye is diverted from one to the other.

Bilaterally symmetrical arrangements are used in *a* and *h,* and a balanced effect above and below is maintained in the simple arrangements of *b* and *i.* With the excepton of *c* all the remaining designs show a decided effect of motion from lower left to upper right.

Plate 174. Of the four designs from interiors of shallow bowls (*a, b, f,* and *g*), the upper two are static; *a* is bilaterally symmetric on two axes, and *b* on four. In contrast, *f* and *g* are dynamic. The Zuñi feather motif, noted in plate 173, is used to good effect in *f.* With this exception, familiar San Ildefonso motifs are used, among which the four butterfly arrangements in *b* are outstanding. Other motifs are the astroid in *b,* the leaf and volute in *a,* and terraces in *f.* In contrast with the dominant curvilinear forms in *f,* the stark simplicity of rectilinear terraces and dotted checker in *g* is unique in matte design.

Dynamic motifs are used also in *c-e.* In *c,* the appendages of the cloud cluster and rain-far-off are distinctly San Ildefonso in origin, as is also the quaintly distorted bird in *d,* and the anomalous device in *e;* both are from the same vessel.

PLATE 171

255

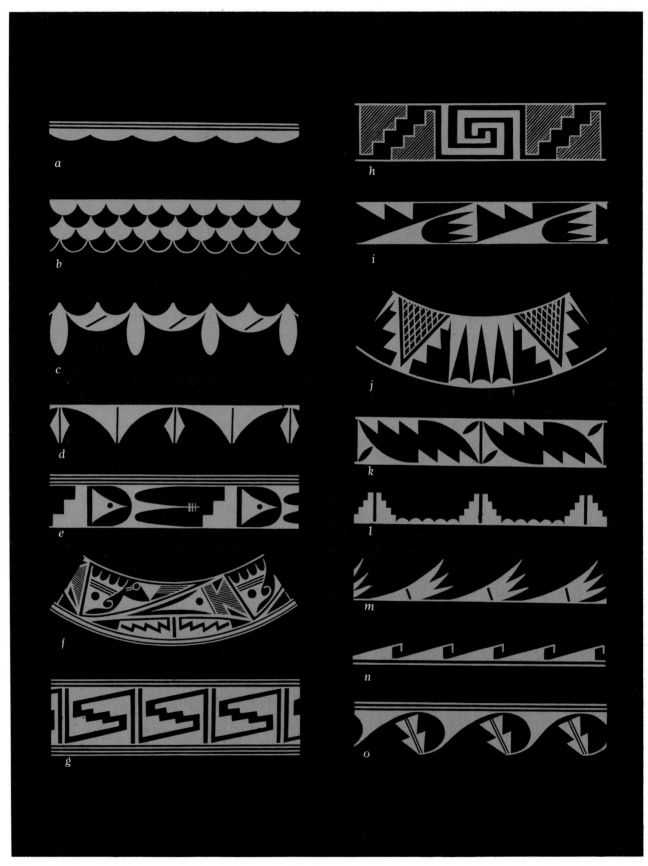

PLATE 172

256

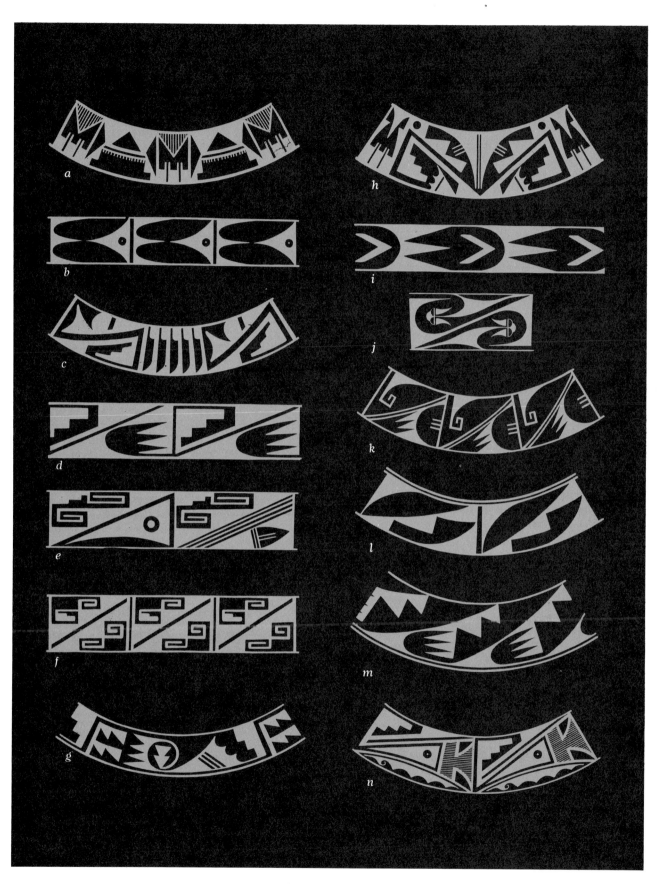

PLATE 173

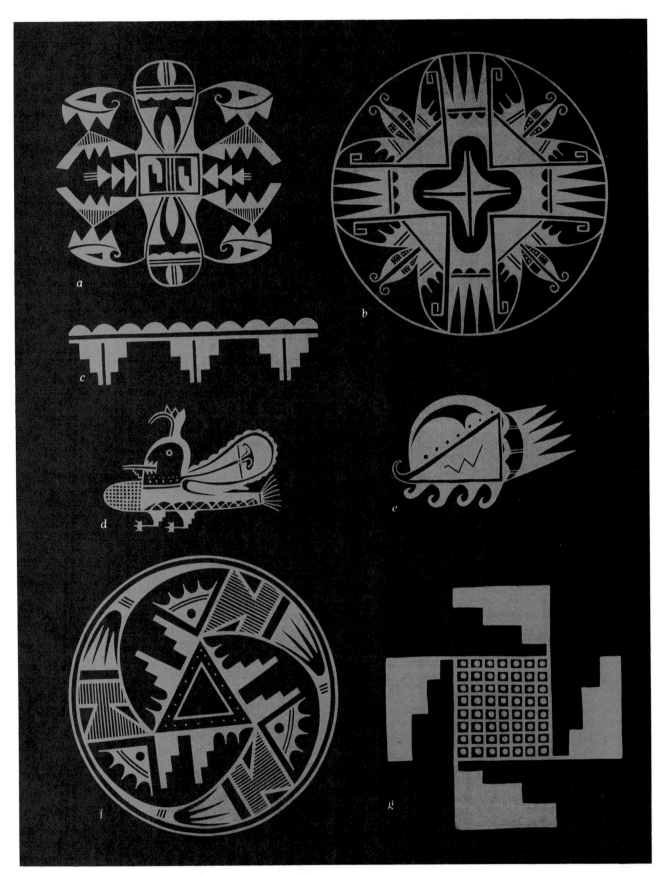

PLATE 174

BIBLIOGRAPHY

Pre-Spanish (A.D. 600-1600)

BANNISTER, BRYANT, AND SMILEY, TERAH L.
1955 *Dendrochronology.* University of Arizona Bulletin Series, Vol. XXVI, No. 2, Physical Science Bulletin No. 2, Tucson, 1955.

CHAPMAN, KENNETH M., AND ELLIS, BRUCE T.
1951 "The Line-Break, Problem Child of Pueblo Pottery," *El Palacio,* Vol. 58, No. 9, Santa Fe, 1951.

COSGROVE, H. S. AND C. B.
1932 "The Swarts Ruin, a Typical Mimbres Site in Southwest New Mexico," Papers of the Peabody Museum, Vol. 15, No. 1, Cambridge, 1932.

FEWKES, JESSE W.
1923 *Designs on Prehistoric Pottery from the Mimbres Valley, New Mexico.* Smithsonian Miscellaneous Collections, Vol. 74, No. 6, Washington, 1923.
1924 *Additional Designs on Prehistoric Mimbres Pottery.* Smithsonian Miscellaneous Collections, Vol. 76, No. 8, Washington, 1924.

HAURY, EMIL W.
1955 *Archaeological Stratigraphy.* University of Arizona Bulletin Series, Vol. XXVI, No. 2, Physical Science Bulletin No. 2, Tucson, 1955.

HEWETT, EDGAR L.
1938 *Pajarito Plateau and Its Ancient People.* Handbooks of Archaeological History Series, University of New Mexico Press, Albuquerque, 1938.

HOLMES, W. H.
1883 *Pottery of the Ancient Pueblos.* Fourth Annual Report of the Bureau of American Ethnology, 1882-83, Washington, 1886.

JEANCON, JEAN ALLARD
1923 *Excavations in the Chama Valley, New Mexico.* Bureau of American Ethnology, Bulletin 81, Washington, 1923.

JUDD, NEIL M.
1954 *The Material Culture of Pueblo Bonito.* Smithsonian Miscellaneous Collections, Vol. 124, Washington, 1954.

KIDDER, ALFRED V.
1924 "An Introduction to the Study of Southwestern Archaeology," Papers of the Phillips Academy Southwestern Expedition, No. 1, Yale University Press, New Haven, 1924.
1931 "The Pottery of Pecos, Vol. I," Papers of the Phillips Academy Southwestern Expedition, No. 5, Yale University Press, New Haven, 1931.
1936 "The Pottery of Pecos, Vol. II," Papers of the Phillips Academy Southwestern Expedition, No. 7, Yale University Press, New Haven, 1936.

MERA, HARRY P.
1935 *Ceramic Clues to the Prehistory of North Central New Mexico.* Laboratory of Anthropology, Technical Series, Bulletin No. 8, Santa Fe, 1935.
1937 *The Rain Bird, a Study in Pueblo Design.* Laboratory of Anthropology, Memoirs, Vol. II, Santa Fe, 1937.

RINALDO, J. B., AND BLUHM, E. A.
1956 "Late Mogollon Pottery Types of the Reserve Area," *Fieldiana: Anthropology,* Vol. 36, No. 7, Chicago Natural History Museum, 1956.

SAYLES, E. B.
1936 "Some Southwestern Pottery Types, Series V," Medallion Papers, No. 21, Gila Pueblo, Globe, Arizona, 1936.

SHEPARD, ANNA O.
1948 *The Symmetry of Abstract Design with Special Reference to Ceramic Decoration.* Carnegie Institution of Washington, Contributions to American Anthropology and History, No. 47, Washington, 1948.
1956 *Ceramics for the Archaeologist.* Carnegie Institution of Washington, Publication No. 609, Washington, 1956.

STALLINGS, W. S., JR.
1939 *Dating Prehistoric Ruins by Tree-Rings.* Laboratory of Anthropology, General Series, Bulletin No. 8, Santa Fe, 1939.

STUBBS, STANLEY A., AND STALLINGS, W. S., JR.
1953 *The Excavation of Pindi Pueblo, New Mexico.* Monographs of School of American Research and Laboratory of Anthropology, No. 18, Santa Fe, 1953.

Tewa (A.D. 1600-1800)

CARLSON, ROY L.
1965 *Eighteenth Century Navajo Fortresses of the Gobernador District.* University of Colorado, Series in Anthropology No. 10, Boulder, 1965.

HARLOW, F. H.
1965 "Tewa Indian Ceremonial Pottery," *El Palacio* (1965), Vol. 72, No. 4, p. 13.
1967 "Historic Pueblo Indian Pottery" (Santa Fe: Museum of New Mexico Press, 1967). "Northern Pueblo Matte-Paint Pottery of the Historic Period" (Santa Fe: Museum of New Mexico Press, in press). "Pueblo Indian Pottery Design" (Santa Fe: Museum of New Mexico Press, in press).

MERA, HARRY P.
1939 *Style Trends of Pueblo Pottery in the Rio Grande and Little Colorado Cultural Areas from the Sixteenth to the Nineteenth Century.* Laboratory of Anthropology, Memoirs, Vol. III, Santa Fe, 1939.

SAN ILDEFONSO (A.D. 1800-1960)

ALEXANDER, HARTLEY BURR
1926 *L'Art et la Philosophie des Indiens de l'Amerique du Nord.* Editions Ernest Leroux, Paris, 1926.

BUNZEL, RUTH L.
1929 *The Pueblo Potter.* Columbia University Press, New York, 1929.

BURTON, HENRIETTA K.
1936 *The Re-establishment of the Indians in their Pueblo Life through the Revival of the Traditional Crafts.* Contributions to Education, No. 673, Teachers College, Columbia University, New York, 1936.

CHAPMAN, KENNETH M.
1916 "The Evolution of the Bird in Decorative Art," *Art and Archaeology,* Vol. IV, No. 6, Washington, 1916.
1922 "Life Forms in Pueblo Pottery Decoration," *Art and Archaeology,* Vol. XIII, No. 3, Washington, 1922.
1924 "The Indian Fair," *Art and Archaeology,* Vol. XVIII, Nos. 5 and 6, Washington, 1924.
1927 "Post-Spanish Pueblo Pottery," *Art and Archaeology,* Vol. XXIII, No. 5, Washington, 1927.
1933 *Pueblo Indian Pottery, Part I.* C. Szwedzicki, Nice, France, 1933.
1950 *Pueblo Indian Pottery of the Post-Spanish Period.* Laboratory of Anthropology, General Series, Bulletin No. 4, third edition, Santa Fe, 1950.

COOLIDGE, MARY ROBERTS
1929 *The Rain-Makers.* Houghton Mifflin Company, Boston, 1929.

DOUGLAS, FREDERIC H.
1930 *Pueblo Indian Pottery Making.* Denver Art Museum, Department of Indian Art, Leaflet No. 6, Denver, 1930.
1933 *Modern Pueblo Pottery Types.* Denver Art Museum, Department of Indian Art, Leaflets Nos. 53 and 54, Denver, 1933.
1935 *Pottery of the Southwestern Tribes.* Denver Art Museum, Department of Indian Art, Leaflets Nos. 69 and 70, Denver, 1935.

DOUGLAS, FREDERIC H., AND D'HARNONCOURT, RENE
1941 *Indian Art of the United States.* Museum of Modern Art, New York, 1941.

GODDARD, PLINY E.
1931 *Pottery of the Southwestern Indians.* Guide Leaflet Series, No. 73, American Museum of Natural History, New York, 1931.

GUTHE, CARL E.
1925 "Pueblo Pottery Making," Papers of the Phillips Academy Southwestern Expedition, No. 2, Yale University Press, New Haven, 1925.

HALSETH, ODD S.
1926 "The Revival of Pueblo Pottery Making," *El Palacio,* Vol. XXI, No. 6, Santa Fe, 1926.

MARRIOTT, ALICE
1948 *María: The Potter of San Ildefonso.* University of Oklahoma Press, Norman, 1948.

SAUNDERS, CHARLES F.
1910 "The Ceramic Art of the Pueblo Indians," *The International Studio,* New York, September 1910.

SPINDEN, HERBERT J.
1911 "The Making of Pottery at San Ildefonso," *The American Museum Journal,* Vol. XI, No. 6, New York, 1911.
1931 *Indian Symbolism.* The Exposition of Indian Tribal Arts, Inc., New York, 1931.

STEVENSON, JAMES
1883 *Illustrated Catalogue of the Collections Obtained from the Indians of New Mexico and Arizona in 1879.* Bureau of American Ethnology, Second Annual Report, Washington, 1883.

UNDERHILL, RUTH
1944 *Pueblo Crafts.* Indian Handcraft Series, Vol. 6, Education Division, United States Indian Service, Washington, 1944.

WHITMAN, WILLIAM
1947 *The Pueblo Indians of San Ildefonso, a Changing Culture.* Columbia University Contributions to Anthropology, No. 34, Columbia University Press, New York, 1947.

WILSON, OLIVE
1920 "The Survival of an American Art," *Art and Archaeology,* Vol. IX, No. 1, Washington, 1920.

260